Beyond Retribution

to
Laurent
and
to my parents

Beyond Retribution

Seeking Justice
in the Shadows of War

Rama Mani

polity

First published in 2002 by Polity Press in association with Blackwell Publishers Ltd, a Blackwell Publishing Company.

Editorial office:
Polity Press
65 Bridge Street
Cambridge CB2 1UR, UK

Marketing and production:
Blackwell Publishers Ltd
108 Cowley Road
Oxford OX4 1JF, UK

Published in the USA by
Blackwell Publishers Inc.
350 Main Street
Malden, MA 02148, USA

ISBN 0-7456-2835-4
ISBN 0-7456-2836-2 (pbk)

A catalogue record for this book is available from the British Library and has been applied for from the Library of Congress.

Typeset in 10.5 on 12 pt Sabon by Kolam Information Services Pvt. Ltd, Pondicherry, India
Printed in Great Britain by MPG Books Ltd, Bodmin, Cornwall

This book is printed on acid-free paper.

Contents

Contents

Section III Synthesis and Recommendations

Abbreviations

ANC	African National Congress (South Africa)
ARENA	Nationalist Republican Alliance (El Salvador)
BWI	Bretton Woods Institutions
CHE	complex humanitarian emergency
CIVPOL	(United Nations) Civilian Police
CSF	Common Security Forum
DPA	(United Nations) Department of Political Affairs
DRC	Democratic Republic of Congo
DTA	Democratic Turnhalle Alliance (Namibia)
ECOWAS	Economic Community of West African States
FMLN	Frente Farabundo Martí de Liberación Nacional (El Salvador)
FRAPH	Front pour l'Avancement et le Progrès d'Haïti (Haiti)
FRELIMO	Liberation Front of Mozambique
HCHR	(United Nations) High Commissioner for Human Rights
HI	Hemisphere Initiatives
HNP	Haitian National Police
HRFOR	(United Nations) Human Rights Field Operation in Rwanda
ICITAP	International Criminal Investigation and Training Assistance Programme (USA)
ICC	International Criminal Court
ICCPR	International Covenant on Civil and Political Rights

ICESCR	International Covenant on Economic, Social and Cultural Rights
ICJ	International Commission of Jurists (*not* International Court of Justice)
IFI	international financial institution
IMF	International Monetary Fund
MICIVIH	Mission Civile en Haiti
	Joint United Nations – Organization of American States Civilian Mission in Haiti
MINUGUA	United Nations Verification Mission in Guatemala
NAMPOL	Namibian Police
NGO	non-governmental organization
NP	National Party (South Africa)
OAS	Organization of American States
OAU	Organization of African Unity (now African Union)
OHCHR	(United Nations) Office of the High Commissioner for Human Rights
OPL	Lavalas Political Organization (Haiti)
OSCE	Organization for Security and Cooperation in Europe (formerly CSCE)
ONUSAL	UN Observer Mission in El Salvador
PNC	National Civil Police (El Salvador)
REMHI	Recovery of Historical Memory (Guatemala)
RENAMO	Mozambican National Resistance
RPA	Rwandan Patriotic Army
RPF	Rwandan Patriotic Front
SAP	structural adjustment programmes
SOE	state owned enterprise
SWAPO	South West African People's Organization (Namibia)
SWAPOL	South West African Police (Namibia)
TCs	truth commissions
TRC	Truth and Reconciliation Commission
UNDP	United Nations Development Program
UNRISD	United Nations Research Institute for Social Development
UNSG	United Nations Secretary-General
UNTAC	United Nations Transitional Authority in Cambodia
UNTAG	United Nations Transition Assistance Group (Namibia)
URNG	Guatemalan National Revolutionary Unity
USAID	United States Agency for International Development
WB	World Bank Group
WIDER	World Institute for Development Economics Research
WOLA	Washington Office on Latin America

Acknowledgements

I thank the many people who supported me intellectually, financially and morally while I researched, wrote and revised this book. For refreshing and rigorous feedback on the manuscript at various stages, I am indebted to Jim Whitman, Nicholas Stockton, James Mayall, Oliver Ramsbotham, Wendy Cue, Andy Knight, Sudanshu Palsule and Ingveld Hestad. Their encouragement was all the more valuable to me in light of their own commitment to integrity and justice in their professional and personal lives.

I extend my gratitude to the over ninety persons I interviewed or held informal discussions with, based on their direct experience and expertise in peacebuilding and justice. I was not able to cite them all in the text, but I thank them without exception for their insights and observations. A large number interviewed were UN officials, and I appreciated their candour and rigour in evaluating their own short-comings. (I have avoided attributing comments directly to their con-tributors to maintain confidentiality, but where necessary I have cited sources, especially to credit an original idea or perspective to its source.) My discussions and interviews with non-governmental or-ganization activists and academics provided challenging insights, for which I am deeply grateful. Some also shared with me valuable documentation I might not have located otherwise. In particular, I thank Ian Martin, Rachel Neild, and Cornelius De Rover.

My observations were tested and my arguments were strengthened by my participation at conferences on the themes of this book, and interactions with other participants, for which I am grateful. I also gleaned insights from the reports and proceedings of certain conferences I did not attend in person. In this new field of enquiry, novel perspectives often emerge from such encounters and exchanges at seminars and conferences, and I express my appreciation to all the participants in these events for helping shape my views and challenge my arguments.

I am grateful to the Common Security Forum for sponsoring a seminar organized on the rule of law, which brought together leading thinkers and actors on the subject and was critical for my analysis. I am particularly grateful to Emma Rothschild, Director of the Forum, for her support, and to Amartya Sen for his encouragement. My thanks to the Faculty of Social and Political Sciences at the University of Cambridge, for its institutional support, and to Girton College, Cambridge, and several other funders, for financial support.

For feedback on pieces of the analysis originally presented as conference papers, I thank James Boyce, Geoffrey Hawthorn, Mahmood Mamdani, Anthony Duff, Toni Erskine and Christian van dan Anker. I am grateful to Michael Pugh for stimulating debate on war-torn societies and for editing two of my earliest journal articles. I would like to thank the excellent team at Polity, particularly John Thompson, for all their support.

I express in closing my debt of gratitude to Laurent, my cherished husband, for his gentle, unswerving commitment; to my parents, Saroja and Mani, for making all my dreams their own; to Jim Whitman, a truly exceptional humanitarian and scholar, for his unfailing encouragement; and to Wendy Cue, phenomenal friend, whose encounters with injustice in Haiti, Rwanda, and Guinea-Bissau paralleled and grounded my intellectual pursuit. Above all, I thank my beloved son, Arjuna, whose unfolding discovery of the world added enchantment to my labours.

Section I
Justice in Theory

1

The Three Dimensions of Justice in Post-conflict Peacebuilding

Introduction: justice, a political and social imperative

Today's wars are devastating in human and material terms. Since the end of the cold war alone, wars have cost over five and a half million lives.[1] The overwhelming majority of war's victims, over 80 per cent it is commonly estimated, are civilians, not combatants. The vast majority of armed conflicts today are located in low-income or developing countries, whose indigent populations and fragile economies are further impoverished in the process. Violent internal conflicts today are no longer distant military and political phenomena fought in remote battlefields, but direct personal events that ravage each household and affect all aspects of social and economic life in war-torn countries. Conflicts in recent decades have occurred primarily within rather than between states, pitting former neighbours, friends or family members against each other. Alongside the loss of life, limb and livelihood, war-torn populations suffer immeasurable trauma and psychological damage prior to, during and long after conflict.

Given the nature of contemporary conflicts, it is as much a political imperative as a social necessity to address issues of justice in the aftermath. Politically, it is difficult if not impossible for rival sides to agree to terminate hostilities and conclude peace until their major grievances are addressed. Socially, the causes, ramifications and effects of conflict on the daily lives and experiences of citizens make it imperative to address their claims for justice. Indeed, it is not only political leaders and combatants who claim redress for injustices in the aftermath of conflict. It is, overwhelmingly, ordinary civilians who suffer and claim redress for the direct and structural injustices inflicted during conflict. The litany of injustices may include discrimination, hate crimes, targeted rape, ethnic cleansing, genocide, involuntary displacement, forced conscription, hunger and disease, loss of home and livelihood, lack of access to economic opportunity and to legal redress.

Rebuilding peace after contemporary conflicts requires not only political will but also civic investment and confidence. If the injustices experienced by ordinary people during and often also prior to conflict are not redressed, it is unlikely that citizens will place their trust in the new peaceful dispensation and participate in efforts to build peace. And peace will flounder as a consequence. As expressed by Guatemalan Nobel Peace laureate Rigoberta Menchu: 'Peace without justice is only a symbolic peace'.[2]

International attention has focused increasingly in recent years on the nexus between rebuilding peace and restoring justice. This book addresses that nexus, and makes two arguments. The main argument made is that after conflict, justice must be restored in an integrated manner, covering all its distinct but interrelated dimensions, and recognizing the complexities of each dimension. It argues that so far national and international 'peacebuilders' have not addressed justice in this integrated multidimensional manner, and have failed to recognize and respond to the complexities of restoring each dimension of justice in low-income war-torn societies.

The secondary argument is that there is a chasm between the concept and practice of justice that is partly responsible for this failure. Justice is a universal concept that has been debated for millennia by political thinkers and philosophers around the world. Yet ironically, today's policy makers and practitioners do not possess or seek to possess a conceptual and philosophical understanding of the dimensions and scope of justice to ground their task of restoring justice on the ground. For their part, contemporary philosophers have lacked interest in addressing the particular challenges of justice posed by low-income societies emerging from conflict. The combined result is that justice is addressed in a skewed, partial and piecemeal manner, as much by practitioners as by scholars, and the attempt to marry peace and justice after conflict remains largely incomplete.

This book addresses the issue of restoring justice in low-income societies emerging from conflict in an integrated manner. First, it identifies the three distinct but interrelated dimensions of justice that are salient in the process of peacebuilding in societies emerging from conflict, in chapter 1. Then, it examines the rift between theories of justice in contemporary philosophy and the reality of injustice in war-torn societies, in chapter 2. The bulk of the book is devoted to evaluating critically the efforts of peacebuilders to address each of the three dimensions of justice in low-income societies emerging from conflict, in chapters 3, 4 and 5, in order to substantiate the main argument. Finally, in chapter 6, it offers a reconceptualization of the three dimensions of justice and recommends ways to bridge theory and practice, and to rebuild peace with justice in societies emerging from conflict.

Widening the lens: three dimensions of justice

Peacebuilders have focused mainly so far on redressing direct injustices committed against individuals during the period of hostilities, that is, gross human rights violations, war crimes and crimes against humanity. These human 'consequences' of conflict are grave. They impel some form of redress in the transition to peace. Cases in point are South Africa's Truth and Reconciliation Commission, and the *ad hoc* international tribunals for former Yugoslavia and Rwanda, all of which received considerable international attention and support.

The connection between conflict and injustice, and the consequent linkage between restoring peace and justice, goes far beyond these human consequences, I would argue. Injustice is not just a *consequence* of conflict, but is also often a *symptom* and *cause* of conflict. To restore justice after conflict, that is, to re-link peace and justice after conflict has torn them apart, all three dimensions of injustice embedded in and related to the symptoms, causes and consequences of conflict need to be addressed.

- The first dimension of justice that needs to be addressed is legal justice or the rule of law. The need to address legal justice stems from the rampant legal injustice, exemplified by the breakdown or corruption of the rule of law and absence of legal redress, that is a common symptom preceding and during most conflicts.
- The second is rectificatory justice. The need to address rectificatory justice arises from the direct human consequences of conflict in the form of injustices inflicted upon people including gross human rights abuses, war crimes and crimes against humanity.

- The third is distributive justice. The need to address distributive justice stems from the structural and systemic injustices such as political and economic discrimination and inequalities of distribution that are frequently underlying causes of conflict. These three dimensions are explained below.

Legal justice or the rule of law

Legal justice, or the rule of law as it is referred to here, and the entire apparatus of the justice system, is usually either delegitimized, debilitated or destroyed during or prior to conflict (as in South Africa, Haiti and Rwanda, respectively). The rule of law needs to be reformed or rebuilt entirely. There are compelling rationales for restoring the rule of law after conflict, both as an immediate priority and as a long-term goal. Restoring the rule of law may serve as an indication to combatants and civilians in war-torn societies of a return to security, order and stability. A rule of law regime assures the population that the government is formally subject to the law, and is no longer above it. It implies that all citizens, regardless of their identity, affiliation and background, are considered equal before the law. Additionally, by upholding principles and regular procedures that are resistant to corruption, the rule of law may act as a deterrent to future conflict, by signalling to conflicting groups that future perversions of the law are not permissible. Courts provide a forum for settling disputes without resort to violence, which is of prime importance after conflict. The rule of law is also intended to safeguard personal freedom and enshrine human dignity. Furthermore, it provides a necessary framework for rectificatory and distributive justice to be meted out. These rationales are additional to the arguable *duty* of governments to provide their citizens with the administration of justice, and their international treaty obligations to this effect.

Recently international donors and agencies have become increasingly interested in restoring the rule of law in societies emerging from conflict. Nevertheless, legal scholars diverge in their interpretation of the concept of the rule of law, as examined in chapter 2. Practitioners on the ground also have confused and divergent understandings of what is required to restore the rule of law in the aftermath of conflict, leading to contradictory outcomes, as examined in chapter 3. Concerted efforts are needed to clarify the conceptual confusion, and to understand the requirements of a regenerated rule of law in low-income war-ravaged societies.

Rectificatory justice

Rectificatory justice refers here to the question of dealing with injustice in terms of direct physical violence suffered by people during conflict. This category typically includes gross violations of human rights, crimes against humanity and war crimes, and is exemplified by the Jewish Holocaust and war crimes during the Second World War. Victims in countries emerging from dictatorship or state repression have also sought rectificatory justice for abuses committed by past regimes, most notably in South America in the 1980s. It is commonly acknowledged today that some established process of reckoning is needed for societies transiting out of political conflict or various forms of repression, to move beyond past trauma and begin constructing lasting peace.

Transitional societies have adopted a variety of approaches to deal with past abuses based on their specific needs, capacities, culture, history and political realities, as well as their legal systems.[3] These approaches have included truth commissions, trials and prosecutions, non-judicial sanctions such as purges, 'lustration' or removal from office, compensation, and symbolic gestures such as commemorations and memorials.

There are distinct legal, political, and psychosocial rationales for addressing rectificatory justice after conflict.

The legal rationale hinges on three arguments under international law, as elaborated in chapter 4: state responsibility under international treaty and customary law, including the responsibility of successor governments for abuses committed by former regimes; the non-derogability of fundamental human rights, even during emergencies; and victims' rights to redress. Therefore, even in the tense aftermath of conflict, states are legally bound to respect their international obligations and prosecute past abuses.

The political rationales for addressing past abuses have been debated often throughout the past five decades, as various societies have undergone transitions from conflict, authoritarian rule or dictatorship to peace and/or democratization.[4] They include the need to combat impunity, to deter future abuses, to establish the legitimacy and credibility of the new regime, to stabilize peace, and to strengthen democracy and the rule of law. However, political constraints may impinge upon these rationales.[5]

The psychosocial rationale stems from the need to understand and heal the trauma of victims and survivors of conflict. Psychiatrists and psychologists have devoted considerable attention since the Holocaust to the profound trauma and victimization undergone by survivors of repression, torture and violence. In addition to the long-term effects of trauma on direct victims and survivors, intergenerational transmission to their offspring has also been noted, for example in Holocaust survivors. Increasingly, aid agencies recognize that the long-ignored question of psychosocial healing must be addressed to promote reconciliation within communities and to consolidate peace.[6]

Rectificatory justice has received far more academic and political attention since 1945 than the two other dimensions of justice identified here. This attention has included analyses of the Nuremberg and Tokyo trials following the Second World War, and the treatment of human rights abuses in the democratic transitions in Southern Europe, Latin America, and, more recently, Central and Eastern Europe.[7]

Nevertheless, insufficient attention has been directed to date to the specific needs and constraints of low-income, less-developed societies emerging from violent internal conflict in restoring rectificatory justice.[8] In these societies pressing demands for rectificatory justice are counterbalanced and constrained by the devastation and depletion of human, material and financial resources and the breakdown of the rule of law. Attempts to restore rectificatory justice must compete on the one hand with the demands of economic rehabilitation to avoid economic collapse, and on the other hand with political constraints to avoid a return to arms by disgruntled belligerents. As largely undocumented violations continue in the largely forgotten wars of the world, including Sudan, Colombia and Algeria, there is an urgent and unmet need to understand the parameters and exigencies of rectificatory justice, particularly in low-income war-torn societies.

Distributive justice

The third dimension, distributive justice, entails addressing the underlying causes of conflict, which often lie in real or perceived socioeconomic, political or cultural injustice. While it would be erroneous to claim that issues of distributive injustice are the fundamental cause of or a necessary underlying feature in all current internal conflicts, they emerge as salient facilitating factors in the terrain of internal political conflicts. The United Nations identified 'the deepest causes of conflict' as 'economic despair, social injustice and political oppression'.[9] Scholars observe that where deep inequalities particularly between groups exist and are not readily justifiable, they are easily exploited by leaders to mobilize groups around shared grievances, on ostensible claims of identity, ethnicity, religion or other factors.[10]

The concern of distributive justice is how post-conflict societies deal with grievances such as inequitable distributions of and access to political and economic resources that underlie conflict. The rationale for addressing distributive justice is both to prevent a recurrence of conflict and to build the foundations of peace. Redressing underlying causes of conflict located in real and perceived distributive inequalities can help to avert a relapse into conflict and prevent future conflicts, and also to consolidate peace.

Until recently the attention accorded to issues of distributive justice and the demand for greater economic equity and political equality was largely rhetorical. The Guatemalan peace accords mark a potential turning point, as unprecedented attention was paid during the peace process to identify underlying structural and systemic causes of conflict, and redress social and distributive injustices. There is an urgent need for scholars and practitioners to accord greater priority to the underlying causes of conflict linked to distributive inequities, and to address distributive justice issues coherently when rebuilding war-torn economies.

The interdependence of the three dimensions of justice

The three dimensions enumerated above capture the central demands of justice that become both pertinent and pressing after internal political conflicts, although they may not be exhaustive. The relative salience and urgency of each of the three dimensions varies between countries, but in most cases some combination of the three is present.

The tendency today to focus primarily on rectificatory justice (and neglect the other two) is ill-advised, I would argue, as, although distinct, the three dimensions of justice are interdependent and mutually reinforcing, specifically in the post-conflict context. The process of rectifying past wrongs through the criminal justice system is vitally dependent on a functioning rule of law. To arrest suspects, a competent police force is required; to incarcerate them securely, an adequate prison system is needed; and to try suspects, an independent and impartial judiciary with trained lawyers and judges is essential. Abuses cannot be rectified and impunity cannot be countered without restoring the institutions and ethos of the rule of law.

Rectificatory justice also depends on distributive justice. Indirect violence inflicted on civilians through systemic and structural injustice usually falls outside the remit of formal rectificatory justice measures. Consequently, to address the generalized systemic and structural injustice suffered by targeted groups or by the population at large, some simultaneous measure of distributive or social justice is necessary. Many South Africans recognize today that the Truth and Reconciliation Commission was not designed to address the institutionalized injustice of apartheid that faced all blacks daily. They recognize too that justice will remain incomplete till the deep socio-economic inequalities produced over generations of apartheid are eliminated. Distributive justice, such as economic equality between races in South Africa, could bring a partial rectification to the larger society that suffered injustice indirectly and collectively. Narrowly defined and targeted measures of rectificatory justice undertaken by states such as trials or truth commissions do not provide such recompense.

Distributive justice is also intrinsically dependent on the rule of law. However, equity in resources and power cannot be meaningfully instituted unless the normative and institutional framework of a rule of law regime is put in place to safeguard equitable distributions. For example, this may include a constitution guaranteeing equal treatment to all citizens and defending socio-economic, cultural and political rights.

The interdependence of the three dimensions is testified in practice, as in Rwanda. Faced with the enormity of genocide in Rwanda, the new government set up by the victorious Rwandan Patriotic Front (RPF) arrested all suspected *génocidaires* with the aim of prosecuting them. However, the debilitated penal system was unequipped to incarcerate such numbers, and the devastated legal system was unprepared to prosecute them. It proved impossible to provide rectificatory justice under the criminal justice system in Rwanda without simultaneously rebuilding and reforming the rule of law. Nevertheless, even when the rectificatory measures undertaken by national trials and the international tribunal are completed, 'justice' will remain incomplete until the persistent political and socio-economic inequalities that preceded and underlay Rwanda's prolonged conflict and culminated in the 1994 genocide are also redressed. In Namibia and South Africa overturning apartheid's racially discriminating legislation was a first step towards distributive justice for the majority black population – that is, legal justice provided an avenue for rendering an initial measure of distributive justice. Police reform in various post-conflict countries including Namibia, Haiti and El Salvador was necessary not only to restore the rule of law, but also to implement rectificatory justice and safeguard distributive justice.

The three dimensions of justice may also be mutually reinforcing when they are addressed concurrently after conflict. The rule of law was shown above to be a necessary fulcrum for rectificatory and distributive justice measures. Similarly, the process of restoring rectificatory and distributive justice serves to test and strengthen the principles and institutions of the rule of law, such as the equality of all citizens before the law, the guarantee of humane treatment to prisoners and the right to a fair trial.

The interdependence and mutual reinforcement between the three dimensions of justice make it desirable and even necessary to address all three simultaneously in the aftermath of conflict. The time frame for the realization of each dimension may differ. Often, rectificatory justice is treated as a relatively short-term order. Nevertheless, in some cases the issue is taken up only years or decades after the end of conflict, as for example in the current attempt to prosecute Khmer Rouge leaders in Cambodia.[11] In others, the issue continues to be addressed over many decades, as with the prosecution of Nazi war criminals even today in Germany, France and elsewhere. Restoring the rule of law in its plenitude and instituting distributive justice measures are longer-term objectives. These measures are usually initiated shortly after conflict formally terminates, but may not be fully effective for some time.

The three dimensions of justice identified here are important and urgent after conflict, but they cannot be addressed in a vacuum. The endeavour to restore justice is shaped by the exigencies of peacebuilding in societies emerging from conflict.

The context: peacebuilding in 'post-conflict' societies

This discussion must begin with a clarification of the term 'post-conflict'. The term is at best a simplification to describe countries that have nominally terminated hostilities, either through negotiation or on the battlefield, and that have not – or not yet – relapsed into violence. However, violence and conflict rarely end with formal settlement. Continued political tension, social instability, economic disruption and heightened crime often mark what are described as 'post-conflict' societies. Insecurity and violence frequently arise with arms proliferating through 'post-conflict' societies and into neighbouring countries, as former combatants sell or use their weapons to earn their livelihoods. In El Salvador, owing to soaring crime, the death toll rose after conflict formally concluded with a final peace agreement in 1992.

Many 'post-conflict' countries have relapsed into political conflict either rapidly, as in Angola and Sierra Leone, after the failure of their negotiated peace agreements, or only gradually, as in Zimbabwe after two decades of 'peace'. It has become commonplace to describe societies that formally conclude hostilities as 'post-conflict societies'. The term is used with caution and humility in this book in full recognition of the insecurity and instability that continue to mark these countries, and the ever-imminent possibility of a relapse into political violence.

The concept and scope of peacebuilding

A quarter-century ago, the peace researcher Johan Galtung drew the distinction between three approaches to peace: peacekeeping, peacemaking and peacebuilding. Galtung described peacebuilding as the associative approach, peacekeeping as the dissociative approach, and peacemaking as the conflict resolution approach. Peacebuilding, in his view, seeks to identify the 'structure of peace': 'Structures must be found that remove causes of wars and offer alternatives to war in situations where wars might occur.' He describes peacebuilding activities as directed at 'building structural and cultural peace'. In Galtung's description,

$$\text{Peace} = \text{direct peace} + \text{structural peace} + \text{cultural peace.}[12]$$

While peacemaking and peacekeeping are long familiar in UN terminology and practice, peacebuilding formally entered the UN lexicon only in 1992. In the Secretary-General's 'Agenda for Peace' that year, post-conflict peacebuilding was described as 'actions to identify and support structures which will tend to strengthen and solidify peace in order to avoid a relapse into conflict'.[13]

From a peace research perspective, peacebuilding, as defined above by the UN, has two distinct but related and complementary objectives. Peace research distinguishes between *negative peace*, which represents an absence of direct violence such as a cessation of hostilities; and *positive peace*, which represents the removal of structural and cultural violence. Accordingly, the 'negative' task of peacebuilding is that of 'preventing a relapse into overt violence'. This can be distinguished from the 'positive' tasks of peacebuilding, which include 'aiding national recovery and expediting the eventual removal of the underlying causes of internal war'.[14]

Striving for the balance between these twin objectives is seen as a defining feature of peacebuilding as conceptualized in this book. We discussed earlier how prone 'post-conflict' societies are to relapsing into violence. If peace is defined solely as the absence of violence, and if peacebuilding limits its goal to ending hostilities, it will lack foundation and will face failure all too often, as in Angola. Peacebuilding has to aim to achieve its objectives of negative and positive peace simultaneously – and not consecutively – in order to be sustainable. It must constantly attempt to balance its task of maintaining the absence of open violent hostilities with the parallel task of deepening and consolidating peace to make a relapse into hostilities ever-less probable. This is not an easy or natural task, as often the two tasks may seem to contradict each other. Often political imperatives may lead peacemakers to prioritize negative peace, such as obtaining or maintaining a cease-fire agreement, in the short run. The challenge here is to ensure that such imperatives do not allow the parallel task of positive peace to be overlooked or marginalized. The twin objectives of peacebuilding and the necessity to balance them constantly is of particular relevance for the pursuit of justice which is often caught in the cross-fire between the two, as will be seen in chapters 3, 4 and 5.

Lederach emphasizes the associative, social and cultural aspects of peacebuilding. Like Galtung, Lederach views peacebuilding as a dynamic process: 'metaphorically, peace is seen not merely as a stage in time or a condition. It is a dynamic social construct'. Lederach defines peacebuilding as 'a comprehensive term that encompasses, generates and sustains the full array of stages and approaches needed to transform conflict towards sustainable, peaceful relations and outcomes'. Lederach proposes a conceptual framework offering 'a comprehensive approach to the transformation of conflict that addresses the structural issues, social dynamics of relationship building, and the development of a supportive infrastructure for peace.'[15]

Boutros-Ghali also underlines the social and economic aspect of peacebuilding. Peacebuilding is the 'construction of a new environment', which not only avoids a relapse into conflict, but also aims to 'advance a sense of confidence and well-being among people'. Boutros-Ghali specifies that 'only sustained, co-ordinated work to deal with underlying economic, social, cultural and humanitarian problems can place an achieved peace on a durable foundation', and most writers acknowledge the importance of the socio-economic dimension.[16]

An important characteristic of peacebuilding is its political nature. Earlier, the approach to peacebuilding consisted primarily of developing an inventory of necessary tasks and functions to be performed.[17] In recent years, there has been a gradual but growing recognition within international circles and in the UN that successful and sustainable peacebuilding requires not merely technical expertise to execute a checklist of tasks but political direction as it is essentially a political undertaking.[18] Some scholars have articulated 'peacebuilding as politics': 'At its base, and at its best, peacebuilding should bolster the possibility of vibrant, responsive political life in societies where politics has been supplanted by military contest and violence.'[19]

This political conception of peacebuilding is intimately dependent on the simultaneous revival of civic life. Peacebuilding needs to be domestically rooted and 'owned' by the local population, and not imported or imposed. Lederach emphasizes 'the need to build on the cultural and contextual resources for peace and conflict resolution present within the setting'. Cockell observes that 'a sustainable peace can only be founded on the indigenous, societal resources for intergroup dialogue, cooperation and consensus,' and identifies indigenous capacity as one of four criteria for success.[20] Operationally, this need is often translated through attempts by international peacebuilders to revitalize civil society and engage civic actors in peacebuilding.[21]

If peacebuilding is described primarily as a domestic task and initiative, it raises the question of what role, if any, there is for international actors. Based on the conceptualization presented here, there is a definite but circumscribed role for international actors in peacebuilding. Countries that undergo violent conflict are very often low-income or middle-income countries that are severely set back during hostilities. They urgently require international financial assistance and expertise to rebuild. However, the goal of peacebuilding is 'moving a given population from a condition of extreme vulnerability and dependency to one of self-sufficiency and wellbeing', where the society can govern itself peacefully and resolve conflicts without recourse to violence.[22] Consequently the international role must be to *facilitate* peacebuilding, but not to impose or dictate its terms. Lederach points to the need for the international community to 'adopt a new mind-set', and to move beyond what he describes as: 'A simple prescription of answers and modalities for dealing with conflict that come from outside the setting and focus at least as much attention on discovering and empowering the resources, modalities, and mechanisms for building peace that exist within the context.'[23]

The UN General Assembly passed a resolution as early as 1993 clarifying that 'each situation in which post-conflict peacebuilding may be undertaken is unique and therefore should be considered on a case-by-case basis'.[24] Yet in practice, the international community's attempts at peacebuilding have been sharply criticized, and described as 'an enormous experiment in social engineering' that 'involves transplanting Western models of social, political and economic organization into war-shattered states in order to control civil conflict'.[25]

These critiques underline the need for external actors to exercise caution and cultural sensitivity and eschew 'one-size-fits-all' standardized approaches to diverse post-conflict situations. As envisaged by the General Assembly above, and expressed by Cockell, 'successful peacebuilding is context-specific'.[26]

Combining the perspectives presented above, peacebuilding is defined for the purposes of this study as follows:

- Peacebuilding is a dynamic process with the twin objectives of consolidating peace (building positive peace) and averting a relapse into conflict (preserving negative peace), which must be balanced.
- Peacebuilding aims to identify, alleviate and if possible eliminate underlying causes of conflict, in the interest of conflict prevention.
- Although comprising many technical elements, peacebuilding is essentially a political task; it depends critically on domestic or indigenous initiative, capacity and political will, while requiring international support to facilitate the process.
- Peacebuilding is also a social and associative process that rebuilds fractured relationships between people and is 'survivor'-focused.

Pre-conflict and post-conflict peacebuilding

The term peacebuilding was originally used to describe both pre-conflict preventive peacebuilding that precedes or pre-empts the outbreak of conflict, and post-conflict rehabilitative peacebuilding that follows the termination of conflict. In the depiction of Gareth Evans, former Australian Foreign Minister, 'peacebuilding strategies are those that seek to address the underlying causes of disputes, conflicts and crises; to ensure either that problems don't arise in the first place, or that if they do arise, they won't recur'.[27] In 1995 Boutros-Ghali also adopted a broad definition encompassing both aspects, although he had initially used the term preventive diplomacy to describe the former and post-conflict peacebuilding to describe the latter.[28] Subsequently, however, Kofi Annan, United Nations Secretary-General (UNSG), returned to the original idea of peacebuilding as an activity restricted to the post-conflict stage.[29] Some writers like Lederach and Cockell support the broader definition of peacebuilding encompassing preventive and post-conflict dimensions, and argue that peacebuilding needs to begin before a peace settlement is reached.

There is clearly an overlap between the two stages, and between the concepts of peacebuilding and conflict prevention.[30] The aim in both is similar: consolidating peace and ensuring that conflict does not break out. The difference is in timing: one precedes the outbreak of violent conflict and the other follows it. In this study, the focus is on the latter, for it is in societies that have already undergone conflict that all three dimensions of justice are pressing and pertinent. Justice issues may be pertinent in pre-conflict preventive peacebuilding as well: it may be effective to address distributive justice issues and remedy shortcomings in legal justice in order to prevent conflict. However, it is in post-conflict societies that all three dimensions become pressing simultaneously within the context of peacebuilding. Here, while an argument is made for a broad, dynamic and encompassing definition of peacebuilding, the analysis of justice focuses on the post-conflict stage.

The practice and relevance of peacebuilding

The concept and practice of peacebuilding have developed rapidly since 1992. A range of UN agencies and departments, and innumerable regional, bilateral and non-governmental organizations have undertaken various peacebuilding tasks.[31] Many recent studies have criticized peacebuilding's record in practice, especially shortcomings in the UN's performance in this new and unprecedented enterprise, as noted earlier.[32] In my view, these critiques do not weaken the concept of peacebuilding, but rather indicate the inevitable difficulties of translating into practice an evolving, dynamic and ambitious concept.

Many terms have been employed to describe the task facing societies that emerge from conflict. The World Bank talks of post-conflict reconstruction, while UN agencies refer to post-conflict rehabilitation or rebuilding.[33] The terms 'complex peacekeeping operations', 'new peacekeeping' or 'peace support operations' have been used to describe multidimensional missions that facilitate the initial transition from conflict to peace. Led by the UN and / or regional organizations, these operations usually comprise civilian monitors, police officers and military personnel, and have short-term mandates.[34] Peace maintenance is an innovative concept that proposes to address the challenge of instituting legitimate and integrated international political authority in war-torn countries. Its concern is the comprehensive effort the UN must undertake in states where domestic capacity for governance is destroyed, or where an interim international authority is required to safeguard the transition to peace.[35]

While many valid terms exist, in my view peacebuilding as defined in the discussion above is the concept that best encapsulates and most adequately responds to the requirements of societies emerging from conflict. Peacebuilding does not preclude either peacekeeping or peace maintenance: it encompasses and goes beyond them. Peacebuilding seeks to identify and address comprehensively the many levels at which peace needs to be built in societies torn by violent internal conflict.

Conflict, as noted in the introduction, is not only a political phenomenon affecting politicians and combatants, but equally a social phenomenon with a direct and usually devastating impact on civilians. This reality provides the backdrop for peacebuilding. A settlement that achieves political accommodation and ends hostilities between belligerents will provide a necessary but insufficient foundation for peace, as this achieves only the 'negative peace' objective of peacebuilding. Peace arrangements need to address not only the political grievances of opposed groups and factions but also the concerns of ordinary inhabitants of society, as the 'positive peace' objective of peacebuilding attempts to do. Peace will be sustainable only if it is founded on the interests of all inhabitants of a society, irrespective of their roles during the conflict.

The concept of peacebuilding as defined here suits societies emerging from conflict because it recognizes and responds to the dual function of building both political peace, between opposed leaders, and social peace, between hostile and estranged citizens. Peacebuilding recognizes that fractured interpersonal relations, as much as damaged infrastructure and disrupted economies, need to be rebuilt after devastating conflict. It is for this reason that this book roots the endeavour to restore justice in the aftermath of violent conflict within the context of peacebuilding as the concept is defined here.

Restoring justice within the parameters of peacebuilding

Ramsbotham proposes a conceptual framework for post-conflict peacebuilding. He identifies three interlinked deficit areas that positive peacebuilding aims to address: political/constitutional incapacity; economic/social debilitation; and psychosocial trauma.[36] The three dimensions of justice correspond to these three deficit areas. Rebuilding legal justice or the rule of law is an essential component of political/constitutional reconstruction; distributive justice is the *leitmotif* of the socio-economic programme undertaken in post-conflict reconstruction; rectificatory justice is the central component in psychosocial rehabilitation.

Situated within the context of 'post-conflict' peacebuilding, then, the tasks of restoring justice and rebuilding peace are complementary and overlapping, and even mutually reinforcing. The tasks of building peace and restoring justice both stem from a combined political and social imperative. Both processes must strive to balance political goals with societal ones, within the stringent material and political constraints faced by low-income post-conflict societies. Yet although some component parts of the three dimensions of justice have been addressed in peacebuilding, the integral nature of justice and the dynamic linkages between its three dimensions have not been consciously acknowledged or addressed by either scholars or practitioners.[37]

Despite their compatibility in theory, the parallel tasks of building peace and restoring justice often come into conflict in practice. Although peace and justice seem inseparable natural allies in peacetime, their relationship is fraught in the aftermath of conflict. Political and material obstacles are frequently encountered in seeking to restore peace and justice simultaneously. Politically, addressing issues of justice after internal conflict is inevitably contentious and riddled with dilemmas. The end of hostilities and the onset of peace often impose requirements that contradict the requirements of justice; the demands of justice sometimes contradict the conditions necessary to maintain (negative) peace. For example, legal justice may require dismantling a corrupt judiciary; rectificatory justice might require prosecuting popular national leaders; distributive justice may necessitate redistributing land more equitably. Such 'just' changes may seem to threaten negative peace and short-term stability by provoking obdurate resistance from powerful groups and institutions, such as the military, the political leadership or the economic elite. Nevertheless, ignoring justice claims may cause discontent and frustration among disenfranchised groups, and undermine positive peace. It may endanger negative peace as well, if unmet grievances degenerate into renewed violence.[38]

Practically, a significant constraint and limit to actions to restore justice stems from the poverty and material limitations of most post-conflict countries. The task of addressing justice issues must compete with the multitudinous tasks of economic recovery and reconstruction that are often considered higher priority to get a war-torn country back on its feet. Addressing questions of justice and winning public confidence in peace are a bulwark of sustainable peacebuilding, but they may get short shrift when attention is focused on immediate tasks of recovery which yield quicker material results. Addressing issues of justice within the peacebuilding process in low-income post-conflict societies is eminently important but also inordinately difficult.

Restoring justice in practice: drawing on recent experience

This introductory chapter has so far laid out the aims of this book, identified the three interdependent dimensions of justice, described the concept of peacebuilding and situated the task of restoring justice within the peacebuilding process in war-torn societies. The next chapter will demonstrate the current disconnect between theory and practice by examining theories of legal, rectificatory and distributive justice within the field of contemporary philosophy.

Thereafter in chapters 3, 4 and 5, we will move to the main thrust of this book to substantiate the arguments made through an evaluation of the experiences and challenges of restoring justice in practice in societies emerging from conflict. In order to do so, this book draws primarily on the experiences of a small number of developing countries that have emerged recently from violent internal conflict or political crises. The countries were chosen based on the salience of one or more of the dimensions of justice before, during and after conflict. They are: El Salvador, Haiti, Namibia, Mozambique, Cambodia, Rwanda, South Africa and Guatemala. These countries were not studied exhaustively or systematically across all three dimensions of justice, but only insofar as their individual experiences in one of the three was relevant to the aims of this study. The examples drawn from these countries are demonstrative rather than comprehensive, as they are intended to substantiate the arguments made in this book. Occasional reference is made to other societies undergoing or emerging from conflict that are relevant to the themes of this book, such as former Yugoslavia or Ethiopia.

All eight countries experienced significant international involvement in post-conflict peacebuilding, and often also during peace negotiations. This was a deliberate choice to evaluate the performance of international actors, particularly the United Nations (UN) and the Bretton Woods Institutions (BWI), in addressing justice issues within peacebuilding, and to draw lessons for the future.

All except two – El Salvador and South Africa – are classified as low-income countries by the World Bank. El Salvador is classified as a lower-middle-income country. South Africa is classified as an upper-middle-income country.[39] However, on a range of socio-economic indicators, 'if South Africa's indicators were restricted to include only the African population, black South Africa fares as badly as a much poorer country like Kenya', making it comparable to the other low-income cases.[40] Although El Salvador and South Africa are marginally better off than the other cases, they are nonetheless developing countries with similar socio-economic constraints. Again, this choice of developing countries was deliberate as this book intends to illustrate the particular difficulties faced in restoring justice after conflict in resource-poor settings that middle- or high-income countries might not face.

Conflict was formally terminated in or before 1994 in seven of the eight countries enumerated through either a negotiated agreement or battle victory. This general cut-off date of 1994 provided a short period to evaluate the initial 'post-conflict' peacebuilding process. The only country referred to here whose conflict ended after 1994 is Guatemala, where final peace agreements were signed only in December 1996. Nevertheless, the salience of all three dimensions of justice in Guatemala's peace negotiation process and, consequently, for peacebuilding, make the case important for this analysis. However, due to the short time-lapse since the termination of conflict, most references to Guatemala are to the negotiation process and aspirations expressed in the peace agreements, with only passing reference to post-conflict implementation.

The choice of cases and the limited passage of time since their conflicts formally concluded does not reflect a presumption that peace is irreversible in these countries and a relapse into conflict is precluded. As discussed earlier, countries described nominally as 'post-conflict' are almost without exception insecure and volatile, and this is borne out in most of the eight cases used here.

In Cambodia, political crisis peaked in April 1997 when then-joint Prime Minister Hun Sen staged a palace coup, only conceding to elections in July 1998. Yet, political violence again scarred campaigning for the first ever local elections in February 2002,[41] in which Hun Sen's party won a landslide victory amidst complaints of irregularities by foreign election monitors. Political turmoil and violence persist in Haiti despite the internationally assisted ouster of the dictator Raoul Cédras's violent regime in 1994. Jean-Bertrand Aristide, erstwhile torchbearer of social justice, is now suspected of nursing dictatorial ambitions. Since retaking the presidency in opposition-boycotted elections in November 2000, Aristide refuses to concede to opposition and international pressure to call new elections, and accuses the opposition and former army of plotting a coup.[42] Political uncertainty and conflict continue in Rwanda. Alleged hostilities by the Interahamwe forces who perpetrated the 1994 genocide and by former soldiers of Forces Armées Rwandaises (ex-FAR) continue in the north-west, providing the ostensible rationale for Rwanda's military involvement in the war in the Democratic Republic of Congo (DRC). Increasing defections or departure of senior Hutus and moderate Tutsis from government and Kagame's consolidation of power have shaken political stability and raised ethnic tensions.[43] In Namibia ten years of relative tranquillity were broken in August 1999 by the challenge of the small separatist Caprivi Liberation Army in the north, and the South West African People's Organization (SWAPO) government has been criticized for its heavy-handed response. Namibia is also involved in two of the worst wars on the African continent, in Angola and in DRC. After three terms in office facilitated by a constitutional amendment, President Nujoma seems to want a fourth, casting doubt on Namibia's democratic credentials.[44] Tension has risen within and between political parties in South Africa, particularly since Mandela's passage from power, as has criminal violence and insecurity. El Salvador has seen gains in relatively peaceful bipartisan politics, with the former rebels now exercising political responsibility at local and federal level, but personal insecurity is high owing to violent crime. Even Mozambique, the cherub of the donor community, has been marred by recurrent political violence since general elections in 1999 that were won by the ruling Liberation Front of Mozambique (FRELIMO) with only 52.3 per cent of the vote, and continue to be contested virulently by Mozambican National Resistance (RENAMO) supporters.[45]

In all eight countries, despite instability, a relapse into full-fledged conflict has so far been avoided, and relative peace prevails in some form. Countries where there was a relapse into war before peacebuilding could take root, such as Angola, or where hostilities have not ended decisively, such as Algeria, were not included.

It should be noted that this book does not address transitions to democracy, and consequently does not address the literature on democratization. We refer here to a diverse range of countries emerging from conflict in varied circumstances. Some countries were already functioning or nominal democracies prior to and/or during conflict, like El Salvador. Some transited to democracy via elections as part of peace agreements or after conflict terminated, as in Mozambique. Some averted the democracy question altogether, for instance, when conflict ended through victory in battle, as in Rwanda. 'Peace' and 'justice' as addressed here are irreducible to and distinct from 'democracy' and 'human rights', which more often receive attention in post-conflict transitions.

Conclusion

Experiences and perceptions of injustice underlying or driving conflict do not disappear when peace is concluded. Restoring justice after conflict is not only a political task but also a social and personal imperative in the process of peacebuilding. The stakes involved in peacebuilding are high. The cost of relapse into conflict can be devastating in human and material terms. And such reversals are a real risk. Angola is a case in point: an internationally brokered peace agreement and UN-led multidimensional peacekeeping missions to oversee a peaceful transition have not sufficed to this day to end hostilities.

The call for justice arouses charged political and personal sentiments that are aggravated by the nature of the excesses committed during conflict. Perpetrators and their victims are obliged to live within the same borders in most cases. All survivors of conflict within a society rarely share a common conception of justice, and nor do the international actors involved. The process of restoring justice after conflict is, inevitably, contentious, all the more so when the means to restore justice are limited as in developing countries.

Post-conflict *re*construction and *re*habilitation do not need to imply a return to the *status quo ante*. This is recognized even by traditionally conservative agencies. The World Bank notes that 'conflict can present an opportunity to develop new social, political and economic systems that can better serve the needs of a changing society'.[46] The UN Development Program (UNDP) observes, 'The insights and lessons learned from crisis provide opportunities for constructive change and future reform. They are new points of departure on the path of innovation and sustainable development. Emergencies are often springboards for progress.'[47]

Addressing issues of justice is controversial even in peaceful societies, as it pits opposing conceptions of state, society and wellbeing against each other. The end of conflict and the transition to peace may seem the least promising time to forward the cause of justice. Yet this transition may also provide a watershed opportunity for societies to achieve greater justice while building peace.

2
Concepts of Justice in Contemporary Philosophy

Introduction: three dimensions of justice, an Aristotelian categorization

In chapter 1 three dimensions of justice – legal, rectificatory and distributive – were identified as relevant, interdependent and mutually reinforcing in the aftermath of conflict. This chapter overviews these three concepts of justice drawing on political and legal philosophy.[1] In doing so, it demonstrates the gap between philosophical theories or approaches to the three dimensions of justice on the one hand, and on the other hand the realities of injustice and the challenges of restoring justice in societies emerging from conflict.

This study mainly examines contemporary philosophy, as it is concerned with the reflections of current-day philosophers on the issues of justice raised here. However, a historical note is in order first on the origin and tradition of the concepts of justice discussed here. The three dimensions of justice identified correspond to Aristotle's categorization of justice in *Nicomachean Ethics*.[2] Aristotle divided justice between that which was 'lawful' and that which was 'fair'. The former he described as complete, universal or general justice. The latter he described as partial, particular or special justice. He further subdivided particular justice into two kinds, rectificatory and distributive justice.

Complete justice, for Aristotle, corresponded to what was lawful and is often translated as 'legal justice' or 'the rule of law'. In Aristotle's definition, complete justice 'consists in the exercise of the whole of virtue in our relations with our fellow men'. It required compliance with laws because 'the great majority of lawful acts are ordinances which are based on virtue as a whole: the law commands to live in conformity with every virtue and forbids to live in conformity with any wickedness'.[3] The task of rehabilitating the violated norms and debilitated institutions of the rule of law in societies emerging from conflict corresponds to restoring what Aristotle described as complete or legal justice.

Rectificatory justice, the first category of special / particular justice, was described by Aristotle as that which had a 'rectifying function in private transactions / exchanges'. Exchanges could be voluntary or involuntary. Aristotle subdivided involuntary exchanges into clandestine exchanges and forced exchanges. In clandestine exchanges / transactions he included 'theft, adultery, poisoning, procuring, enticement of slaves, assassination, and bearing false witness'. Involuntary exchanges / transactions under constraint included assault, imprisonment, murder, violent robbery, maiming, defamation and character smearing.[4] The task of addressing and rectifying violations committed during contemporary internal conflicts is comparable to Aristotle's rectificatory justice, particularly for involuntary clandestine and forced exchanges.

Aristotle described distributive justice as 'the distribution of honours, of material goods, or of anything else that can be divided among those who share in a political system'. Distributive justice claims hinge on inequality, for, according to Aristotle, 'in these matters it is possible for a man to have a share equal or unequal to that of his neighbour'.[5] The attempt in post-conflict societies to identify and address underlying causes of conflict that are often related to neglected grievances about unequal distributions of wealth, assets and opportunities is essentially an exercise in distributive justice.

In chapter 1 it was noted that the three dimensions of justice are interdependent in post-conflict societies. The three dimensions are also related and symmetrical at the conceptual level.

> There are three sorts of relationship: that of the parts to the whole, that of the whole to the parts, and that of one part to another. Legal justice pertains to the first, since it relates citizens to the State; distributive justice pertains to the second sort, since it relates the State to the citizens. Commutative justice pertains to the third, relating one private citizen to another.[6]

Beyond proposing this categorization, Aristotle also posited certain principles and measures for achieving rectificatory and distributive justice in *Nicomachean Ethics*. Judged by today's standards, many of them would be considered highly controversial at best and unfair at worst, and they are certainly not proposed here as applicable to war-torn societies today. The Aristotelian categorization is referred to strictly for the purpose of indicating that the three dimensions of justice identified as pertinent to war-torn societies have a long philosophical identity and tradition.

The concept of the rule of law

The rule of law has been portrayed in various ways. Some see it as a conceptual political ideal, others as a tangible legal institution. Some consider it the centrepiece of any viable political system, while others demonize it as the enemy of democracy. For some it is a current reality, for others a distant aspiration.[7] Its place in intellectual discourse is often traced back to Aristotle's popular injunction that the rule of law was preferable to the rule of man.[8] Despite the concept's recent resurgence in academic debate and international practice, and its popularity with aid donors in post-conflict and post-communist states, confusion persists about its meaning and scope among scholars and practitioners alike.[9]

The controversy over definition is partly attributable to the centuries-old dichotomy in legal philosophy between the traditions of natural law and positive law. The natural law tradition draws on Thomas Aquinas and his stipulation that 'a Law, properly speaking, regards first and foremost the order to the common good'.[10] Natural lawyers insist that the law has a necessary correlation to morality. Consequently, what the law 'is' cannot be separated from what the law 'must be'.[11]

In contrast, legal positivists stress what the law is, rather than what it ought to be. For positivists the source and formal criteria of law rather than its content is determinant. If it fulfils established criteria of legality, a bad law is still law. As articulated by the nineteenth-century lawyer John Austin, 'the existence of law is one thing; its merit or demerit is another'.[12] Legal positivists would clarify that they do not disregard morality, but simply place it afterwards. In their view naturalists, who deny that bad law is still law, are in fact denying or ignoring the moral questions raised by bad law, which, they would claim, positive law is better equipped to confront.[13]

It should be noted that some scholars dilute strict divisions between normative and factual judgements. Furthermore, newer approaches like critical legal studies, sociological jurisprudence and legal realism challenge the pre-eminence of these two schools of thought. Nevertheless, the opposing views of positive and natural law remain influential in legal philosophy.

While people use the term 'rule of law' without differentiation, on closer scrutiny one observes at least two quite different interpretations of the concept. The two predominant conceptions mirror positive and natural law respectively, and I describe them as 'minimalist' and 'maximalist'. Other scholars have noted a similar dichotomy. For example, Dworkin separates the 'rule book' conception from the 'rights' conception of the rule of law, and Prempeh distinguishes between the jurisprudence of executive supremacy and the jurisprudence of constitutionalism in Africa.[14] Yet there is little recognition or discussion by either scholars or practitioners of this basic dichotomy, which, I believe, is fundamental to understanding the concept of the rule of law.

The minimalist view

The position that I describe as 'minimalist' is akin to positivism. This view divests the rule of law of substantive and moral content, and draws its definition from the historical origin and role of the concept.[15] Traced back to the writings of Aristotle and Plato and, more recently, to the Magna Carta, the concept of the rule of law was devised as a means of protection from the arbitrariness of 'rule by man' and from the abuse of power by the state. Its main purpose was to subject human conduct to rules and consequently guarantee predictability in legal relationships and all interactions within the frame of law.[16] Typically, the rule of law in a minimalist perspective implies a government which is subject to and operates within the law, and which guarantees the protection of the individual from the state.

Hayek's definition of the rule of law best describes the minimalist position: 'Stripped of all its technicalities this means that government in all its actions is bound by rules fixed and announced beforehand – rules which make it possible to foresee with fair certainty how the authority will use its coercive powers in given circumstances, and to plan one's individual affairs on the basis of that knowledge.'[17] This certitude affords a certain degree of freedom to citizens who stay within the bounds of established rules. 'A predictable action of the state, i.e. its measurable interference, even if oppressive, is to be

Give ORGANIC STYLE and Get a Year for Yourself!

▶ DETACH AND MAIL THIS CARD TODAY! ▶

BUSINESS REPLY MAIL

FIRST-CLASS MAIL   PERMIT NO. 258   RED OAK, IA

POSTAGE WILL BE PAID BY ADDRESSEE

organic style™

PO BOX 8070
RED OAK, IA 51591-3070

Give the gift of organic style™

...and renew your own subscription!

Please enter a 1-year ORGANIC STYLE subscription for my friend below, and send me my own 1-year subscription at no additional cost! Bill me at the special price of just $11.96 for both subscriptions, and send my friend a card announcing my gift.

W4BG124

SEND GIFT SUBSCRIPTION TO:

NAME _____ (FIRST) _____ (LAST)

ADDRESS _____ APT. #

CITY _____ STATE _____ ZIP

BILL ME:

NAME _____ (FIRST) _____ (LAST)

ADDRESS _____ APT. #

CITY _____ STATE _____ ZIP

Send No Money Now. We'll Bill Your Gift After January 1, 2004!
Your friend's gift subscription starts with the new year.

D 10/598 \ 10/598 \ 20/1196   Published 10 times a year.   200192402 / Printed in USA preferred to immeasurable intervention (unpredictable, arbitrary action), even if at one time benevolent, as such immeasurable state of affairs creates insecurity.'[18]

One early manifestation was the *Rechtsstaat* or 'state of law' model, popularized in nineteenth-century continental Europe, which gave primacy to administrative control in a bid to eliminate arbitrariness. A state following iniquitous laws could, nevertheless, be a *Rechtsstaat*. Prominent legal scholars like Dicey, Hayek and Fuller rejected the *Rechtsstaat* as an inadequate and distorted expression of rule of law.[19] The minimalist position described here includes, but is generally broader than, the *Rechtsstaat*.

Minimalist rule of law can be consistent with various political systems besides democracy, such as theocracy or monarchy, as long as established laws and regular procedures to govern are followed. Furthermore, as minimalist proponents themselves concede, the rule of law could coexist with gross human rights violations, and discriminatory laws like apartheid.[20] It should be clarified nevertheless that the minimalist position, like positive law, is not necessarily unconcerned with substantive justice and values like human rights, but regards these as distinct ideals that are independent of the rule of law.[21]

The maximalist view

The position I describe as maximalist rule of law is closer to the natural law position. In this view, the rule of law is an umbrella encompassing structural, procedural as well as substantive elements.[22] In effect, the maximalist position might accept the minimalist position as a necessary starting point for the rule of law, but would find it incomplete.

In the maximalist view, the rule of law is more than mere rule *by* law, and requires more than a mechanistic series of structures and procedures for its realization. For maximalists, it is not possible to separate substantive justice from formal justice, as minimalists would insist. For maximalists, laws are about justice. The nineteenth-century jurist Dicey popularized the notion that the rule of law consisted of more than its institutions and its predictability, and included values like equality and human rights.

> The 'rule of law' . . . which forms a fundamental principle of the constitution, has three meanings. It means, in the first place, the absolute supremacy or predominance of regular law as opposed to the influence

of arbitrary power; . . . [second] equality before the law; . . . [third] the laws of the constitution are . . . the consequence of the rights of individuals.[23]

The rule of law in the maximalist conception is sometimes cast as a Western concept applicable only to liberal democracies or common law countries, but its defenders consider it to be universal and applicable to diverse systems. Maximalists observe that countries as diverse as Canada, India and Zambia champion the rule of law, and argue that it is more rather than less relevant in developing countries.[24]

A lucid contemporary definition of maximalist rule of law as distinct from minimalism is provided by the Organization for Security and Cooperation in Europe (OSCE), which sports a relatively diverse membership in political, historical and cultural terms.

> The rule of law does not merely mean formal legality which assures regularity and consistency in the achievement and enforcement of democratic order, but justice based on the recognition and full acceptance of the supreme value of the human personality and guaranteed by institutions providing a framework for its fullest expression.[25]

Dworkin concedes that his 'rights' conception is less clearly articulated, and consequently more politically controversial and philosophically contestable, than the more straightforward 'rule book' conception, and the same could be said of maximalism vis-à-vis minimalism.[26] The maximalist view is, clearly, more ambitious in scope and aspiration. It is also more dispersed, complex and unclear than the delimited, clearly defined and pragmatic minimalist position. Consequently, maximalist rule of law is more susceptible to failure, or more resistant to success, than the minimalist. This is a consequence maximalists would willingly accept for their insistence that substance supersedes form and justice overrides rules.

Commonality and divergence

Despite their divergence on content, the two positions share some common ground on the form and structure of the rule of law. Both positions require conformity to principles of the rule of law or legality. These principles require that laws be general; promulgated; clear and open; non-contradictory; prospective; constant and relatively stable; possible; and that official action be congruent with declared rule.[27] Both positions would agree that courts should be easily accessible, and that principles of natural justice should be observed, such as open and fair hearing, absence of bias, and due process, to ensure the impartial and regular functioning of the legal order. Both would also concede that courts should have judicial review powers over legislation and administrative action.[28]

The OSCE catalogues the 'elements of justice' that constitute requisite conditions to establish the rule of law. They are: representative government with an accountable executive; a government acting in compliance with the constitution and the law; clear separation of powers between the government and political parties; a civilian-controlled military and police; an independent judiciary; an independent bar association and protection of legal practitioners; public procedure in the adoption of legislation; publication of administrative regulations as a condition for their validity; effective and publicly known means of redress to citizens against administrative decisions. So far, this list could be consistent with both views, although it is primarily 'minimalist' in subjecting government to rules and eliminating arbitrariness. However, the OSCE document goes further: it explicitly includes in its conditions the guarantee of human rights and fundamental freedoms, and consciously links the rule of law to democracy.[29] This gives the OSCE's articulation a distinctly maximalist orientation, which the minimalist position would reject.

The outstanding difference between the maximalist and minimalist views concerns not the form of the rule of law but its fundamental ethos. The crux is whether the substantive and moral content of laws is and should be a determinant or rather a peripheral feature of the rule of law, and whether the concern should be with form or substance. This apparently minor conceptual divergence has major practical implications. In the absence of a single clear, dominant conception of the rule of law, and the absence of debate about divergent views, practitioners remain confused as to whether rebuilding the rule of law requires rehabilitating its structures or reconstituting its substance.[30]

Human rights and the rule of law: an overlap?

The boundary between the rule of law and human rights is unclear both in theory and practice.[31] The minimalist view regards human rights as entirely separate from and unrelated to the rule of law. In contrast, the maximalist view considers human rights and values to be a fundamental underpinning of the rule of law. Maximalists typically restrict the purview of the rule of law to political and civil rights. A more extreme maximalist depiction of the rule of law is as: 'A dynamic concept... which should be employed not only to safeguard and advance the civil and political rights of the individual in a free society, but also to establish social, economic, educational and cultural conditions under which his legitimate aspirations and dignity may be realized'.[32]

Human rights and the rule of law are linked historically and functionally. Both concepts emerged, albeit at different times, as responses to the threat of state abuse of power, in order to defend citizens' rights and security. The two are also functionally interdependent. Fundamental human rights encoded in international covenants like the International Covenant on Civil and Political Rights (ICCPR) can be protected only if institutions of the rule of law function effectively. For example, to guarantee rights to life, and freedom from arbitrary arrest, degrading punishment, and torture, a state requires an independent judiciary, a disciplined civilian police force and an efficient prison system. Procedural requirements encoded in the ICCPR like the right to fair trial, the presumption of innocence, and the non-applicability of retroactive laws echo principles of legality and can be fulfilled only in a rule of law regime.

International treaties and declarations draw a clear link between human rights protection and the provision of a rule of law framework to safeguard these rights. The preamble of the Universal Declaration of Human Rights states: 'It is essential, if man is not to have recourse, as a last resort, to rebellion against tyranny and oppression, that human rights should be protected by the rule of law.'[33]

In practice, human rights promotion constitutes an important aspect of international peacebuilding efforts in post-conflict societies. Practitioners adopting a functional view falling somewhere between the maximalist and minimalist positions might consider the rule of law to be instrumentally necessary to achieve human rights objectives. Until recently, human rights promotion primarily entailed monitoring government behaviour. Today human rights programmes include assistance to governments in strengthening rule of law institutions and procedures that are necessary to protect human rights. Programmes also include human rights education to institutions and officials responsible for the rule of law and law enforcement – to government and civil administration officials, judges and lawyers, the police and the military. Consequently, in practice, the rule of law and human rights tend to overlap and theoretical boundaries between the two become unclear. Once in the field, there is a tendency in some programmes to link the two, and some practitioners even refer to the two terms interchangeably.

Despite the overlap, the two concepts are not identical. The rule of law, in both minimalist and maximalist forms, is more than a vehicle to protect individual human rights. It is also a check on effective governance, and an independent, non-partisan forum for non-violent conflict resolution. It is often suggested that a human rights framework is desirable and even necessary for the operationalization of the rule of law, especially in post-conflict societies. Even if this were accepted, it is necessary to distinguish human rights objectives from rule of law objectives so that the two are not subsumed into one another. One danger in subsuming the two is that distinct human rights objectives may be overlooked in an overall attention to the rule of law. Practitioners note that today both recipient countries and donors prefer the more neutral language of rule of law to the accusatory discourse of human rights. Governments find it more palatable to accept assistance to rebuild the rule of law than to accept an international presence monitoring their human rights performance.[34]

In conclusion, this discussion revealed the impasse between two predominant and divergent conceptions of the rule of law, and an undefined relationship to human rights. Legal and political philosophy does not provide conceptual clarity and guidance to practitioners seeking to rebuild the rule of law in war-torn societies. The maximalist position must determine how to integrate human rights without reducing rule of law to rights or being subsumed by them. The minimalist position must reconsider whether the theoretical separation of justice and rights from law is tenable in practice, particularly in war-torn societies experiencing massive injustice. The current impasse needs to be bridged.

The concept of rectificatory justice

Rectificatory justice is about righting wrongs committed against, or harm done to, other individuals. The concept of rectificatory justice as such has attracted scant scholarly attention since its identification by Aristotle in *Nicomachean Ethics*. The term itself was soon discarded from philosophical discourse. Finnis describes how Thomas Aquinas, 'purporting to interpret Aristotle faithfully, silently shifted the meaning of Aristotle's second class of particular justice, and invented a new term for it: "commutative justice"'. This new term was taken to cover 'the whole field in which ... the problem is to determine what dealings are proper between persons (including groups)'.[35] However, commutative justice so defined is too unspecific to be relevant or applicable to the context of post-conflict societies, as it does not refer to righting wrongs. We are interested in Aristotle's original term, rectificatory justice, which addresses precisely the correction of harm done, in our case, in the course of conflict. An obstacle to applying the concept of rectificatory justice in post-conflict societies lies in the difficulty of locating a body of relevant philosophical literature on the subject, as described below.

In legal, political and social philosophy, *punishment* has come to be treated as the primary and necessary response to wrong done, and, in that sense, offers a substitute to rectificatory justice in philosophical literature.[36] Punishment is defined as 'the imposition of some kind of suffering, pain, restriction, or burden' for harm done.[37] Punishment has been studied for centuries across a variety of disciplines, generating diverse opinions between thinkers about how to justify, determine and apportion punishment. The two dominant views are, first, retributive punishment, often referred to as 'backward-looking', and, second, consequentialist or utilitarian punishment, referred to as 'forward-looking'.[38] The two positions differ in their responses to three basic questions: why punish, who to punish and how much to punish.[39]

Utilitarian punishment

Utility or the 'greatest happiness principle' is the central tenet of utilitarianism espoused by its founders Bentham and Mills.[40] Utilitarianism is a consequentialist or teleological approach that 'recommends a choice of actions on the basis of consequences, and an assessment of consequences in terms of welfare'.[41] Consequentialism justifies policies and institutions based solely on their social consequences.

Utilitarian punishment answers 'why' punish by identifying three social benefits. The first is deterrence: preventing similar abuses by other potential offenders. The second is incapacitation: distancing the criminals from the society they may harm and preventing them from repeating the offence. The third is rehabilitation: reforming or correcting individuals and their conduct through re-education.

In response to 'who to punish', utilitarians say that punishment should be administered only when warranted by the utility principle, that is, only when punishing someone will serve some social good. On strict interpretation, this implies that innocent persons may occasionally be punished, accidentally or deliberately, for the public good. In calculating how much to punish, utilitarians are seen to neglect proportionality. This is not entirely accurate: as Bentham noted, 'the value of the punishment must not be less in any case than what is sufficient to outweigh that of the profit of the offence'.[42]

Utilitarian punishment is 'forward-looking' because it is less concerned with the crime itself than with the effect of punishment on society. It is inherently a preventive and deterrent view of punishment rather than one aimed at meting out to offenders their 'just deserts' for past misdeeds. Utilitarian punishment is sharply criticized by retributivists and liberals. Retributivists accuse utilitarians of treating people as means rather than ends by punishing them for societal utility, rather than out of reprobation for harm done and suffering caused. Retributivists object fiercely to the implicit danger in utilitarian punishment of punishing innocent individuals for the common good. They feel that the utilitarian urge to incapacitate or rehabilitate offenders treats people as animals or as sub-human.[43] Retributivists strongly oppose punishments based on rehabilitation and therapeutic treatment of offenders. They claim that attempting to reform offenders robs them of their autonomy and denies the equal worth of all humans.[44] Liberal thinkers also oppose utilitarian objectives of rehabilitation and incapacitation. Regarding rehabilitation, liberals argue that 'the state has no right to subject a citizen to treatment against her will for her own supposed benefit'. Regarding incapacitation, liberals argue that 'people are detained not for what they have done but because of what they might do if not detained', again undermining their freedom and moral agency.[45]

Newer versions of utilitarianism like liberal utilitarianism attempt to respond to these critiques, and argue that retributivism does not respond better to these critiques either.[46] Nevertheless, these critiques have weakened utilitarian punishment, and strengthened retributive punishment.

Retributive justice

Retribution is a deontological or duty-based approach, strongly influenced by Kantian and Hegelian philosophy. For Kant, 'Both the love of man and respect for his rights are duties, but the former is only conditional, while the latter is unconditioned and inevitably obligatory.'[47] The basic retributive urge is that wrongdoing must be punished simply because the wrongful act merits condemnation and punishment. A retributivist is someone who insists that it is a moral obligation to inflict suffering on a wrongdoer regardless of society's symbols or conventions.[48] Retributive justice is 'backward-looking' because its *raison d'être* is rooted in the past, in the commission of the act.

The response to 'why punish' derives from Kant's stricture that the penal law is a 'categorical imperative'.[49] Kant insisted it was both society's right and its duty to punish the offender. According to Hegel, it was also the offender's right to be punished: 'The injury which is inflicted on the criminal is not only just *in itself*...; it is also a *right for the criminal himself*, that is, a right *posited* in his *existent* will, in his action.'[50] Retribution offers two answers to the question of who to punish. Positive retribution holds that only the guilty (that is, those proven culpable) should be punished. Negative retribution holds that the innocent should not be punished. To determine how and how much to punish, retributivists use the principle of *ius talionis* or retribution/restitution, and emphasize proportionality in punishment. Kant insisted on capital punishment for murderers: 'If he has committed a murder, he must *die*. No possible substitute can satisfy justice.'[51] Kant believed that the state could never transfer its sovereignty, particularly regarding its duty to punish offending citizens. Several retributivists soften Kant's position by saying that proportionality does not imply 'an eye for an eye', but simply that the punishment must fit the crime by being severe enough to match the crime and the 'just deserts' the criminal merits.

In the 1950s 'the retributive theory of punishment appeared dead', and utilitarianism and welfare served as the basis for the justification and design of penal punishments.[52] However, retributivism was revived in the 1970s by Anglo-Saxon thinkers who objected increasingly to utilitarian punishment and concern for offenders' rights. Renewed retributivism was also fuelled by anxiety over rising crime and widespread perceptions of the latitude of utilitarian-based criminal justice systems. In *Wild Justice*, Jacoby captures the popular rise of retributivism. Legal and penal institutions seek to repress retributive sentiments by distancing victims from offenders, and provide institutional responses to natural impulses to seek revenge. Indeed, Jacoby describes how 'the very word "revenge" has pejorative connotations', and is considered barbaric and uncivilized.[53] Yet Jacoby notes that weak punishments only aggravate desires for revenge. She observes rising support, particularly in the USA and Europe, for harsher responses to crime, and popular disdain for and disappointment with criminal justice systems that let criminals off too lightly. Retributivists note that 'retributive hatred' is in fact the natural and appropriate response to certain kinds of wrongdoing, and that it can be morally inappropriate to overcome such natural resentment in the attempt to forgive.[54] Consequently, alongside concern for offenders' rights, 'a dominant slogan of the new retributivism of the 1970s was "just deserts"', which was defended as the central and perhaps the only aim of punishment.[55] Several lawyers, philosophers, criminologists and legislators began to see trials as the necessary retributive response to violations.[56]

Some retributivists defend the symbolic or expressive value of punishment. They note that retributive desires flow not only from the so-called primitive 'desire to "strike back" at one's assailant', but also 'from the need to restore "something missing" – a sense of physical and emotional integrity that is shattered by violence'.[57] An offender's act, whether intended or unintentional, 'sends a false message about the value of the victim relative to the criminal', and makes the victim feel worthless.[58] As Hampton argues, a retributive response is required to reverse this effect symbolically, and punishment functions as a revalidation of the victim's worth. Lawyers too have used retributive arguments to defend trials as a way of vindicating victims by demonstrating that societies care about their suffering.[59]

Some retributivists, like Duff, believe that punishment must be essentially communicative. Punishment must go beyond mere expression, 'which requires only an expresser', to communication, which 'by contrast is essentially a two-way rational activity'.[60] Penance is the second central notion in Duff's conception. 'A penance is, ideally, a punishment which a wrongdoer imposes on herself – a painful burden to which she subjects herself because she has done wrong.' Punishment in this conception is both retributive, in imposing suffering on the offender, and forward-looking, in aiming to induce 'the process of repentance, reform and reparation which will restore the offender's moral standing in the community whose values she flouted'.[61] It is a narrower view of 'forward-looking' punishment than utilitarianism, as it focuses on the individual offender rather than on societal benefits.

Some scholars base their approach on community values rather than prevalent liberal thinking that underlines individual accountability. Both Duff's and Hampton's positions incorporate notions of community. Lacey goes further in proposing a 'community conception' of punishment explicitly based on communitarianism. Her vision is: 'A society genuinely committed to pursuing with equal concern the welfare and autonomy of each of its citizens, and of creating an environment in which human beings may flourish and develop, whilst acknowledging the role of the community in constructing the values and human interests which it seeks to defend'.[62] Some scholars who propose ideal theory or community-based conceptions recognize the divide between ideals and reality. Duff concedes that his conception is ideal theory that is suited only to perfect systems where there is a genuine sense of community; where this is absent Duff proposes radical social change 'to transform ourselves into the kind of community that could justly punish'.[63]

Retributivism faces serious challenges despite its renewed popularity. Retributivists cannot avoid the question of whether states today have the moral authority to mete out retributive punishment. Duff and other scholars recognize the failings and frequent injustice of penal and criminal justice systems and prevalent social injustice in many societies. If societies are themselves not legally and socially just, state-imposed punishment could represent an added injustice on offenders who are themselves victims of structural injustice. Murphy questions the right of societies to punish offenders. He critiques the Kantian view of a gentlemen's club of equals, where an offender breaks known and accepted rules, and, consequently, deserves and *calls for* his own punishment. As Murphy notes, criminal offenders are often people who have been excluded and marginalized from their societies and feel no sense of belonging to a society or adherence to its rules.[64] Many retributivists accept this critique. Hampton acknowledges the dubious 'moral credibility' and hypocrisy of state punishment which ignores the fact that punished offenders are often 'themselves far more victimized'.[65] Retributivism is also susceptible to the criticism that it is not a viable social theory as it does not provide adequate justification for the social institutions of punishment. Retributivists believe in the moral obligation to punish and the expressive or communicative value of punishment, but overlook that punishment in practice is often difficult to justify for the reasons outlined above. Hart's hybrid theory stemmed from his recognition of the need to combine retributive and utilitarian principles to justify punishment.[66] The retributive argument will remain incomplete until it adopts a hybrid approach and provides better justification for punishment.

Informal justice

The variety of alternative approaches to punishment described as 'informal justice' emerged in the 1970s from the dissatisfaction of penal practitioners and reformers with existing punitive mechanisms, including utilitarian and retributive approaches. The underlying belief was that 'more informal forms of dispute processing' would 'provide a greater level of participation and access to justice while overcoming some of the major deficiencies of the formal legal process'. Proponents

of informal justice believed it would be more flexible and accountable, and also 'of benefit not only to the offender and victim but also
to the wider community'.[67] Informal justice was characterized by
responses which were 'informal, ... noncoercive, ... nonbureaucratic,
decentralized, relatively undifferentiated, and non-professional', and
rapidly became 'a phenomenon of international provenance and
rapidly growing significance'.[68] Informal justice aimed to be reparative, reconciliatory and restorative, in contrast to retributivism and
utilitarianism.[69] Some forms adopted techniques of mediation.
'Victim–Offender Reconciliation Programmes' (VORPs) were one
popular experiment using mediation.[70] Other versions borrowed
principles of conflict resolution.[71] Some emphasized co-operative
problem solving.[72] Punishments in the community were often preferred to custodial punishments.

The ill-defined relationship between formal and informal justice
has created confusion. It is unclear whether informal justice measures
are intended and viable as complements or as alternatives to formal
legal measures. Abolitionists within informal justice wish to dispense
with legal mechanisms altogether, while other proponents see informal measures like VORPs functioning in parallel to and supported by
legal institutions.[73]

The reliance of many informal justice measures on community is
both its originality and its weakness. Informal justice has received
similar criticism to ideal theories of communitarianism, like Lacey's,
noted above. Critics question the relevance and feasibility of community-based informal justice at a time when the widespread reality in
most societies is observed to be fragmenting communities and crum-
bling values. 'Reconciliatory justice is possible and appropriate only
between neighbours or friends (in a broad sense of that term); between people whose lives are structured by shared values and mutual
concerns.' Furthermore, informal community-mediated justice can be
more violent, repressive and conflictual than court-ordained measures, as 'communities can, after all, be harsh, hostile and exclusion-
ary'.[74]

Initial optimism generated by radical ideas of informal justice has
dwindled. Critics note that informal justice measures often create a
two-track system that reinforces and even exacerbates the unequal
access to legal justice. Minor cases or poor people's cases go through
informal channels, while formal legal channels remain in the domain
of the rich, as before. They observe, 'not incidentally, alternatives
prevent the use of courts for redistributive purposes in the interest
of equality, by consigning the rights of disadvantaged citizens to
institutions with minimal power to enforce or protect them'.[75] Critics

argue that informal justice's 'substantive and procedural rules are imprecise, unwritten, democratic, flexible, ad-hoc, and particularistic', and could prove as dangerous in practice as they appear promising in rhetoric.[76] In contrast to the stated aims of informal justice, critics observed that in practice: 'Contemporary informal legal institutions clearly do increase state control, although they seek to appear to withdraw it, and are just as clearly coercive, although they try to disguise coercion in the forms of volition.'[77] Although informal justice is still favoured by penal reformers, some scholars like Auerbach find it necessary to 'beware of the seductive appeal of alternative institutions', and prefer the imperfections of formal laws to the incertitude of informal justice.[78]

To summarize, there are no clearly viable responses to rectificatory justice in the available philosophical literature today. If the next best alternative, punishment, is adopted as the rectificatory response, the shortcomings of the main approaches to punishment raise considerable concern. Neither utilitarian, retributive nor informal conceptions of punishment offer an adequate substitute to the concept of rectificatory justice, none offers a robust response to the challenge of rectifying harm done, and none appears particularly applicable to war-torn societies emerging from conflict. Effectively, as Duff notes, 'there is no course of action available to us that is completely justifiable or free from moral wrong'. Consequently, 'The radical imperfection not only of our existing legal institutions, but also of our own moral capacities ... should induce a salubrious humility and restraint in our treatment of, and our attitudes towards, those who break the law.'[79]

These observations are particularly appropriate in the context of war-torn societies where the imperfections of the law are acute, as we will observe in chapters 3 and 4. This discussion also exposes the linkage between the three dimensions of justice. Even in states with a well-established rule of law, it is questionable whether states are competent and able to mete out just punishment. Second, it is debatable whether states possess the moral authority to administer punishment in situations where offenders are often themselves victims of structural and distributive injustices within their societies. On this note, we turn to the third and last dimension, distributive justice.

The concept of distributive justice

Distributive justice, or social justice as it is interchangeably called, is the most extensively examined of the three dimensions of justice over the centuries, and more particularly since the 1970s, galvanized by Rawls's seminal work.[80] Given the abundance and diversity of contemporary approaches to distributive justice, we focus on aspects relevant to the aims of this book.[81] Therefore, we address only three categories of distributive justice that are salient concerns in developing countries, particularly those emerging from conflict: needs, rights and inequality.[82]

Needs

A pressing distributive concern in developing countries, which is of great relevance in post-conflict societies, is fulfilling citizens' basic needs in conditions of scarcity. Although some philosophers, like O'Neill, recognize that 'a full account of international distributive justice would require a complete theory of human needs', they do not provide it. Consequently, 'much modern ethical thought makes no use of the category of needs'.[83] Three reasons could be posited for the neglect of needs.

First, philosophers have concerned themselves with principles for distributing surplus in society, presuming that needs are already fulfilled. That is, they may recognize, like Sadurski, that 'satisfaction of basic needs is a prerequisite' for theories of distributive justice to be applicable.[84] However, contemporary philosophers do not concern themselves with how this 'prerequisite' condition is fulfilled, perhaps because they operate primarily in high-income rather than low-income societies.

Second, philosophers argue that needs are means rather than ends in themselves. Consequently, 'a political philosopher has to take no special account of needs', because 'the only interesting questions arise in connection with the ends'.[85] This argument might apply to instrumental needs that are means to ends. Intrinsic or basic needs *are* ends in themselves, as they represent the minimum without which individuals cannot survive, and, therefore, ought to elicit philosophical interest.

Last, some philosophers argue that needs constitute a fluid and expansive category, indistinguishable from wants or desires, and therefore a superfluous basis for distributive justice. However, this argument is weak, as scholars have rigorously defined needs, distinguished them from wants, and prioritized them according to importance.[86] Some scholars identify 'basic needs' as the most urgent needs essential for survival, including food, shelter, sanitation, health and education.[87] It is accepted that of the vast category of needs, 'only basic needs unquestionably require social intervention for the sake of justice'.[88]

Despite the importance of need, as Miller concedes, 'it is safe to generalize that in no society has distribution according to need become the main element in a shared conception of social justice'.[89] With few exceptions, distributive justice theories today neither discuss needs nor address the fundamental distributive question in poor societies of how basic needs for survival may be met within scarce means. One possible avenue for addressing needs might lie in Sen's and Nussbaum's related concept of 'capabilities', which are defined as 'a set of vectors of functionings reflecting the person's freedom to lead one type of life or another'.[90] However, so far the 'capabilities' approach has not been applied to concerns of distributive justice in post-conflict developing societies.

Rights

Unlike needs, rights have received considerable attention from political philosophers. Rights-based approaches to justice fall within what is described as the deontological tradition deriving from duty or obligations, in contrast to teleological or goal-based theories like utilitarianism.[91] Rights are sometimes associated with libertarian views of distributive justice, whose main concern is to preserve the entitlements of (usually privileged) individuals from encroachment, particularly by the state.[92] The 'central demand of libertarian justice whether national or international is: do not redistribute'.[93] Libertarianism is irrelevant to this discussion, therefore, and is not considered further.

Various rights are distinguished in political philosophy: prosthetic and conservative rights, legal and moral rights, claim rights and ideal rights.[94] The concern here is with universal human rights enshrined in the International Bill of Human Rights. This includes civil-political rights, encoded in the ICCPR, as well as socio-economic and cultural rights, encoded in the International Covenant on Economic, Social and Cultural Rights (ICESCR). Both sets taken together rightly form the subject matter of distributive justice.[95]

Despite their claim to universality under international law, human rights are controversial in political philosophy. Some philosophers accept the category of civil-political rights which they describe as negative rights, in that they purportedly require no 'positive' action by states to enforce them, but only 'negative' or preventive action to prevent their encroachment. Yet they oppose the concept of socio-economic rights, which they describe as 'positive' rights, in that their fulfilment requires positive intervention and action by the state or other actors.[96] Their main conceptual difficulty with positive rights is the problem of assigning agency, in contrast to negative rights, where agency is easier to assign, typically to governments. These scholars describe positive rights as 'manifesto' rights. As no identifiable agent can be allocated to the corresponding obligations raised by these rights, they create imperfect obligations, and the right 'disappears'.[97]

This distinction between negative and positive rights is misleading. Negative rights, such as the right to life and liberty, or protection from torture, also require positive, resource-consuming action by states, such as the maintenance of a police force, a judiciary, and a penal system to guarantee and protect these rights.[98] That is, a 'positive' action is required even to protect so-called negative rights. There is no valid basis, consequently, for prioritizing negative over positive rights, particularly in impoverished post-conflict countries.

The argument of unassigned agency is also weak, I would contend. In the case of both positive rights, encoded in the ICESCR, and negative rights, encoded in the ICCPR, the manifest agent is the government that ratifies the treaty. If it is argued that positive rights create imperfect obligations, it is not because there is no assignable agent, but because poor countries' governments may simply lack resources and capacity – agency – to fulfil their obligations. The ICESCR itself explicitly recognizes these difficulties, and provides for developing countries to meet their obligations gradually and incrementally. If both negative rights and positive rights require resources, capacity and positive action, then the governments in poor countries will be (and often are) equally incapable of meeting either set of obligations, in which case the distinction between perfect and imperfect obligations no longer holds.

It must be recognized, then, that governments in poor countries have difficulty fulfilling both negative and positive rights. The rights approach to distributive justice will have meaning in developing countries only if both socio-economic and civil-political rights are put on the same footing, and impoverished, embattled governments are assisted in providing both simultaneously. The World Conference on Human Rights in 1993 asserted in its final Vienna Declaration that 'all human rights are universal, indivisible and interdependent and interrelated'. It also asserted that 'the lack of development may not be invoked to justify the abridgement of internationally recognized human rights', and reaffirmed the right to development.[99] International legal opinion holds that both sets of rights enjoy the same legal status and validity, yet lawyers themselves acknowledge that socio-economic rights have been marginalized in academia and international practice in preference for political rights.[100] Although it is common wisdom that providing the basic needs for survival and a decent living through the provision of economic rights is the minimum prerequisite to exercise the political rights to life and liberty that liberals cherish, this interdependence is often neglected.[101] It is arguable that 'the paradigm of rights [is] so narrowly articulated, it has little room for a meaningful notion of justice', particularly when their remit is limited to political rights.[102]

Some deontologists present a *duty-based* approach as an alternative to overcome the shortcomings of rights approaches. The appeal to duties and obligations has gained considerable ethical and political support in recent years, due to dissatisfaction with expanding demands for rights without reference to the corresponding responsibilities of rights claimants.[103] O'Neill proposes a duty-based approach to distributive justice based on a Kantian framework.[104] Reacting to the inadequacies of rights, this approach attempts to encourage governments and other external actors to respond to distributive justice claims based on duty, rather than rights.

O'Neill's duty approach is conceptually appealing. However, I argue that it is impracticable. Duties lack even the limited acceptability and enforceability that rights have acquired gradually, through developments in international human rights law. O'Neill provides an unconvincing account of why governments might feel obligated to act spontaneously based on Kantian duty, when they are unable or unwilling to fulfil even their legally binding international obligations. O'Neill portrays duties as overcoming the imperfect obligation problem encountered by positive rights. However, her argument neglects the fact that duties too, however convincingly demonstrated in philosophical argument, lack 'teeth' if they are not encoded and enforced through domestic law or international treaty. O'Neill effectively substitutes 'manifesto rights' with 'manifesto duties'. Human rights, whatever their shortcomings in theory and practice, are already established in political and legal discourse; they have rapidly expanded and been codified in the last fifty years, and are constantly evolving.[105] The translation of duties into legally enforceable action is not imminent, albeit their popularity in some circles.

O'Neill's rejection of rights undermines her attempt to privilege duties above rights. Although duties/obligations are not as visible as rights in international legal and political practice, they are fundamental to international law, for 'responsibility is the necessary corollary of a right'.[106] Even the leading utilitarian, Bentham, recognized that to have a right is to be the beneficiary of someone else's duty.[107]

The deontological approach is appealing but inadequate in present form. The rights approach pays insufficient attention to socio-economic rights; the duty approach lacks enforceability, but resists association with rights discourse to gain the teeth it requires. Rights and duties are more effective, I would argue, when treated as complements rather than competitors, as they collectively provide a stronger impulsion for action.[108]

We had mentioned earlier retributivist critiques of utilitarian punishment. It is important to note before closing the opposition between deontological and utilitarian perspectives on distributive justice as well, as deontologists explicitly seek to counter utilitarians in their many varieties.[109] Deontologists question the validity of an aggregative theory for what they see as the essentially individual value of justice. Deontologists criticize utilitarians for treating individuals as means rather than ends, and as mere units in a calculus; they reject utilitarianism's sacrifice of individual justice for social welfare.[110] Notwithstanding the ethical basis of these critiques, the categorical rejection of utilitarianism by deontologists is unhelpful to the cause of distributive justice. Despite his anti-utilitarian position, Rawls himself conceded, 'all ethical doctrines worth our attention take consequences into account in judging rightness. One which did not would simply be irrational, crazy.'[111] Miller agrees: 'Even if the basic moral demand of justice is not founded on utility, it may still be a necessary condition of the emergence of justice that it should be socially useful.'[112] In conclusion, then, deontological approaches may need to adopt some utilitarian concerns if they are to be meaningful, especially in resource-scarce developing countries where there is a premium on maximizing welfare.

Inequality

Addressing inequality would appear a logical focus for theories of distributive justice. Yet inequality and equality receive inadequate attention in many current theories. Recent theories of distributive justice have based themselves on one or more of the following principles: contractual arrangements; fairness; mutual advantage; 'desert' or 'to each according to his due'; the contribution principle which justifies differential returns to individuals based on the differing value of their respective contributions to society.[113]

These varied approaches may be conceptually rigorous and theoretically sound, but they lack applicability to the realities of low-income societies and war-torn contexts. The assumptions in contract theories of rough equality between individuals and the exercise of rational free choice make them impracticable in societies where individuals and groups are grossly unequal, and free choice is enjoyed at best by an elite minority. Fairness and mutual advantage are unfeasible bases in societies where individuals have been treated unfairly for generations, or where distributive decisions have been made unilaterally by 'haves' to the deliberate disadvantage of 'have-nots'. Desert is inappropriate for apportioning shares in societies where one's due is determined not by differential merit or talent, but by unequal or politically manipulated access to opportunities. The contribution principle is unsatisfactory as it overlooks the role of society in apportioning differing value to contributions, often based on existing social hierarchies – for example a doctor's contribution being greater than a trash collector's, or a salaried employee's contribution being greater than a community worker's. Rather than seeking egalitarian procedures or outcomes, these theories attempt to explain or justify existing social inequalities, and may effectively reinforce rather than counter them.

A theoretical position can provide a credible and viable framework for distributive justice in a society only if it is embedded within the parameters of inequality and deprivation experienced in that society. Current approaches to distributive justice, as noted above, are not. For instance, many philosophers regard Rawls's contract-based theory, especially the difference principle, as a basis for a globally applicable principle of redistribution. Yet Rawls himself concedes that his theory was applicable only to liberal democracies, and inapplicable elsewhere.[114]

Egalitarianism, in contrast to the theories depicted above, addresses inequality directly and seeks egalitarian distributive principles, which, in particular, might aid the worst-off. The first question facing egalitarians is 'equality of what?', and a variety of responses are offered.[115]

For Rawls, 'primary goods' are the unit of measure for equality, which, in his all-encompassing conception, included 'rights, liberties and opportunities, income and wealth and the social bases of self-respect'.[116]

Dworkin counters Rawls by underlining the distinction between 'treating people equally with respect to one or other commodity or opportunity, and treating them as equals'. Dworkin compares carefully the benefits of pursuing equality of welfare on one hand and resources on the other. He opts for equality of resources, although he concedes that equality of resources is a 'complex' and probably 'indeterminate' ideal.[117]

Walzer introduces a radically different perspective with his concept of complex equality. He observes, 'equality is a complex relationship between persons ... it is not an identity of possessions'. Consequently, he argues, equality requires not a single distributive principle but 'a diversity of distributive criteria that mirrors the diversity of social goods'.[118] Walzer bases his account on the differing values and meanings diverse societies seem to attribute to different goods. Walzer is sharply criticized by his peers like Dworkin. Nonetheless, Walzer's insight that a single distributive principle may not suffice even within an individual society is deeply instructive, and is particularly relevant in the context of poor, war-torn societies with deep, complex and multifaceted inequalities.

Sen cuts through these diverse accounts by observing that all theories of distributive justice, whether egalitarian or libertarian, seek equality of something. With Nussbaum, Sen argues that the goal should not be the pursuit of some equality of possessions or of end-states (wellbeing), but rather the equality of *freedom* to pursue capabilities. Sen notes that most philosophical accounts discount the diversity of humans, and presume uniformity. Sen's and Nussbaum's approach attempts to be sensitive to endless human diversity. It 'concentrates on our capability to achieve valuable functionings that make up our lives, and more generally, our freedom to promote objectives'.[119] This approach has already been applied to analyse inequalities in developing countries, and Sen argues that freedom to pursue capabilities is the key to development.[120] It could usefully be developed further to address the specific exigencies of distributive justice in developing countries emerging from conflict.

It should be noted that egalitarian theories are persistently attacked on two grounds. The first is the overwhelming concern, primarily among economists, that equality is not efficient. Sen, both an economist and a philosopher, has countered forcefully that equality can be efficient, and does not need to be detrimental to society and economy.[121] The second ground is that equality is at odds with liberty, which, if justified, poses a significant moral concern for philosophers. This concern prompted Rawls to prioritize liberty above his egalitarian difference principle.[122] However, some liberal egalitarians disagree. Dworkin demonstrates why liberal thinkers must take on the challenge of equality, and he argues forcefully that liberty and equality are allies, not enemies, as long as neither is pursued to an extreme.[123]

Despite the strength and moral appeal of egalitarian arguments, it should be noted that equality and egalitarianism remain neglected in both theory and practice today. Even in Western societies, where inequalities are less steep and contentious than in many war-torn developing societies, as Taylor notes, 'there is great strain...between the drive for equality on the one hand and the sense of justified differentials which the contribution principle yields on the other'.[124] The fall of communism and its professed if unsuccessful prioritization of need-based equality and socio-economic above civil-political rights and the concomitant rise of globalized market economies may have strengthened the trend to justify rather than diminish distributive inequalities, and to overlook needs, rights and equality as criteria for distributive justice.

In conclusion, despite the wealth of literature on distributive justice, very few scholars address the three criteria most relevant to developing societies emerging from conflict – need, rights and equality. Consequently the dimension of justice that is the most richly studied in political philosophy has little to offer as a viable conceptual basis for addressing distributive injustice in low-income post-conflict societies.

In lieu of a conclusion: a commentary on philosophy and justice after conflict

This chapter provided an overview of the three concepts of justice in political and legal philosophy. To summarize, the discussion of legal justice revealed the dichotomy between minimalist and maximalist rule of law, and the overlap with human rights, and demonstrated the deep confusion that marks understanding of the concept. The discussion of rectificatory justice noted that this term was discarded and largely replaced by punishment. Yet all three major approaches to punishment – retributive, utilitarian and informal – exhibit serious flaws and fail to provide adequate responses to rectificatory justice's objective of correcting harm committed. The discussion of distributive justice limited itself to three criteria pertinent to low-income post-conflict societies: needs, rights and equality, and demonstrated that these criteria receive only marginal philosophical attention. The inapplicability of prevalent theoretical approaches like desert and contribution to low-income, unequal societies was noted. The strength and potential of egalitarian approaches were contrasted to the current aversion in theory and practice to redistributive equality.

Before proceeding further, it is necessary to clarify the approach to justice and human rights adopted in this book. Justice, as understood and addressed in this book, is not reducible to rights. The linkage between justice and rights was noted in all three dimensions. In legal justice, the distinction between the minimalist and maximalist positions hinged on their treatment of human rights and values, and it was noted that the Universal Declaration of Human Rights treated the rule of law as a prerequisite for human rights. Rectificatory justice effectively concerns how various abuses of human rights committed during conflict are to be addressed. In distributive justice, political and socio-economic rights are one important criterion for just distributions. Yet I would argue that the scope of justice goes beyond rights discourse and the coverage of specific human rights treaties and covenants. Rights are a partial but incomplete expression of justice, and this book is about justice broadly defined, and exemplified in the three dimensions identified here.

The inadequacy of present accounts in legal and political philosophy to address justice claims in the three dimensions that arise in low-income post-conflict societies requires some commentary. Most theoretical and philosophical discussions of justice are state-centric. They are conducted within the national context, taking national boundaries as the natural demarcation of human communities within which questions of justice are determined.[125] This may explain in part why contemporary philosophers, who are predominantly Western-based, have not yet turned their attention to problems of post-conflict justice arising outside their own boundaries, although they have addressed polemical issues within their own societies, such as racial segregation and wage differentials.

This may yet change: the nascent field of international or transnational justice breaks from this tradition and extends beyond national borders to address contemporary international problems, including ecology, inter-generational equity and even humanitarian intervention.[126] A salient focus is an enquiry into the obligations of rich countries towards poor people in developing countries.[127] The three dimensions of post-conflict justice particularly in developing countries have not so far been addressed specifically. However, the field of international justice may provide fertile soil for rigorous ethical and philosophical enquiry in this area, and it is pressing that scholars of transnational justice respond to this need.

Transnational justice will not, however, overcome the greatest hurdle to developing and applying philosophical approaches to justice issues in post-conflict developing societies. This is the predominance of Western-generated theories and the absence of non-Western philosophical discourse. The predicament is well described by one British scholar:

Although justice is agreed to be a universal ideal, whenever it is
elaborated for use in social practice or examined at length theoretically,
it appears as a concept constituted by a limited context. And since the
literature results largely from experience and theory developed in
Western societies, nearly all discussion is . . . specifically related to Western forms of social order.[128]

Inevitably Western philosophers are inadequately attuned to the
conditions found in non-Western societies. An illustration is Rawls's
theory of justice which many Western philosophers regard as universally applicable. Yet this is refuted from a non-Western perspective. It
is argued that Rawls's two principles are individualistic and grounded
in liberty. Consequently, they are inappropriate for non-Western societies in Africa and elsewhere which do not prioritize liberty. In such
societies, membership of a closely woven social group may be preferred to individual liberty, or opting out of such membership and its
concomitant obligations may not be a choice.[129]

Non-Western scholars who still live and work in their home countries have little voice in Western-dominated academic debates and
limited access to established publishing houses with global reach.
Consequently, there is a serious paucity of published philosophical
literature in the West generated by non-Western philosophers, particularly those living and working in resource-poor and war-torn
societies where injustice has its own forms and particularities. This
is a troubling imbalance or 'injustice' in the study of justice that needs
to be redressed.

The two points made above touch at the heart of the ongoing
debate between communitarian and cosmopolitan or liberal thinkers
in international relations and political theory. While the full scope of
that debate cannot be captured here, its relevance to this discussion is
briefly mentioned. The unanswered question in all three dimensions
of justice is whether there exists a single, universal set of values and
ideas about justice which may be applied uniformly across different
societies and cultures, including post-conflict developing countries,
that is, a cosmopolitan or universal vision; or, alternatively, whether
the values and ideas informing justice are and must be articulated
within and by each community, based on its specific realities and
needs, that is, a communitarian vision of justice. Liberal and cosmopolitan theorists like Dworkin, Barry, Rawls and Beitz would argue
that there is necessarily only one universally acceptable set of values
about justice, whose domain is worldwide. However, a growing body
of philosophers like Walzer, McIntyre and Lacey defend a communitarian vision, where the whole or part of a given society's conception

is determined and articulated internally, based on its specific cultural and societal needs.[130]

However, our discussion indicates that neither position on its own provides a satisfactory answer. O'Neill notes that both accounts fail 'the distant poor and vulnerable'. Cosmopolitan and liberal accounts 'are often fellow-travellers with old and ugly forms of imperialism, and sometimes rely on exaggerated, indeed false, assumptions about human rationality, independence, and self-sufficiency'. Communitarian accounts 'have nothing much to say about action towards those who are distant or different, since they exclude "outsiders" from the domain of justice'. Further, she notes that many liberal accounts of justice 'have a cosmopolitan surface, but are fundamentally statist', while genuine cosmopolitanism requires a wider domain for justice.[131]

Returning to our discussion, cosmopolitans with their universal vision find it unproblematic to apply principles of justice devised in the Western societies they predominantly inhabit to fundamentally different low-income and post-conflict societies. Yet cosmopolitan assertions of universality are weakened by the commonly observed existence of cultural specificities in the forms of injustice and treatment of justice across different societies. Communitarians would reject cosmopolitan principles as invalid, and insist that only locally rooted articulations of justice elaborated within post-conflict developing societies are valid. Yet such articulations are difficult to obtain in the near-absence of philosophical discourse generated by and within non-Western, low-income and war-torn societies.

I would argue that in reality a compromise between cosmopolitan and communitarian positions is both appropriate and necessary, not just in theory but particularly in practice.[132] As we turn to practice, it is possible to discern opposed but unarticulated cosmopolitan and communitarian attitudes and approaches. However, this opposition is unhelpful. If ideas and institutions about as fundamental and personal a value as justice are imposed from the outside without an internal resonance, they may flounder, notwithstanding their assertions of universality. If these concepts are articulated internally, there must be some universal standard against which to evaluate them, to ensure that they do not entrench unjust principles or discriminate against weak groups under the guise of respect for traditional cultural values.

In conclusion, we noted in chapter 1 that a firm understanding of the three concepts of justice could provide vital grounding to practitioners in the field confronting the realities of injustice in war-torn societies. Yet this chapter revealed the gaps between contemporary approaches to justice in all three dimensions and the realities and needs of low-income countries and war-torn societies. This chapter has lifted the lid on the first problem faced in restoring justice in war-torn societies. It is the lack of conceptual clarity about the nature and scope of justice on the part of practitioners, and the parallel disinterest of philosophers in addressing post-conflict justice and providing such conceptual coherence.

Turning from theory to practice, it is little surprise that on the ground the technical skills of practitioners applied to restoring justice in all three dimensions may often be compromised by lack of coherence and direction resulting from their conceptual confusion. We will now examine empirical experience in the three dimensions of justice in turn in chapters 3, 4 and 5.

Section II
Justice in Practice

3

Legal Justice:

Re-establishing Order or Restoring the Rule of Law?

Introduction: pursuing order or justice?

Aphoristic notions that law is a prerequisite for peace and a tacit promise of stability have imbued the rule of law with a panacean quality for peacebuilders.[1] The re-establishment of the rule of law is increasingly viewed by the international community as 'the most fundamental requirement, and a primary objective, of a lasting peace'.[2] Consequently, in recent years, a panoply of international actors – UN and bilateral agencies, regional and non-governmental organizations, development banks and other international financial institutions – have started addressing the breakdown of the rule of law in post-conflict societies.

This attention is not unproblematic and raises one serious question: do the various rule of law reform programmes undertaken by international and national actors really provide legal justice to citizens in post-conflict societies? This chapter argues that peacebuilders tend to treat the rule of law as a mechanism for establishing order rather than as a vehicle to restore justice within society. While the motivation for doing so may emerge from their urgent search for security after the uncertainty and chaos of conflict, current efforts by national and international agencies risk bolstering only short-term negative peace to the neglect and detriment of just and sustainable positive peace.

This chapter provides a background to rule of law reform undertaken by international actors. It identifies and briefly surveys achievements and obstacles in the three main areas addressed: police, judicial and prison reform. Thereafter, it provides a critical evaluation of international actors' efforts in undertaking rule of law reform after conflict, and identifies three major flaws in the international approach: it is, first, technical rather than politically sensitive; second, a one-size-fits-all approach; and third, it represents what we describe as 'programmatic minimalism'. As a combined result of these fundamental shortcomings, it is demonstrated how international efforts to reform the rule of law miss their objective of restoring justice and instead merely serve to establish order.

The emergence of rule of law reform in the peacebuilding arena

The attention to rule of law reform is recent, and was triggered in good part by the experience of the UN Transitional Authority in Cambodia (UNTAC), whose mandate included helping Cambodia's Supreme National Authority with judicial reform in the lead-up to elections. Yet the inadequate attention and resources accorded to rule of law reform by UNTAC, despite Cambodia's debilitated justice system, led to only modest and disappointing results. This experience led legal experts involved to propose the idea of UN 'justice packages' to accompany peacekeeping and post-conflict peacebuilding operations.[3] Although the concept of justice packages has not been adopted formally by the UN, there is widespread acceptance today amongst international donors and agencies that a minimal legal framework is essential to put a war-torn society back on its feet. What was still an alien notion to many international actors in 1994 became accepted practice by 1996 for organizations as disparate as the World Bank Group and the UN Office of the High Commissioner for Human Rights (OHCHR).

National efforts are, naturally, of considerable importance in shaping and determining the success and longevity of rule of law reform. Nevertheless, as rule of law and judicial reform require substantial and long-term investment and expertise, most impoverished post-conflict societies are deeply dependent on external assistance and legal expertise. This chapter focuses on international actors, because of the decisive role they play in rule of law reform in most countries emerging from conflict.

A panoply of international actors is involved in various aspects of rule of law reform. They include: UN agencies and departments, like the OHCHR, UN Crime Prevention and Criminal Justice Division, and UNDP, particularly its Emergency Response Division; regional organizations like the OSCE, the EU, the Organization of American States (OAS) and the Organization of African Unity (OAU); international financial institutions like the World Bank and the Inter-American Development Bank; bilateral donor agencies like the US Agency for International Development (USAID) and the Canadian International Development Agency; international non-governmental organizations (NGOs) such as the International Commission of Jurists (ICJ) and International Human Rights Law Group. This list is not exhaustive but indicates the number and diversity of organizations involved.[4] Donor agencies are not spread uniformly in all post-conflict countries across the globe but focus on countries where they have an institutional mandate or historical interest, such as OAS and USAID in Latin America, and EU in Africa and East and Central Europe. Often, consequently, entirely different sets of actors confront each other in every post-conflict society. These actors cannot necessarily build on prior shared experiences, lessons and relationships.

The recently restructured human rights branch of the UN, the OHCHR, has the broad responsibility of 'coordinating system-wide attention for human rights, democracy and the rule of law'. The High Commissioner is mandated to 'accord high priority to the technical cooperation activities undertaken with the Centre with regard to the rule of law'.[5] However, the OHCHR, with its modest budget and staff as compared to larger agencies like USAID or the World Bank, is a minor player with little influence.

Rule of law programmes are varied and diverse. The earlier-mentioned 'justice packages' proposed for post-conflict peace maintenance operations identify six 'core objectives': 'create a functioning criminal justice system; establish an independent, impartial and competent judiciary; appoint public prosecutors and defenders; train a responsible, respected police force with a strong sense of public service; build humane detention centers; and conduct legal education'.[6]

International agencies use different names to refer to their programmes in this area, such as 'administration of justice', 'judicial reform' or 'legal reform' programmes, with 'rule of law reform' being an umbrella term of sorts. Agencies tend to focus on different aspects of the wide-ranging tasks of rule of law reform, according to their own expertise and interests.[7] The diversity of rule of law programmes often reflects the divergent mandates, interests and agendas of donor agencies as much as the needs of the country in question. To some extent this is perhaps unavoidable, as institutions are bound by their official mandates. For example, the World Bank's assistance to countries in the field of legal reform must conform to the Bank's mandate specified in its Articles of Agreement, of 'assisting a member country to stabilize or revive its economy and thus enhance or facilitate investment for productive purposes in its territory', without interfering in or influencing the politics of member countries.[8] This contrasts with OHCHR, which, as noted earlier, was designated by the UN as the 'focal point' for the rule of law. Therefore, although both agencies belong broadly to the UN system (the OHCHR's mandate in the rule of law area is explicitly linked to and framed by human rights objectives, whereas the World Bank's is limited to economic development and investment, and explicitly divorced from political objectives) Rule of law programmes deriving from such divergent mandates often bear only an extended family resemblance to each other.

The 'tripod' of institutions of the rule of law

Three interdependent institutions emerge as the most salient in rule of law reform, and are referred to as the tripod or triad of the justice system – the judiciary, police and prisons. The three are interdependent: once police officers intercept suspects, prisons are required to hold them in safe custody until trial; courts – a functioning and dependable judiciary – are needed to accord fair trial to suspects, and an efficient, humane penal system is necessary to incarcerate guilty offenders for the length of their sentence. If any leg in this triad is weak or inefficient, the work of the other two institutions may be undermined or negated. In Haiti, for example, UN human rights observers noted that the efficiency of the reformed police force was compromised by the persistent weakness of the judiciary and prison system. Police officers report their frustration that when offenders are intercepted they either evade prison because the penal system is dysfunctional and inadequate, or escape trial because the courts are too inefficient to try them, or so corruptible that suspects can buy their freedom.

Despite the functional interdependence of these three pillars of the rule of law, international interest has focused increasingly on police reform or what is now referred to as 'security sector reform'. Additionally, in all three areas international efforts have focused on material and technical aspects rather than substantive issues. A brief overview is provided of international experience and obstacles in these three areas.

Police reform

The police force is responsible for upholding and enforcing the law, and is the most publicly visible pillar of the rule of law to citizens in their daily life. Yet in post-conflict societies the police institution is often the least trusted by ordinary people. This is because the police force is frequently associated with human rights abuses and violations during conflict rather than enforcement of the rule of law, as for example in Haiti, South Africa and El Salvador. Reforming the police corps is essential therefore, not only to ensure that the rule of law is restored and upheld, but also to regain public confidence in the government's commitment to uphold the rule of law and safeguard its citizens. As noted by a veteran police reformer, 'the way the police interacts with the people and enforces the law will delineate the face of peace and justice'.[9]

Of the tripod, police reform has received the greatest practical and academic attention in recent years, and merits scrutiny. Internationally sponsored police reform programmes have been implemented by a plethora of bilateral, multilateral and non-governmental agencies in the full range of post-conflict countries, from Namibia in 1989 to Sierra Leone more recently. A civilian police (CIVPOL) component features in most international peacekeeping and peace maintenance operations, entrusted with interim policing, training and inducting new recruits. A Civilian Police Unit was established in UN's Department of Peacekeeping Operations to play a co-ordinating role for CIVPOL, and OHCHR provides human rights training to police recruits and CIVPOL in many countries.[10]

The first experiment in internationally assisted police reform in a post-conflict society was in Namibia, which gained independence in 1989. The task was ambitious. The new Namibian Police force, NAMPOL, had to integrate diverse former combatants: the armed wing of SWAPO, namely the People's Liberation Army of Namibia, the South-African controlled forces of the South West African Territorial Force and officers of the disbanded South West African Police, SWAPOL. The last included Koevoet, the dreaded counter-insurgency police unit responsible for apartheid's worst abuses in Namibia.

The fundamental aim was to change the values and quality of service of the organization, while maintaining much of the structure and leadership of the old SWAPOL, an ambitious project given its pervasive abuses during apartheid. A British advisory team provided training to transform 'oppressive policing to policing by consent', while 'tactical on-the-ground training aimed to facilitate socialisation between black and white members of the force, to reduce the culture of racial harassment prevalent on both sides'.[11] The return of many white former SWAPOL police to South Africa facilitated the process by leaving spaces for black recruits.

Predictably, there have been difficulties. Some black police officers are disgruntled that leadership remains largely in white hands. They complain that change has been cosmetic, after the high expectations that accompanied liberation and the end of apartheid. They resent the government's enforced policy of reconciliation and national unity which retained jobs for white bureaucrats, and offered other reconciliatory measures to the white community to encourage them to remain in Namibia. However, despite challenges, observers note that the process has been generally successful, in terms of integration and camaraderie between white and black policemen, and public confidence in NAMPOL.[12]

Obstacles and dilemmas

Despite accomplishments, internationally assisted police reform programmes face considerable obstacles and dilemmas in post-conflict societies.[13] The greatest obstacle is de-linking the police and military institutions. The major dilemma concerns the recruitment and composition of the new police force.

It is critically important to de-link the military and police in the transition from conflict to peace because, in many countries, the two institutions become closely associated preceding or during conflict. States turn increasingly to the military to shore up the capacity of the police to maintain internal order during civil unrest and conflict. The distinction between internal order and external security becomes blurred. Sometimes the military comes to dominate the police formally or informally, and the police becomes de-civilianized and militarized.

De-linking the two institutions is essential but has proven difficult in practice. When conflicts are formally settled, a diminution in the size and status of the military is usually stipulated, and demobilization of both government and opposition forces often forms a critical part of peace arrangements.[14] Often governments themselves may find it politically and/or financially expedient to downsize the military. However, military leaders in these countries stiffly resist any reductions in their institution's budget, size, status and influence. When, in addition, the elimination or reduction of the military's hold on the police and politics is sought through re-civilianizing both police and political power, the military leadership often mounts obdurate opposition. El Salvador is a case in point.

The peace agreement in El Salvador called for the National Civil Police (PNC) to be 'a new force, with a new organization, new officers, new education and training mechanisms and a new doctrine'.[15] The police had earlier been entirely dominated by the military, controlled by the Ministry of Defence and trained by military personnel. Additionally, it had a pernicious history of human rights abuses. Arguably the best way for the opposition FMLN (Frente Farabundo Martí de Liberación Nacional) and external negotiators to ensure implementation of police reform by the Nationalist Republican Alliance (ARENA) government was to call for an entirely new police, and specify the requirements meticulously in the agreement.

Substantial assistance was directed to police reform, principally by bilateral donors, the USA, Norway, Spain, Sweden and Chile. This included forty advisers and instructors to constitute the International Technical Team at the new National Police Academy. The USA, the biggest donor, committed US$20m in 1992–4. The International Criminal Investigation and Training Assistance Programme (ICITAP) of the US Ministry of Justice played an exclusive role in the reform process, upon the request of the ARENA government.[16] The UN Observer Mission in El Salvador (ONUSAL) was mandated to assist the process, and it provided valuable logistical, training and monitoring assistance.

Despite the peace agreements, international assistance, and close monitoring by ONUSAL and NGOs, the military repeatedly interfered with police reform and tried to infiltrate the new PNC, unrestrained – and perhaps abetted – by the ARENA government.[17] The military was 'singularly uncooperative': it refused, for example, to hand over the designated site for the new Police Academy, and finally did so only after stripping the building of all equipment, doors, windows and light bulbs. It also refused to hand over police posts which it had earlier controlled, as well as equipment, vehicles and weapons. The military and government consistently frustrated international organizations' efforts, and particularly ONUSAL's, to assist and monitor the PNC.

The peace agreements clearly specified that former armed forces officers could not be inducted into the PNC, but conceded that screened former National Police (NP) officers could. Yet it was discovered in October 1992, early in the implementation process, that eleven of eighteen senior-level NP officers presented by the government for induction into the PNC were actually former military officers.[18] In 1993 a former military officer appointed by the government to a leading PNC post began to remilitarize the PNC by introducing military personnel and transferring military units to it, in violation of the agreement, before he was forced to resign following US pressure and ONUSAL complaints. Furthermore, a rising crime wave led the government and military to deploy armed forces along national highways to perform policing functions. This action ran contrary to the spirit of the peace agreements which strove to separate the military and police doctrines, and risked again blurring the distinction between police and military, allowing the latter to encroach on the former, as in the past.[19]

Despite these considerable challenges, observers note, 'there is no doubt that today, El Salvador has a police force that, far from inspiring fear in the general public, is a source of confidence and security', and it is acknowledged that 'without the active participation of the international community...[the PNC] would not be what it is today'.[20] El Salvador's police reform has survived military obstruction, but the experience has underscored both the need for and the difficulty of demilitarizing the police.

An extreme case of a militarized police force was Haiti, where, historically, the military and the police were not two separate institutions but a single entity called the Security Forces, with men simply changing uniforms according to the occasion.[21] Furthermore, this entity was deeply distrusted by ordinary people because, 'for most of Haiti's 193-year history as an independent nation, its security forces have served as an instrument of repression'. In this context, 'the creation of a professional, civilian police force in the form of the Haitian National Police offer[ed] the hope of breaking this cycle of repression and impunity'.[22] International donors directed substantial aid to the process. From 1994 to the end of 1996, total assistance, including monitors, exceeded US$100m. The main external actors were the USA (acting through ICITAP), Canada and the UN through CIVPOL and the UN Support Mission in Haiti.[23] The process was rushed through with only a four-month initial training to inexperienced recruits, criticized by some as inadequate for Haiti's volatile situation.

The *de facto* abolition of the Security Forces by Aristide's government was the most decisive step for police reform. Aristide was determined that the old Security Forces who were responsible for the bloodiest coup in Haiti's violent history and decades of abuse should play no part in the new dispensation. Although some international actors expressed fears of a rise in insecurity and crime,

Aristide remained inflexible. Given the Security Forces' historic domination of political and civil life, their abolition was described as 'the single greatest reason for optimism about the endurance of democracy in Haiti'.[24]

Despite the government's demonstrable political will, even abolition did not entirely succeed in eliminating the influence of former security forces on the new Haitian National Police (HNP), into which 130 former military officers were incorporated subsequently, many in top positions, supposedly owing to lack of leadership. Many more were inducted at lower levels, feeding fears of a remilitarization of the police.[25] However, its *de facto* abolition diluted the influence of security forces over the police in Haiti compared to El Salvador.

The record of the reformed HNP is mixed. Human rights abuses; high crime rates; a major drug trafficking problem; continued paramilitary activity; and institutional weaknesses continue to dog the force. Yet some observers praise it: it is seen to be a genuinely civilian institution, recruitment is observed to be relatively apolitical, and recruits as well as police authorities are reported to be motivated, qualified, and untainted by the repressive habits of the military.[26] Haiti's deteriorating political and economic condition since its nominal return to civilian rule in 1994 has deeply discouraged the international community.[27] Yet its police reform process largely succeeded in overcoming the greatest hurdle of dissociating the police from the military and from an oppressive past.[28]

The dilemmas of recruitment and composition of new police corps are not unrelated to the military–police nexus. The challenge of reintegrating demobilized combatants is a serious one in most countries emerging from war. If the military is to be downsized as part of peace arrangements, the natural option of integrating opposition forces into the military is limited or closed. As employment must be found for demobilized government soldiers as well as opposition ex-combatants, a convenient option is the police institution. However, if ex-combatants trained for warfare are inducted into the police precisely at the moment when the military and police need to be de-linked, police reform will lack credibility. Former soldiers and militants may have difficulty adjusting from making war to maintaining a civil peace, and the public may not trust a police institution comprising ex-combatants to protect internal peace. Yet if the option of recycling ex-combatants in the police is closed, few other openings may remain in economically debilitated societies. Finding employment in a field where they feel their skills and background are being put to relevant use may reduce the grievances of unemployed and disgruntled ex-combatants, which might otherwise find violent expression.

However, hiring ex-combatants risks reinforcing the nexus between police and military doctrines, and perpetuating the military's influence over the police.

A further recruitment dilemma is whether former police officers, implicated in earlier police abuses, should be retained in the new police.[29] Clearly, the public will lack confidence in a police corps composed of familiar violators, and it may be traumatic for victims to see their past oppressors policing their streets despite new-found peace. Yet if recruitment were restricted only to fresh cadets without an incriminating police past, they would lack requisite police experience to deal with the rampant insecurity and crime found in most countries emerging from war. Insecurity could rise during the interim period while new recruits are being trained and deployed. Furthermore, the greater cost of training entirely inexperienced recruits rather than retraining experienced – albeit abusive – police staff may affect recruitment decisions taken by governments and donors facing budgetary constraints.

The spectre of rising crime provided an excuse to the government in El Salvador to keep investing in the old, discredited National Police and to delay its demobilization stipulated by the peace agreements.[30] In Haiti, largely on US insistence, a 5,500-strong Interim Public Security Force was trained by the US and deployed to provide interim policing and control crime during transition. Comprising former security forces, the IPSF's performance was severely flawed. The public feared that it might provide a conduit for former security forces to infiltrate the new HNP. Resented and rejected by the public, it was completely abolished when the HNP was deployed.[31]

A frequent practice is screening former police officers purportedly to establish their 'human rights credentials' before recruitment. This is often unsuccessful. In El Salvador the peace agreement called for a screening process. As former armed forces were barred from recruitment to the new PNC by the peace agreement, but former NP police officers were not, as noted earlier, several military officers were transferred to the NP to circumvent the agreement and pave the way for their entry into the new PNC.[32] In Haiti 'a fundamental concern of the Haitian government was that no person involved in human rights violations be allowed into the National Police'.[33] Aristide's government insisted on scrupulous human rights screening. In what is noted as 'an improvement on US policies in other countries', particularly El Salvador, the USA as the key donors agreed.[34] Yet despite screening, former Security Forces officers have found their way into the HNP, as noted earlier, and the police were found responsible for at least ninety-two killings by the end of 1997 half of which were reported as human rights violations.[35]

Training in human rights is seen as another way of overcoming this problem and now forms an integral part of police reform. Yet it may be inadequate. As experienced police reformers observe, human rights violations by police officers are not caused by their ignorance of the law. Whether they are formerly abusive police officers, ex-combatants trained for warfare, or new cadets with no previous police experience, a human rights module in their training course may not inculcate in police officers a sense of responsibility to uphold justice and the rule of law.

It should be noted that the police do not suffer a tainted reputation in all war-torn countries. Police officers are usually proud of their profession and believe they are fulfilling their mandated duty to the nation, and protecting citizens against considerable odds. For example, in South Africa many former police officers express anger and humiliation at being made to feel guilty and ashamed for what they believed to be simply fulfilling their duties as required by the apartheid regime.[36]

Less common but vital are exercises that bring police and communities closer to each other, so that the police's genuine commitment to generating and upholding the rule of law is made evident to a fearful, distrustful public. In Namibia relations with the public were taken seriously at NAMPOL's creation. A media campaign publicizing the police's new orientation was launched, Public–Police Relations Committees were established throughout the country, and police leaders addressed townships and rural communities innumerable times.[37] Community policing has often been suggested as a way to improve police–public trust and co-operation, although it has had mixed results, as for example in Haiti.[38]

Police reform or 'security sector reform' enjoys great popularity with donors today. Alongside this enthusiasm, it should be noted with concern that more attention is given to technical aspects of police training than to the difficult questions raised here like police–military relations, recruitment issues, police–community relations and public confidence. It should also be acknowledged that international enthusiasm for police reform is linked largely to the police's role in enforcing the law and maintaining order, which are seen as essential after conflict. The police are seen as the coercive arm of the state mandated to enforce security, and they are trained accordingly; hence the emphasis on 'security sector reform' in international parlance. Populations in war-torn societies often have suffered serious abuses at the hands of state law-enforcement officials, police and security forces. In these settings, as I have argued elsewhere, it is necessary and appropriate to treat and train police as guarantors of justice and law, and protectors of peace, rather than coercive enforcers of security.[39]

Reforming the judiciary

'Without fundamentally changing how justice is administered, human rights guarantees will be fragile and the rule of law a pipe-dream.'[40] This observation made in Haiti rings true for all post-conflict countries. Across a range of post-conflict countries, international actors have provided material, technical, legal and training assistance to judicial reform. The World Bank, for example, lists ten separate elements of judicial reform in developing countries, including: building an independent judiciary; protecting the security of judicial officers; simplifying judicial procedures and improving judicial management; selecting and training judicial officers; providing institutional facilities and legal information systems; facilitating access to courts; and making available arbitration and other alternative facilities.[41] International assistance in this area is not negligible, as noted in Rwanda and Haiti.

In Rwanda, in the chaos accompanying the flight of the government and Forces Armées Rwandaises following genocide in 1994, the legal system was plundered and destroyed: 'The Ministry of Justice building, courthouses and prosecutors' offices were stripped bare. Windows were blown out, case files burned, telephones stripped... typewriters and computers stolen... There were literally no pens, paper, legal forms or other basic material which allow an office to function.'[42] The new government set up by the victorious Rwandese Patriotic Front possessed no human or material resources to initiate the restoration of the rule of law. International assistance responded to these needs. The UN Human Rights Field Operation in Rwanda, HRFOR, identified eight tasks: refurbishing material needs; transportation; basic supplies; legal texts; recruiting and training judicial personnel; technical assistance; prisons; judicial and legal reform. International donors provided legal advice and training to the Justice Ministry, as also substantial material assistance to rebuild courthouses and provide the Justice Ministry with basic supplies and legal texts.[43] International aid has helped rebuild the institutions of the rule of law, but its ethos is yet to be restored. The international community has not publicly addressed the increasingly skewed trend of recruitment into the justice system that seems to favour Tutsis and largely exclude Hutus, although this threatens to undermine the ability of courts to administer impartial justice.[44]

Debilitated under successive dictatorships, Haiti's justice system was dealt a devastating blow during the brutal military regime of Raoul Cédras between 1991 and 1994. In late 1993 the UN–OAS

Joint Civilian Mission in Haiti (MICIVIH) identified eight serious deficiencies in the judiciary. These were: the military's utter domination of the judiciary; endemic corruption and extortion; poorly trained and unmotivated judges and prosecutors with inadequate legal training; 'monumental' shortage of essential materials, leaving courthouses in 'complete disrepair'; lack of respect by the people for rule of law officials; and impunity of military and civilian leaders.[45]

Despite the paucity of resources and lack of government oversight, MICIVIH did a respectable job in evaluating and strengthening the judiciary in Haiti. Additionally, a full range of international donors undertook judicial reform, with USAID the most prominent. Progress was made due to concerted efforts by international actors. However, the judiciary remains weak and inefficient and impunity prevails, largely attributable to poor or absent governance and lack of oversight.[46]

Obstacles

The technical aspect of providing training and materials to judiciaries is straightforward, and it is this area that international efforts focus on. More elusive is the task of restoring to the judiciary the two vital traits it requires to function under the rule of law: independence and impartiality.[47] The greatest obstacle to judicial reform in many countries is eliminating the influence of the executive branch of government. Equally tenacious in militarized societies is the hold of the military establishment over the judiciary. As the Salvadorean example illustrates, political, military and economic elites usually resist any diminution of their influence over a judiciary they have long manipulated and enjoyed impunity from.

The nature and scope of the UN-negotiated peace agreements in El Salvador were unprecedented, and judicial reform was addressed directly. The San José Agreement of July 1990 was the very first in a long series of peace agreements and it was devoted exclusively to human rights and justice reform issues.[48] This agreement established ONUSAL, specifically to verify the observance of human rights, and to support Salvadorean judicial authorities 'to help improve the judicial procedures for the protection of human rights and increase respect for the rules of due process of law'.[49] The Mexico Agreement of April 1991 addressed the critical weaknesses of the justice system and attempted to promote the rule of law.

The Supreme Court urgently needed reform, as it wielded enormous centralized power, was highly politicized and deeply corrupt. Accordingly, under the Mexico Agreement procedures for electing Supreme Court judges, the Attorney-General and the Chief of State

Counsel were changed. Additionally, the National Council of the Judiciary was restructured, 6 per cent of the state budget was allocated to the judiciary, and the office of National Counsel for the Defence of Human Rights was instituted.

The government undertook a binding commitment to respect the peace agreements and to implement the recommendations of the UN Truth Commission established by the agreements. Yet when the Truth Commission recommended that the Supreme Court should resign in its totality, little was done to enforce this. The Supreme Court steadfastly resisted all attempts to reduce its entrenched power. The Supreme Court President, Mauricio Gutierrez Castro, and his judges compromised the commission's work by refusing to co-operate with its enquiries. They rejected and resisted the Truth Commission recommendation to resign.[50] The ARENA government that had installed the Supreme Court's judges did little to weaken Gutierrez's intransigence, demonstrating its own reluctance to respect its commitments under the peace agreement. The debate dragged on and a tense struggle ensued in the legislature between political parties for control over the election of judges and choice of a Supreme Court President. It was only in July 1994 that a new and more representative Supreme Court was elected following the new procedure.[51] After this pitched and politicized struggle, the general opinion of observers today is that the judiciary is undoubtedly far superior, more independent and less partisan than before.[52] Nevertheless, the UN reports that despite 'considerable achievements', 'persistent deficiencies in the judicial system' still remain.[53]

This experience in El Salvador illustrates that, although reforming the judiciary is essential for restoring the rule of law, this is an arduous task in volatile post-conflict societies, where unexpected political ramifications may sometimes obfuscate the intentions and frustrate the technical or legal expertise of international actors.

Prison reform

Prison reform was the last of the tripod to receive international attention. As recently as 1992, donors were unaware of or unwilling to address this issue. During UNTAC's mandate in Cambodia, new prisons were urgently needed to satisfy human rights criteria by providing humane treatment to prisoners. Yet 'many foreign governments had difficulties in accepting requests for funds to build prisons in Cambodia after all the tyranny the Khmer people had endured in such places'.[54] It was only subsequently that donors realized the discrepancy between their objective of promoting human rights and the rule of law – which included the rights and treatment of prisoners – and the absolute inability of existing prisons in impoverished and battered post-conflict societies to fulfil this objective. Today donors are less hesitant to address the appalling condition of prisons and treatment of detainees, in Haiti and Rwanda for example, and realize how critical it is to their objectives of rule of law reform and human rights protection.[55]

Obstacles and dilemmas

The new attention by international actors to prisons has its own problems. The goal pursued by the UN and international donors is that prisons conform to universal human rights standards. This is frequently beyond the resources and capacities of post-conflict countries. When foreign assistance is directed at prisoners and prison conditions, locals view this as favouring 'criminals' over 'victims', and increasing the legitimacy of prisoners.[56] The UN-built prisons in Arusha for those detained to be tried in the International Tribunal for Rwanda highlight this issue.[57] Rwandans understandably complain that while the worst *génocidaires* are held in the comparative luxury of UN jails, petty perpetrators in Rwandan prisons suffer illness, overcrowding and death; furthermore, impoverished survivors feel neglected alongside this attention to prisoners' welfare. In Cambodia too, the UN was perceived by the population as giving more resources to prisoners than to prison guards and the villagers around the prisons. Prison reform is unquestionably important for restoring the rule of law. Nevertheless, the Cambodian and Rwandan experiences have brought UN officials to the realization that the UN and other actors need to assist – and be seen to assist – the entire population and not just one section of it, in order to have public credibility. And this is a cost that rule of law reform programmes can rarely meet.

To summarize, starting only in 1989 with Namibia, international assistance to the three areas of rule of law reform – police, judiciary and prisons – has burgeoned. It is widely accepted today that the rule of law is a prerequisite for consolidating peace after conflict, and the need for 'a minimum legal framework', 'justice packages' and police reform are now familiar if not official concepts. It has also been proposed that rule of law reform be included in peacekeeping missions in countries still in conflict, and not restricted to the post-conflict stage.[58]

Can it be concluded, then, that international efforts to restore the rule of law have been successful? Have they provided appropriate and adequate responses to the needs and contexts of low-income war-torn societies? Have they provided people with legal justice, and laid the foundations for both negative and positive peace? I argue that they have not.

A critical evaluation: three fundamental flaws

International assistance in reforming the rule of law in war-torn societies is important. Most low-income societies emerging from conflict would be unable to undertake this crucial, time-consuming, resource-intensive task without external assistance. Admittedly, there are largely technical drawbacks in many rule of law programmes which international practitioners themselves are often the first to point out. These include a severe lack of co-ordination, overlap and duplication, low competence and high pay of international staff, inadequate legal training of lawyers involved, and insensitivity to local culture and politics.[59] However, it is fair to regard these as teething problems of what is still a fledgling and evolving practice. Ongoing efforts, such as the proposal of the UN High Commissioner for Human Rights (HCHR), Mary Robinson, for 'a comprehensive United Nations programme of assistance for the rule of law', could lead to improvements.[60]

What is more important is to identify whether there are any fundamental rather than functional problems besetting the current direction of rule of law reform, and to question whether these programmes actually restore legal justice and contribute to building a just peace.

My contention is that international rule of law programmes suffer from three fundamental and interlinked shortcomings. The first is that their implementers regard their task as a mainly technical one and ignore its political ramifications. Second, there is a tendency for these programmes to be 'one-size-fits-all', that is, standard and uniform. Third, and following from the two above, rule of law programmes embody 'programmatic minimalism', that is, they seem to target the institutions and structures rather than the substance and ethos of the rule of law. Owing to these shortcomings, current internationally driven efforts to restore the rule of law risk missing their central objective.

Technical rather than political approach?

A fundamental problem with international rule of law programmes arises from the tendency of their executors to treat the rule of law primarily as a technical task and to ignore or sideline its political implications. A wry comment by a senior official in Rwanda captures the problem: '"Restoring justice" became a question of how to give computers to the Justice Ministry.'[61]

Understandably, some aspects of rule of law restoration do call for technical expertise, and technical responses are appropriate here. More often, rule of law reform is too technical and legalistic, but not adequately politically sensitive or culture-specific. The need for rule of law reform to be undertaken by 'more than just lawyers' to ensure a wider interdisciplinary approach has commonly been reiterated by practitioners.[62] The observation made in the context of Rwanda rings true for many post-conflict societies:'The real challenge [in restoring the judicial system] is not of marshalling sufficient human and technical resources, but of institutionalising a new political culture in which differences are settled through discussion, accommodation, and sound civil institutions and not through bloodshed.'[63] Serious difficulties have arisen from the insensitivity of international actors to the political nature and ramifications of their task. Reforming the rule of law is a process that is crucially dependent on the political context. It requires political commitment, but the process can easily become too politicized and partisan.

In El Salvador the main problem we saw earlier was the 'over-politicization' of the rule of law, by a government and military that manipulated the Supreme Court, and by judicial officials who were themselves deeply corrupt. In Haiti, on the contrary, the main problem stemmed from 'under-politicization' or political paralysis, due to the political vacuum and consequent lack of government oversight over rule of law. Following the internationally assisted ouster of the dictator Raoul Cédras, Aristide had hoped to seek a second presidential term in 1995's elections despite a constitutional ban, having lost three years of his presidency in exile. However, he was pressurized, especially by the USA, to step down. Although Aristide's own Lavalas Political Organization (OPL) won in 1995, and his close ally René Préval became President, severe infighting rocked the OPL and paralysed government, owing partly to Aristide's alleged political manoeuvring and non-co-operation.[64] Haiti had no prime minister from June 1997 to January 1999, during which period a fractious and disarrayed parliament rarely made quorum when it assembled, and consistently refused to approve any of the prime ministerial candidates proposed by Préval. In January 1999 Préval dissolved Parliament and appointed Jacques-Edouard Alexis as Prime Minister without parliamentary approval.[65] The results of long-delayed legislative elections in May 2000, giving Lavalas victory, were sharply disputed and never recounted, and limbo persisted. Aristide's return to presidency in the November 2000 elections has aggravated rather than calmed matters, as the opposition boycotted the elections and accuse Aristide of plotting dictatorship.[66] In the long absence of political leadership and oversight, many donors grew tired of expending resources in a seemingly meaningless exercise of reforming the rule of law, and withdrew their aid. Other donors used the opportunity to step in and fill the vacuum themselves, with mixed outcomes.[67]

Both over- and under-politicization can affect rule of law reform, and international actors need to be politically sensitive and astute to know how to respond. A technical approach ignores the basic reality that the success of rule of law restoration is influenced by and depends on the political will and capacity of national leaders to carry it through. As noted earlier, success also hinges on whether the process wins public confidence, but political will and capacity are prerequisites. The outcome of a project or programme depends necessarily on the starting point at which it is initiated, and this point can vary widely between cases according to the degree and combination of political will and ability of post-conflict governments to carry through rule of law reform.

The police reformer Cornelius De Rover uses a framework in police training to assess the entry point and exit level of police cadets and measure outcomes:[68]

Willing / Able	Willing / Not Able
Able / Not Willing	Not Able / Not Willing

De Rover explains that the grid presents four distinctly different entry level points, which rationally calls for at least four entirely different management styles to achieve the desired outcome – a logical step from a management point of view. Yet the international community, he suggests, seems to act as if a single uniform management style will work for all four diverse situations, and accords them the same treatment. This framework lends itself well to assessment of the political starting point of post-conflict societies regarding rule of law reform.

Willing /Able   South Africa and Namibia present examples of countries both politically willing and materially able to conduct rule of law reform. The new post-apartheid governments possessed the credibility and legitimacy afforded by electoral victory to support their drive for a newly legitimized rule of law to overturn the illegitimacy of the apartheid system, and both countries had available resources to back this political commitment with requisite capacity. As will be seen in the next chapter, Namibia's political will to see legal justice restored stood in contrast to its lack of political will to address rectificatory justice issues.

Willing/Not Able   In Rwanda, although lacking the requisite capacity after the devastation of genocide and conflict, the government set up by the RPF initially possessed the political will and commitment to see the rule of law restored, as UN human rights officials observed. The government seized the opportunity of a supportive international donor community to rebuild the shattered legal apparatus. Illustrating government determination, the Ministry of Justice decided to use funds from a foreign aid project to increase the low salaries of Rwandan judges, prosecutors and other legal employees, rather than as originally proposed – to pay the high international salaries of fifty foreign advisers.[69] Over time, however, the government's commitment wavered. Insurgency by Hutu extremists led to continued war in the north-west, and a preoccupation with the conflict undermined the government's respect for legality and human rights. The government gradually became more Tutsi-dominated, excluding Hutus from positions of power.[70] The resignation of the Hutu President Pasteur Bizimungu and Prime Minister Pierre-Celestin Rwigema, and appointment of the Tutsi leader Paul Kagame as President in March 2000 are disquieting indications of deepening Hutu exclusion.[71] The government once intent on replenishing fully the rule of law effectively narrowed its sights to restoring the minimal institutions and procedures of the rule of law.

Able/Not Willing   El Salvador is a case where internal resources and generous external assistance made the necessary reforms to the rule of law feasible from a financial and material point of view – that is, ability was not lacking. Yet the ARENA government and judiciary lacked the political will to see the rule of law restored, and obfuscated the process, as discussed earlier.

Not Able/Not Willing   This is the nadir of the grid, and Cambodia well fits this scenario. Ability was visibly lacking in Cambodia. This was due to the destruction of the country's resources during its prolonged conflict, the extermination of legal personnel during Pol

Pot's regime, followed by the manipulation of the judiciary by the government of the Cambodian People's Party. Preceding and following elections, Cambodian leaders paid lip service to the idea of the rule of law as a key political and economic objective.[72] Yet there was an absence of genuine political will, particularly on the part of joint-Prime Minister Hun Sen. Some early progress demonstrated by a relatively high standard of human rights and government co-operation was noted by human rights officials until 1994. But the nascent rule of law was gradually eroded by government inroads. Political will degenerated dramatically in the period culminating in Hun Sen's palace coup in April 1997, and has been only partly restored since disputed elections in July 1998 that returned Hun Sen to power.

Haiti too fits here in the grid. Following Aristide's return to constitutional rule in 1994, his government initially demonstrated genuine will to reform the rule of law, availing itself of substantial international aid, as noted by legal experts.[73] But this evaporated during the long political paralysis described above. The conspicuous absence of political will is seen to be the greatest obstacle to rule of law reform today in Haiti.

As the Haitian case illustrates, external actors have the ability to bolster weak capacity with their assistance and expertise. However, they cannot invent national political will, and are severely hampered in its absence. In approaching rule of law reform mainly as a technical task, international actors largely ignore the political context and its influence on their programmes. They do not factor in varying levels and combinations of political will and capacity in designing their programmes. Technical expertise cannot substitute for the political sensitivity and astuteness required in rule of law reform.

One size fits all?

The attitude of most international rule of law efforts is aptly depicted in the observation made by a veteran police reform expert: 'If you only have a hammer it is very tempting to see every problem as a nail, rather than developing different tools to deal with different problems.'[74] As discussed above (rule of law programmes typically focus on the tripod of institutions and focus on technical, material and training requirements.) Each agency tends to have a standard and fairly uniform programme that it applies with minor adaptation in entirely different countries. This 'one-size-fits-all' approach is unlikely to succeed because the state of the rule of law at the termination of conflict is quite markedly different across countries.

States of disrepair

At least three separate scenarios could be identified and described as 'states of disrepair' in which the rule of law finds itself at the end of conflict, depending on the nature, causes, duration and intensity of conflict in a particular country, in addition to other factors. They are: (illegitimate but functional; corrupt and dysfunctional; and devastated and non-functional.[75]) These three categories are not intended to be comprehensive or definitive, and each category is not exclusive and impervious, but porous and overlapping. Countries may not fit neatly within a single category, and may bear characteristics of more than one. Conceivably, alternative categories could be identified, based on other criteria.

Illegitimate but functional   In this scenario, ('the rule of law' is observed or claimed to remain operational at some level throughout the conflict or emergency. Certain core legal institutions continue to exist and function; there is a judiciary, a written law that is more or less upheld, legal personnel are appointed and hold office, detainees including rebels may even be tried in court and sometimes acquitted.) However, the rule of law adhered to is, at best, a 'minimalist' rule of law. While minimal principles of legality are not transgressed, the law itself is iniquitous, and bad or unjust law is passed and enacted. As protested by Nelson Mandela in his Rivona trial in 1972, in such situations, 'the law as it is applied is...immoral, unjust and intolerable'.[76] (In minimalist vein, human rights may be violated by laws that discriminate against the population or sections of it, while the state claims to uphold the rule of law procedurally.) As expressed by Thabo Mbeki, the South African apartheid regime 'declared freedom from poverty, from suffering, from degradation, and human equality without discrimination...to be illegal and criminal in its eyes'.[77]

When besieged by conflict, the state increasingly uses law and the rule of law as a weapon in its arsenal, subjugating both the courts and the legislature to its purposes. A partisan judiciary becomes complicit with – or, at best, blind to – government's use of the law to repress a section or even a majority of the population. Oppressed populations might feel, as Mandela expressed it, that their 'consciences dictate that [we] must protest against it, that [we] must oppose it and that [we] must attempt to alter it'. Yet the illegitimate rule of law may criminalize protest, leading to a bizarre situation where, as former Norwegian Prime Minister Brundtland put it, 'normality is criminalised and criminality normalised'.[78]

The apartheid regimes in both Namibia and South Africa fit this description well, as the references above illustrate. The National Party's apartheid policy and its war against anti-apartheid activists were greatly aided by the weapon of law. However, other legal systems than apartheid could qualify here as well, such as Guatemala's.[79]

It should be noted in this scenario that the judiciary may sometimes exert some independence. In South Africa and Namibia some anti-apartheid activists were actually acquitted after reasonably fair trials, despite the government's obvious opposition, demonstrating that a vestigial commitment to the rule of law did prevail in the judiciary. In Namibia in 1978, the original deadline for independence, most judges and tribal courts were seen to be entirely manipulated by the South African colonial state. According to one international lawyer long involved in Namibia, this changed by 1989, and Namibia acquired at independence an 'extremely independent Supreme Court', whose four white judges were highly committed to preserving human rights.[80]

Corrupt and dysfunctional   In this scenario, some of the features of minimalist rule of law are maintained. A judiciary and legal system exist in name throughout the conflict; the Justice Ministry and Supreme Court exercise their functions. The problem is not primarily illegitimacy, as above. Rather, the rule of law is progressively emasculated over time. Its structure and facade remain, but the rule of law loses most of its defining characteristics and principles.

The most significant failing is the judiciary's loss of independence and impartiality, as it is manipulated by the executive branch of government and, often, the military. The judiciary is controlled largely by the executive, and becomes a tool for the benefit of the political, military and economic elite. Legal justice is inaccessible to the ordinary population, while it is bought and sold by the rich and powerful. Approximating Prempeh's jurisprudence of executive supremacy, 'the state is thus subject to only such restraint as it chooses to place upon itself, while the citizen has only such rights as the state may allow'.[81] Therefore, although some of its institutions function in name, the rule of law is seriously dysfunctional as it caricatures legality, and loses public trust. The rule of law in El Salvador and Guatemala at the end of their respective conflicts are cases in point.

A vivid illustration of the depth of corruption of the judiciary and the dysfunction of the rule of law in El Salvador was provided by the verdict of the UN Truth Commission in El Salvador. Although its painstaking enquiries led to the identification and naming of the most prominent human rights abusers in its report, the Commission decided not to call for trials against them. In its opinion, 'Public morality demands that those responsible for the crimes described here be punished. However, El Salvador has no system for the administration of justice which meets the minimum requirements of objectivity and impartiality so that justice can be rendered reliably.'[82]

Devastated and non-functional   In several cases, owing either to long-term neglect or manipulation (Haiti), or the devastation wreaked by war (Rwanda), or a combination of both (Cambodia), the entire formal legal apparatus of a society collapses. The rule of law disintegrates, and slips from dysfunctional to non-functional. Sometimes vestiges of prior justice systems remain: courthouses emptied of legal codes and furniture, or divested of qualified lawyers and judges; justice ministers and ministry buildings with little or no staff. Only a 'phantom' rule of law remains.

Haiti exemplifies this scenario, where in 1994 it was observed that 'Haitian justice lacks everything: resources, competent personnel, independence, stature, trust.... Courts lack even rudimentary materials necessary to do its work.' Furthermore, 'although Haitian law creates elaborate proceedings governing arrests, detentions, and prison inspections and monitoring, all these procedures and protections are systematically breached' due to the breakdown of the system.[83] Sometimes even these vestiges are erased, pillaged and destroyed during conflict, as described earlier in Rwanda.[84]

Although the centralized and official administration of justice collapses, sometimes a partial alternative may emerge. Koranic law or customary law may be dispensed by elders, local chiefs or warlords, as in Somalia. Popular justice may be exercised by communities or civic groups. The recent public trials and lynching of suspected murderers in Guatemalan villages in the perceived absence of state-provided rule of law, even after conflict, are illustrative.[85] These informal alternatives may facilitate or hamper the restoration of the rule of law, depending on their nature. The potential and the risks of informal justice discussed in chapter 2 are relevant here. International and national actors must pay careful attention to how they deal with them.

The three scenarios are not hermetic or exhaustive, but their depiction illustrates the significant differences in conditions and needs across post-conflict societies, and underlines why a uniform rule of law package might not be applicable to such disparate situations. Countries emerging from conflict may share some generic problems, but each is a unique or *sui generis* case, as illustrated in the preceding discussions. It is a short-sighted strategy to attempt to treat such countries alike, and replicate a successful programme in a different post-conflict situation without careful adaptation to its specific context and needs. Admittedly, it may be a cost-effective and time-saving measure from the point of view of donors and recipient governments. However, the chances of reproducing 'success' in very different political contexts with a uniform programme are slim at best.

A frequent common denominator across the three scenarios is the population's lacking or lost trust in the rule of law. Consequently, winning back popular confidence may be the touchstone of success in all three cases. However, public trust may have been lost for different reasons and in different ways in diverse societies, and therefore a one-size-fits-all approach is unlikely either to regain public confidence, or restore the rule of law.

'Programmatic minimalism'?

The direction and impact of current international efforts suggest an inclination towards a minimalist conception of the rule of law in programmatic terms, which I describe as 'programmatic minimalism'. The majority of international programmes focus on the institutions and mechanics, the form and structure, of the rule of law, while evading the substantive content – the *ethos* – of that rule of law. They focus on resurrecting the standardized and replicable pillars of the rule of law – the judiciary, police and prisons – rather than addressing the content of the laws upheld by them. They focus on law *enforcement* – as illustrated by the preoccupation with police reform – rather than the *generation* of the rule of law and of public confidence in it. They shy away from knowledge and integration of cultural and historical specificities and needs of individual societies, and engage local populations only minimally in their programmes. While focusing considerable effort on rehabilitating legal institutions, international actors do not appear attentive to the countervailing necessity of ensuring that the rule of law is firmly anchored in the society and enjoys political commitment and public trust. Perhaps most important, the programmes and their sponsors are largely silent as to whether the rule of law is designed to provide citizens with their right to justice and to safeguard their dignity, or merely to provide order in society.

Several factors could explain why rule of law programmes and their executors have adopted this apparently minimalist focus, three of which are outlined here. The first may be pragmatism: it is possible that, based on the scant ability and lack of political will in many

post-conflict countries, international actors come to a realistic decision to reduce expectations and focus on the minimum. UN human
rights experts concede that 'rights and norms are universal, but their
application varies', and that 'movement towards the full application
of norms must take account of the base line at which a country
begins'. Consequently, international experts, once on the ground in
war-shattered societies like Cambodia, realize that 'the high standards
of administration of justice and human rights must be adjusted and
brought down to a *"juste niveau"* – a level that is acceptable in the
region', in order to be 'closer to reality'.[86]

A second factor may be an awareness on the part of international
actors of their own limitations in understanding the complexities and
nuances of a foreign political history and culture, and integrating
these into their programmes in order to form a substantively viable
rule of law. Chastised for their insensitivity to the cultural and political context, as in Cambodia, international actors may decide to leave
the substance and direction of the rule of law to national authorities.
They may opt to focus instead on the technical aspects, and the
replicable institutions like courts, police and prisons. Here, technical
expertise rather than cultural sensitivity and political *savoir faire*
seem to be called for, and it may appear possible to follow standardized templates without the worry of transgressing cultural norms.

A third reason may stem from their perception of priorities. The
danger of a costly relapse into conflict and the pressure to forestall it
may make international actors more concerned with the need to build
institutions that promise security and order and less concerned with
the need to restore to citizens confidence in justice.

This tendency is dangerously implicit in donors' preference for the
term 'security sector reform' rather than rule of law reform and for
their prioritization of police reform above judicial and prison reform,
as noted in earlier sections. The term security automatically connotes
external security, and implies a role for the military.[87] El Salvador's
peace agreements recognized the common confusion between security
and defence, and tried to clarify this and relegate the military's role to
the latter.[88] Civilian survivors in many countries have suffered police
brutality and military oppression in the name of state security. In this
context it is insensitive to treat the rule of law as a tool to maintain
security and to refer to it as the security sector. It is also politically
perilous to do so, as the ambiguity between internal and external
security may once again be manipulated leading to the remilitarization of society, as discussed above. By using the term 'security sector
reform', international actors risk creating public fear rather than
public confidence in the rule of law.

High crime and insecurity, frequently ineluctable in conflict's aftermath, are due to many factors: a surplus of cheap weapons; vestiges of underground war economies; high unemployment; disgruntled, and often armed, ex-combatants. If the rule of law is treated primarily as a mechanism to restore order and security, and if its main objective is seen as maintaining and enforcing negative peace rather than simultaneously deepening positive peace, several consequences may ensue. The police may backslide towards the use of excessive force. Courts may violate legality and impose unjust and unduly harsh sentences to curtail crime. Prisons may violate prisoners' rights. In the purported interest of security, and in the name of the law, the rule of law may be violated. If courts, police and prisons are seen to constitute the security sector, it risks making the law subservient to the needs of security and order rather than justice. Yet the urge to restore security and entrench order appears today to be a motivating force behind donors' rule of law reform efforts, as is manifested in their preoccupation with enforcing rather than generating law.

The dangers of programmatic minimalism
Whichever of these reasons may explain the current tendency to focus on 'programmatic minimalism' – and the justifications may well vary according to the actors and their diverse mandates and objectives – this approach may be fraught with dangers in the post-conflict context.

If the motivation is pragmatism, there is a difference between reducing universal standards to realistic and acceptable levels and achieving them in an incremental fashion, and simply setting low goals and standards in a minimalist way. Yet it is easy to confuse the two, miss this distinction, and effectively settle for a minimalist approach, in the turbulence following conflict. Even if the base line may be low in a developing country particularly after conflict, its citizens are equally deserving and demanding of the same right to justice and dignity accorded to 'all human beings' under international covenants, and the country legitimately can aspire towards this longer-term goal.[89]

The justification for adopting programmatic minimalism may be a desire on the part of external actors not to meddle in internal politics and domestic culture out of a sense of their own limitations. However, a host of dangers might flow from this relinquishing of responsibility for the substantive content of the rule of law. Can international actors be confident that left to its own devices the government in question will have the necessary political will to put in place a 'maximalist' rule of law that is appropriate to the needs and aspirations of its society, and cognizant of its cultural realities and traditions? Can it trust that opposition parties and independent civil society groups will be strong enough to voice their opinion and sufficiently influence the process, even if the government is not so inclined?

Not all conflicts, we know, end with 'free and fair' elections. In many countries, the regime which conducts the war remains in power after the transition (El Salvador, Guatemala). In others it is a victorious army that forms the government, often possessing little notion of democratic governance (Rwanda, DRC, Ethiopia). In still others, democracy may as yet be so weak, and the might of the military and elite so strong, that leaders can do little to exercise independence (Haiti). Or elections may be rigged by political leaders, despite international scrutiny (Cambodia). For whichever of these reasons, if the government that takes charge after transition is not the popular, democratically elected representative of its people, then the wishes of its people may not be its guiding concern. Even when democratically elected, the government may not dispose of sufficient political authority or financial means in the immediate aftermath of conflict to act in favour of its electorate.

In any of these cases, governments – abetted by other institutions with vested interests like the military or the judiciary – may undermine rule of law reform, despite painstaking efforts by the UN and other international actors, as occurred in El Salvador. In countries where international actors relinquish the responsibility of influencing the rule of law in substance and not just in form, national leaders may be even more reluctant to imbue the rule of law with justice, if it is not in their interests or within their ability to do so.

The hesitation on the part of international agencies may stem from a desire to avoid cultural rather than political interference. International programmes have been sharply criticized, often by the practitioners involved, for their tendency to ignore local cultural and legal traditions, systems and customary laws, and to exclude the local communities from the design of the rule of law which they are then expected to adopt, trust and respect.[90] Sometimes external actors have treated post-conflict societies as blank slates. In Cambodia the peace agreements accorded sweeping administrative authority to UNTAC during the transition to electoral democracy.[91] This included a mandate to assist the transitional Supreme National Council in conducting judicial reform and restoring the rule of law.[92] The rights encoded in UN covenants are already present in Buddhist culture, and have been known for generations to the Khmer people.[93] Yet foreign legal experts arriving in Cambodia concluded that 'any legal culture has been completely absent in Cambodia in legal history'. They believed 'there was no tradition of a competent independent judiciary. There was no legal culture where Courts could stand as dispensers of criminal justice independent of political direction.'[94] Confronted with what they saw as a legal vacuum from a Western standpoint, foreign legal experts felt uninhibited and justified in treating Cambodia as a *tabula rasa* and importing foreign legal practices drawn mainly from their own systems. They were oblivious to the affront this caused ordinary Cambodians who felt that their own legal traditions had been overlooked.[95] They were equally oblivious to the probability that Cambodians would not feel beholden to respect laws they neither understood nor trusted.

Sometimes this attitude may result simply from a lack of interest on the part of international actors, rather than benign neglect. More often, it may be due to a genuine shortage of time and resources to investigate fully the local culture, history and conditions; ignorance of local languages; and the difficulty of identifying and interacting with reliable local interlocutors in devastated and turbulent post-conflict situations. If they do have the time, resources and inclination to investigate local legal traditions, international actors may encounter a more significant impediment: that of unpacking complex, contested and fluid customary laws and traditions and deciding how to integrate them in the rule of law programmes they propose. The question of customary law has been inadequately considered in the context of rule of law reform, and is given more detailed attention below.

Whatever the reasons for this cultural diffidence, it is questionable whether the international community can renounce all responsibility in this area. It is not certain that post-conflict governments will be more willing and able than external actors to achieve the right balance of modern and customary laws, and of universal norms and cultural traditions. It is debatable whether governmental efforts, free of external involvement, will be able to engage and consult local voices in order to achieve a rule of law that is acceptable to their populations and inspires their confidence.

It is not claimed that international actors have not at all been involved in the substantive content of laws. In Cambodia, in the absence of functional laws, UNTAC officials wrote much of the criminal code and constitution – although to mixed effect, as noted earlier.[96] In Namibia too, it was the Western Contact Group in the Security Council that drafted and obtained agreement between opposed factions on the Constitutional Principles that served as a basis for the elected Constituent Assembly in drafting the Constitution. Nevertheless, SWAPO leaders insist that the Constitutional Principles were accepted only because they replicated SWAPO's own principles.[97] In Rwanda foreign legal experts helped the government find ways of dealing with its overwhelming caseload resulting from the 1994 genocide. The genocide law finally passed by the government was drafted with assistance mainly from North American lawyers, loosely based on the US plea bargaining system.[98] However, as experts involved themselves acknowledge, international lawyers engaged in drafting substantive laws have largely referred to and replicated their own legal systems, rather than catered to and built on local realities and needs.[99] Therefore foreign involvement in this substantive area so far has reinforced rather than mitigated the minimalist direction of rule of law programmes. Guatemala is the first example of a post-conflict country where the peace agreement specifically calls for the integration of indigenous Mayan customary law into national law. The outcome of this experiment – which has provoked controversy and opposition – may prove decisive for dealing with future cases.[100]

Contending with customary law and legal pluralism

A significant impediment facing donors and legal experts undertaking rule of law reform is to find out, despite conflict's disruption and destruction, what the content of local legal culture is, in order to assess how it might be integrated with the legal framework they propose. This predicament is roughly analogous to that confronted by frustrated nineteenth-century colonial administrators seeking the roots of 'native' customary law in African colonies: 'The difficulty after a period of disintegration is to find out what their [legal] system was. *They* know perfectly well but, for one reason or another, they may not tell you.'[101]

It is inordinately difficult in most post-conflict situations to find living, present, informed interlocutors with expertise in customary or formal domestic law, who, moreover, have sufficient trust and confidence in external actors to confide in them. The majority of potential interlocutors may have fled or been killed, and those left behind may have valid reasons to shy away from this responsibility. It may be equally confounding to ascertain what are considered 'authentic' and 'accepted' customary laws and legal traditions. As African scholars observe, not all customary laws are necessarily benign, as they have undergone their own troubled history and evolution, and their content may not necessarily be uniformly acceptable to all citizens or communities in the country.[102]

Colonial administrators in nineteenth-century Africa often opted for indirect rule in their attempt to establish the rule of law and find effective laws to govern and control native populations. To simplify governance, they acknowledged the authority of traditional chiefs and invested them with judicial authority as well as a degree of executive power to settle disputes according to customary law. They co-opted chiefs into colonial administrations by establishing Native Authorities. This was the origin of legal dualism, a precursor to current-day legal pluralism, where one set of modern laws applied to the white, mainly urban, colonizers and another set of customary laws applied to the 'native', mainly rural, population. Chieftains invested with relatively unquestioned authority to arbitrate according to customary law, backed by the power of the colonial state when necessary, did not necessarily dispense this authority benevolently. Chieftains possessed arbitrary power to decide the content of customary law, and many manipulated this power to suit their own purposes: 'Conferred the power to enforce their notion of custom as law, chiefs were assured of backup support from colonial institutions – and direct force, if need be – in the event they encountered opposition or defiance. Customary law thus consolidated the non-customary power of colonial chiefs.'[103] This process did not always produce 'laws which were well designed to achieve justice'.[104]

The simplistic and erroneous assumption made by colonial administrators about customary law – that it is static and uniform – is often repeated by rule of law reformers today. In reality, 'the customary was not opaque but porous, not stagnant but dynamic'.[105] 'Customary law has long existed but never been static. It has always been in processes of development and adaptation.'[106]

Given this background, customary and traditional laws and practices may be particularly difficult to integrate with modern law in the aftermath of conflict. It was noted earlier that when official administration of justice collapses during conflict or political emergency, local alternatives often arise, based in many cases on traditional practices and customary law. Authority often reverts back to traditional chiefs, as in Afghanistan, or to warlords, as in Somalia.[107] This could have a stabilizing effect on society and partially fill the vacuum left in legal justice. However, it is also potentially dangerous, as the chief's authority is unsanctioned and arbitrary, and as the customary law reverted to may not be acceptable to all parts of the population. It has been observed that such informal or 'traditional' individuals or institutions that emerge during or after conflict 'are normally reflections of local power structures, with no necessary commitment to egalitarian principles. Simply because they exist outside the control of the state does not guarantee that they embody any qualities of morality or concern for the greater good.'[108] As a UN human rights official observed, 'It is trendy to say the voice of locals is crucial. But sometimes it is very negative. We need to test which voices we really want to hear and help.'[109]

Beyond the problem of integrating customary law lies that of dealing with legal pluralism. In the intermediate years of post-colonial independence, many governments embarked on radical legal reform to integrate customary with modern law. Their responses took a few different forms in the African context. On one end of the spectrum, a limited, conservative response sought to retain customary law as a valuable cultural expression, and consequently retained the dual colonial structure of customary and modern courts, linking them only at the apex through a single integrated review process. This was done, for example, in Chad, the Central African Republic and Zaire. The more radical states undertook bolder reform. They aimed to unify the court system either by integrating the substantive customary and modern laws into a single legal code called state law, as in Ghana and Senegal, or by simply abolishing customary courts, as witnessed in Nigeria, Mali, Côte d'Ivoire and Tanzania, where legal reform was most far-reaching.[110]

This led to different forms of legal pluralism which persist in African states today. State law pluralism refers to cases where the official state law accepts both customary and modern laws. Deep legal pluralism refers to cases where both operate separately, customary law on the one hand and state law on the other. Western countries are governed by a 'legal universe consisting of unified, coherent, clearly demarcated bodies of norms, institutions and practices'. By contrast, in non-Western societies peacebuilders must contend with '[m]any so-called legal systems, including those of states, as derived from multiple sources of validity, potentially full of inconsistencies, and merging by imperceptible degrees into other bodies of laws, many of them non-state laws, around them'.[111] International actors often must contend, therefore, not only with customary law in its varied forms and indefinite substance, but also with the vestiges of post-independence legal systems and varieties of legal pluralism. Understandably, it is not an easy task for them to understand and integrate these within their rule of law reform efforts. Nevertheless, it is a responsibility they cannot shirk.

Anchoring public confidence

For the astute ear, the recurrent whisper through this examination is public confidence. The blatantly missing element in rule of law reform is engagement of the populations inhabiting war-torn societies. The realization born of experiences like those in Cambodia is that 'ultimately, success is determined by public confidence in the . . . system to deliver justice', for which 'ensuring community participation is essential'.[112] Based on his experience in Haiti, Rwanda and elsewhere, the human rights lawyer O'Neill contends that engagement with the population is the fourth pillar of the rule of law, alongside the traditional tripod.[113] Rule of law reform can improve and meet its objective only if it recognizes and adopts this fourth leg.

To achieve public confidence, it is necessary that substantive laws be grounded in notions of justice germane to that society and in legal practices familiar to and accepted by its population. Further, it requires that individuals and groups in community be actively engaged in the process, and that they voluntarily accept the proposed rule of law. However, a careful balance is required. Alongside the difficulties of discovering customary law and cultural traditions in post-conflict contexts, there is the risk of unwittingly reinforcing iniquitous practices or undesirable power authorities, out of deference to local customs, culture and leaders, as noted above. As Plunkett observes, 'Criminal justice systems initiated and designed by the UN [and other external actors] must therefore be culturally sensitive and acceptable to the population concerned, and must at the same time accord with basic UN standards.'[114]

The difficult question for external actors is how to integrate universal or Western notions and frameworks of the rule of law with indigenous culture, legal traditions and customary laws, when so little is known about them. Without such integration public trust may not be won. No society is devoid of its own concepts of justice and its practices of law and peaceful resolution of disputes, however battered by conflict. The difficulty for international actors today is translating such realizations into practice.

Conclusion

Ultimately, a rule of law framework will be acceptable and sustainable if it responds adequately to the needs and realities specific to each society. Despite the notable achievements of international actors in rule of law reform, their programmes tend towards programmatic minimalism. They are largely replicable, standardized, culturally in-offensive and politically 'neutral' or uninformed; they focus on tech-nical procedures and institutions rather than law's substance and ethos.

There are two concurrent and countervailing needs operative in post-conflict situations: order and justice. There is, admittedly, a pressing need in the post-conflict context to restore security and stability after the destabilization of conflict. This need to restore order is urgently felt by governments and the international donor community. They are apprised of the price of a relapse into conflict, and the necessity of preserving negative peace deploying limited human and financial resources. And they view the rule of law as an instrument to achieve this goal. As expressed vehemently by the former legal prosecutor for Cambodia, 'A young democracy without an established rule of law may soon degenerate into a people ruled by warlords and tribalism. A fragile government without an independent and adequately resourced judiciary may soon perish . . . a lasting peace is not achievable unless it carries with it the imperative of law.'[115]

On the other side, however, are populations progressively stripped of justice and human dignity by violent conflict, and by illegitimate, dysfunctional or non-functional states of rule of law offering neither legal protection nor redress. For ordinary people, restoring the rule of law will be meaningful only if it is synonymous with justice, with protecting their rights and dignity so that they can live safe from humiliation and fear. The demand of people in post-conflict societies, in effect, is not just for order and 'negative peace' which national and international governments have their sights focused on, but simultan-eously for legal justice and 'positive peace' to cement and consolidate it. In this context, where the need for law and order hangs as heavy in the balance as the demand for legal justice, it must be asked whether programmatic minimalism is an appropriate and sufficient response, and whether it will contribute to building a just peace.

As noted, some post-conflict societies do have a minimalist rule of law regime that functions throughout conflict, as in South Africa. Nevertheless, South Africa's legal system of apartheid was considered to be illegitimate not only by the majority of its own population but also by the international community. As underlined in this chapter, it is not outward institutions and structures that inspire public trust in legal justice and popular engagement in the reconciliation process. Rather, what will inspire public trust is the actual substance of the laws and the state's explicit commitment to them; what will regain public confidence is the state's performance in upholding these laws and guaranteeing legal justice and human dignity to all its people without distinction. Admittedly, substance without form has no meaning. However, the maximalist vision is not unmindful of form. It merely says that form and structure are inadequate unless underpinned by the appropriate ethos. If the rule of law is restored only in form without any reference to its substantive content, and if that substantive content is devoid of justice, it may succeed temporarily in underpinning order and preserving negative peace, but it will provide an insubstantial foundation for consolidating a just peace.

Yet it would appear that, for the present, international actors have cast their lot with programmatic minimalism. For all their technical achievements in this crucial aspect of peacebuilding, the efforts of international actors in restoring the rule of law are designed primarily to secure order, with justice being a second-order priority. This is potentially dangerous in post-conflict situations. An observation made in the context of nineteenth-century colonization in Africa is ominously apposite to current experience: 'As the substance of the law was subordinated to the quest for order, the claim to be bringing the "rule of law" to Africa became handmaiden to the imperative to ground power effectively.'[116] This is not to suggest any similarity between the objectives of today's peacebuilders and those of nineteenth-century colonial administrators, but only to underline the similar risk faced today. International actors must be wary lest the quest for legal justice is supplanted by the imperative of order, and negative peace is paid for at the cost of positive peace.

4

Rectificatory Justice:

Punishing Perpetrators or Vindicating Victims?

Introduction: the lure and dangers of simplification

Rectificatory justice contends with the claims for justice arising from violations committed during the course of conflict. Its concern is the immediate human consequences of conflict in terms of the direct violence inflicted on people – gross human rights abuses, crimes against humanity and war crimes. International and national attention has focused on this dimension of justice recently, as countries emerged from protracted internal conflicts, notably Bosnia, Rwanda and South Africa.

International attention has helped highlight issues of post-conflict justice. However, it could be questioned whether this flood of interest clarifies or, rather, obfuscates the exigencies of rectificatory justice in war-torn low-income societies. I argue in this chapter that the complex claims of rectificatory justice in war-torn low-income societies have been oversimplified by peacebuilders; rather than understand and respond to complexity, they have sought to find a single definitive solution that could be applied, with minor adaptation, across disparate cases. Shaped by past experiences of democratic transitions in other parts of the world, scholars, activists and practitioners as yet possess an incomplete understanding of the distinctly different circumstances of less-developed post-conflict countries, and the specific needs, constraints and dilemmas they face.

I argue instead that rectificatory justice issues in these countries are complex and contentious, and elude simple, universal solutions. My argument has three strands. First, I contend that a single officially sponsored mechanism cannot resolve rectificatory justice claims definitively, in any country. Rather, a combination of measures that includes but goes beyond the criminal justice system is required. Second, the preferred mechanisms in use today are inappropriate because they target individual perpetrators and victims, and sideline the wider community of survivors affected by injustice. Although the law requires identifying individual perpetrators and victims, rectificatory justice requires a broader and more comprehensive response, engaging all survivors within a given society. Third and in conclusion, I argue that rectificatory justice, divorced from its organic and functional interdependence with legal justice on the one hand and distributive justice on the other, is incomplete and precarious.[1]

In search of definitive solutions: trials or truth commissions?

Catalysed by the horror of the Nazi Holocaust, international treaty law developed rapidly after the Second World War. The Nuremberg and Tokyo trials set up by the victorious Allied forces after the Second World War, although not entirely successful, were a dramatic manifestation of the world community's determination that gross human rights violations, and particularly war crimes and crimes against humanity, could not escape some form of reckoning.[2] Thereafter, international law spread its coverage rapidly: the Genocide Convention (1948); the Universal Declaration of Human Rights (1948) and the two covenants (1966); the Geneva Conventions on laws of war (1949) and the two additional protocols (1977); Conventions against racial discrimination (1966), apartheid (1973), and torture and degrading punishment (1984).[3]

Yet until recently 'Nations have honored these obligations largely in the breach'.[4] It was only in recent years that the international community acted forcefully to defend these principles, by setting up *ad hoc* international tribunals to try war crimes in the former Yugoslavia and Rwanda, and accepting with ninety-eight signatures the Rome Treaty of 1998 to institute an international criminal court.[5]

Although dormant in international practice until recently, the challenge of dealing with human rights abuses remained alive at the national level. As countries exited from dictatorship and authoritarianism in Southern Europe (1970s), Latin America (1980s), and Central and Eastern Europe (late 1980s), scholars and politicians deliberated on issues of transitional justice: how to balance the legal and moral imperative of rendering justice for past violations with political constraints imposed by transition.[6] Amnesties for past human rights abuses were the order of the day in the 1980s, especially in Latin America.[7] More recently the preference of human rights organizations, victims' groups, certain UN agencies and several bilateral donors is for prosecution and punishment. Simultaneously, 'truth commissions' have gained currency, and the establishment and public acknowledgement of the truth about past atrocities is regarded by many scholars and practitioners as an essential complement to trials or as a second-best alternative where trials are impossible.

The immense popularity of both mechanisms – trials and truth commissions – and the strong support they receive from the international, human rights and donor communities have created an implicit obligation for countries newly emergent from conflict to adopt one or both. Often this obligation is written into peace agreements, as in El Salvador and Guatemala, both of which were bequeathed truth commissions. In other cases, human rights activists and donors pressure governments to institute trials or truth commissions as means to counter impunity and establish accountability, as in Sierra Leone. There are forceful arguments in favour of both options. However, proponents of trials and truth commissions accord less attention to the difficulties of applying these two mechanisms in low-income post-conflict societies, and to their shortcomings in these politically and materially constrained contexts.

Prosecution: legal imperatives and practical difficulties

The legal case for prosecution for past violations is strong and rests on three primary arguments. The first, state responsibility, is clearly elaborated in international law.[8] Under international treaty law and international customary law, the duties of states to provide redress for specific violations committed during conflict are clearly established. Successor states are expected to fulfil their duties even if violations were committed by a prior regime. Under international customary law, these duties apply even to states that are not parties to specific treaties in application.[9] Second, victims' rights to compensation and redress are specified in human rights covenants and relevant treaties, and establish clear obligations on states.[10] Additionally, a strong legal case is made for establishing individual criminal accountability for certain crimes under international criminal law.[11] Third, international law strictly circumscribes the mitigating circumstances under which derogations are permissible. Article 4 of the ICCPR discusses derogations during emergencies, and Article 4 (2) states that no derogation is possible for the right to life, protection from torture, degrading punishment and slavery.[12]

The argument for prosecution and punishment is also strongly defended on moral grounds by human rights activists and moral philosophers.[13] As noted in chapter 2, rectificatory justice is often interpreted today as retributive justice, based on the Kantian model of punishment. Proponents of trials put forward retributive justifications for trial and punishment, or utilitarian arguments of punishment as a form of deterrence.[14] Psychologists and scholars of procedural justice who have studied victims of the Holocaust, state repression and torture note that victims derive more satisfaction from the way the procedure is conducted and its symbolic value than from its actual outcome.[15] Victims want above all a fair procedure where they can be heard by an impartial arbitrator, as this allows them to express their loss, and goes further towards restoring their sense of dignity and giving value to their suffering. For these reasons, studies of procedural justice suggest that victims prefer formalized proceedings such as court trials and tribunals to out-of-court settlement, as the latter denies them the opportunity to voice their grievances. These moral and psychological arguments strengthen the legal case for trials.

However strong the legal and moral arguments in favour of prosecution, formidable obstacles confront the attempt to prosecute in practice in less-developed, war-shattered countries with overwhelming legacies of atrocities. The difficulties faced are, first, political; second, related to the state of the rule of law; and third, financial and material.

Political obstacles
Current literature on political obstacles focuses mainly on Latin American transitions in the 1980s, where the constraint to action was 'determined primarily by the residual power retained by forces of the old order', notably the military.[16] Although partly valid in some countries, like El Salvador, Guatemala and Haiti, it is more often the case that no party or institution is solely culpable, as all sides commit violations. In Mozambique, for example, although most atrocities are attributed to the rebel RENAMO forces, the government led by FRELIMO is not guiltless.[17] In Rwanda, although the 1994 genocide was planned and perpetrated by the Hutu extremist Interahamwe, the government formed by the victorious RPF also committed excesses

against suspected Hutu extremists and collaborators, and innocent villagers in north-western Rwanda, which it has tried to conceal.[18]

The political task is to get opposing factions who have committed atrocities against each other and against an innocent civilian population to come to a peaceful settlement. The dilemma for those seeking peace in vicious conflicts today is whether to accept a continuation of hostilities which add daily to the injustices heaped on innocent civilians, or to accept some form of peace, even if it precludes formal justice, at least temporarily. This was the compromise peacemakers initially made in Sierra Leone in July 1999, in concluding a peace agreement that specifically excluded justice for atrocities.[19]

It is extremely difficult during peace negotiations to get leaders to agree to institute trials; such agreement is even harder outside the context of peace negotiations, or after the conclusion of conflict. Leaders on both or all sides are reluctant to accept culpability for their own side's offences, as they would lose credibility with their supporters, and compromise their ambition to exercise political leadership in the post-conflict dispensation. The UN Secretary-General's belated plans to establish a tribunal for Sierra Leone are hampered by the clear amnesty provisions in the peace agreements, and the reluctance of both sides to have their atrocities publicized.[20] The dilemma faced by the African National Congress (ANC) and President Mandela in South Africa over Winnie Madikizela Mandela's alleged involvement in gang activities, and in the murder of a 14-year-old boy, Stompie, exemplifies this. One black South African commented, 'We should be harder on Winnie than on Magnus Malan or P. W. Botha, because she stood for more. She is supposed to be one of us – someone with principles.'[21]

Further, however brutal their tactics, both or all parties to conflict usually believe they are fighting a just cause, and are unwilling to accept that their conduct may be criminal. Despite its well-documented atrocities, Mozambique's RENAMO maintained it was fighting for democracy and religious and economic freedom, and received support from right-wing and religious groups in the USA, Europe and elsewhere on these grounds. Indeed, RENAMO's 1982 'Manifest and Programme' commits to the creation of a multi-party, democratic state, free enterprise and a market economy, and a state respecting human rights, all highly appealing to donors.[22] By contrast, the ANC was willing to subject its own actions to public scrutiny during its outlawed struggle, and set up two truth commissions for this purpose – the only non-state entity to do so.[23] Ironically then, once in government, the ANC was less co-operative with the Truth and Reconciliation Commission (TRC): it resented being held to the same standard by the TRC as the former apartheid government, for violations it may have committed in its struggle against a recognized crime against humanity.[24]

Governments who use violence to repress rebel movements claim – and often believe – they are justly defending their state and citizens from traitors. True of past Latin American dictatorships like Chile, Argentina and Peru, it was also the case in El Salvador, Guatemala and apartheid South Africa. El Salvador's ARENA government was incredulous and dismissive when the Truth Commission's report held it responsible for the vast majority of abuses perpetrated during conflict. The government had agreed to have a truth commission partly because it believed it was no more culpable than the FMLN.[25] Many agents of apartheid are angered at being treated as criminals for doing what they believe was simply their duty. De Klerk, joint-recipient of the Nobel Peace Prize with Mandela, long refused to admit that apartheid was wrong, and only concedes that excesses were committed due to 'bad judgement, overzealousness or negligence of individual policemen'.[26]

The only cases where trials face less effective opposition is where one side emerges victorious and is able to impose 'victor's justice', as in Rwanda and Ethiopia. Yet trials in these cases rarely escape allegations of bias and unfairness, as happened with the Nuremberg and Tokyo tribunals imposed by the victorious Allies.[27] A study based on empirical evidence from thirty transitions since the mid-1970s notes that a government's policy choice on former human rights abuses tends towards trials as outgoing regimes become weaker and away from trials as they become stronger, indicating the resistance of leaders to prosecution.[28]

Recent experiences illustrate the political difficulties of prosecuting perpetrators. In South Africa ANC stalwarts concede that if they had not accepted a partial amnesty to forestall the possibility of trials, the National Party would never have agreed to peace at all.[29] It was an ineluctable political compromise.

The Namibian case is less frequently discussed. SWAPO had long championed the cause of justice against its colonial, apartheid oppressors during its struggle, but performed a *volte face* once elected to office.[30] The SWAPO government defended its decision not to pursue trials – and, in fact, to take no action whatsoever regarding past atrocities – as 'a very conscious process': 'We looked at other past experiences: if we open the past, where will it end? We respect history, we don't want to change or forget it, but we want to forgive, join hands and build the country together.'[31] This attitude coincided with the SWAPO government's policy of national reconciliation, which prioritized national unity and political stability, and attempted to avoid antagonizing the powerful white community, as much for political as for economic reasons.[32]

Nevertheless, SWAPO's decision to turn a blind eye to the past was not based solely on its policy of reconciliation: it was also influenced by the public exposure of its own alleged atrocities during the liberation struggle. Several hundred SWAPO members were detained on charges of being South African spies, and tortured in detention camps in Angola. Several died in custody.[33] The detainee issue became so politically charged during the mandate of the UN Transition Assistance Group (UNTAG) that a UN Mission on Detainees was established by UN Special Representative Marti Athisaari to conduct enquiries at SWAPO's detention camps. In May 1989 201 SWAPO detainees were released.[34] However, detainee groups continued to demand accountability and investigations. The case was sensationalized by the South African-supported opposition party, Democratic Turnhalle Alliance (DTA) in the lead-up to elections, losing SWAPO many votes. Burnt by this scandal and fearing a further loss of credibility from an investigation of its own past, the SWAPO government refused to establish a proposed commission of enquiry, and was reluctant to accept any wrongdoing. In July 1991 the SWAPO government finally allowed the Red Cross to trace missing persons, but not to investigate accountability or culpability. This operation was phased out a year later.[35] The public exposure of the detainee issue made SWAPO the focus of claims for rectificatory justice and deflected attention away from the apartheid state's atrocities. The SWAPO government's unwillingness to expose its comparatively fewer misdemeanours prevented an accounting of the South African apartheid regime's graver systematic injustices against the Namibian population.[36]

In Cambodia the Khmer Rouge regime was responsible for perhaps 1 million deaths between 1975 and 1979.[37] Many unsuccessful independent and international attempts were made during the 1980s to prosecute Khmer Rouge perpetrators.[38] Gregory Stanton's Cambodian Genocide Project proposed that the case be brought to the International Court of Justice; David Hawk's Cambodia Documentation Commission proposed a tribunal as an alternative. Several countries like Australia, Canada, Norway and the UK presented evidence on the genocide to the UN Commission on Human Rights, but were unwilling to take the issue to the International Court of Justice. In 1986 Australia proposed the establishment of a tribunal at the Association of South East Asian Nations (ASEAN), but withdrew the proposal when China and the USA objected. When the opportunity was revived during the peace process, Hun Sen initially insisted on trials of Khmer Rouge leaders as a condition for negotiations. This was firmly rejected not only by other Cambodian factions, but also by China and the USA. Finally, the only acknowledgement of Khmer Rouge atrocities in the peace agreement was: 'Cambodia's tragic recent history requires special measures to assure the protection of human rights, and the non-return to the policies and practices of the past.'[39] Over two decades later, and after over two years of intense lobbying by the UN and the USA, Cambodia has signed into law the establishment of a mixed UN-assisted tribunal to prosecute Khmer Rouge leaders. However, in February 2002, the UN ended its negotiations with Cambodia, fearing that trials would not be fair.[40]

In El Salvador the FMLN too had initially insisted during negotiations that the only adequate redress for human rights violations was trials. It is only when the FMLN realized that the ARENA government would not yield on that score that it settled for an international truth commission as the next best available option. Although the Truth Commission's report did not call for trials and simply identified by name the principal perpetrators, the ARENA government rushed an amnesty through Congress to foreclose the possibility of prosecution of its allies in the military and judiciary.[41] These examples illustrate that political obstacles and resistance to trials can be formidable if not insurmountable in many if not most countries emerging from conflict.

Legal obstacles
The second set of difficulties stems from the state of the rule of law. That is, even when political obduracy does not prevent trials from being carried out, weaknesses of the rule of law may do so. As discussed in chapter 3, the rule of law is often either illegitimate, corrupted or devastated in countries undergoing conflict. In any of the three scenarios portrayed in chapter 3 it is unlikely that trials can be conducted fairly and with due process, if they are conducted at all. When the ethos of the rule of law is weak and its three institutional pillars, courts, police and prisons, are dysfunctional, trials respecting legality are near-impossible.

In Rwanda, despite the devastated state of the rule of law after genocide, the new government initiated national trials. These trials have been criticized for failing to respect the rule of law they set out to defend. When the RPF took power and the Hutu-dominated government fled with its forces, as there was no functioning police force, it was the RPF that arrested suspected perpetrators. Yet it is a violation of the rule of law for a military force to conduct arrests. More seriously, the trials have been accused of not following due process, and failing to provide suspects with a fair trial. Most suspects cannot afford legal defence and, even when they can, they are unable to find anyone to defend suspected *génocidaires*. The lack of a jury and skewed (Tutsi-dominated) recruitment into the judiciary inhibit fair trial.[42]

A central point of contention is the death penalty, which the UN opposes but Rwandan law mandates for murderers. The execution of the first lot of convicted *génocidaires* in mid-1998 led to the breakdown of relations between the government and HRFOR. When negotiations between the two failed, HRFOR withdrew from Rwanda in July 1998, leaving no UN presence to monitor the degeneration of human rights, especially in the north-west province where violent conflict persisted.[43] The difficulties encountered in Rwanda also underline that the restoration of the rule of law, both its ethos and its institutions, are pivotal to the success of conducting trials for past abuses.

The sheer number of atrocities committed in many conflicts creates a paradox. It reinforces the argument for a firm response based on international law to counter impunity, yet it makes this response difficult to operationalize within existing legal systems. In Rwanda international lawyers concede that it would be impossible even for an extensive, well-established legal system to handle the overwhelming caseload faced in Rwanda, which is beyond Rwanda's present capacity. With help from foreign lawyers, the government tried to develop innovative laws and legal mechanisms such as collective trials or plea bargaining to speed up trials.[44] The government passed the Organic Law on 30 August 1996 to deal with the serious backlog of cases. Covering events between 1 October 1990 and 31 December 1994, the law classifies persons accused of genocide according to four categories, ranging from planning and perpetrating genocide in Category One to property offences in Category Four.[45] The law introduces an element of plea bargaining, as anyone not in Category One can confess and name accomplices in exchange for a reduced sentence. Despite innovative legislation, trials have progressed very slowly, as the Organic Law is little known or used by Rwandans. Yet it is bitterly opposed by some victim groups who insist on full accountability via formal justice.[46] Furthermore, even if it were decided to try only Category One cases, it would take an estimated ten to fifteen years to try them all.[47] The same problem/paradox is faced in many other war-torn countries with massive violations, including Afghanistan, Sierra Leone, the DRC and Sudan.

It is not only in extreme cases of total breakdown of the rule of law that trials may become unfeasible. El Salvador is a case where the legal system was deeply corrupt but still functional, as noted in chapter 3. The Truth Commission's recommendation against prosecution owing to the incapacity of Salvadorean legal institutions to provide impartial trial, despite the strong moral argument favouring it, is a case in point. Truth Commissioner Buergenthal, himself a human rights lawyer, maintains this was the best possible option at the time as no trials were preferable to unfair trials.[48] A familiar argument in support of trials is that they reinforce and test the rule of law.[49] Yet unfair trials serve to undermine, not strengthen, the rule of law.

Material obstacles

The third set of obstacles to trials stems from the serious constraints of financial and material resources faced in post-conflict contexts. Even if political and rule of law problems are not insurmountable, the sheer cost of trials often makes this option unfeasible. This is especially so in situations of mass atrocities where perpetrators are numerous, and the resources at the disposal of the state are very limited. International financial support for trials, when received, is usually limited, and may also risk deflecting assistance from other urgent projects of reconstruction. The international tribunal for Rwanda exemplifies the problem: with a budget of US$36m for 1996 alone, it had indicted only twenty-one people by the end of that year.[50] In South Africa it cost 9 million Rand and six court appearances simply to try to get the defiant P. W. Botha to appear before the TRC.[51] Although South Africa is relatively wealthier than other post-conflict countries considered here, the legal costs associated with the TRC have raised doubts among South Africans about the moral justification for so much expense on justice, when people continue to live in deprivation. In Sierra Leone, although the extreme nature and scale of atrocities caught public attention, the UN's proposed tribunal has won only political support from the UN Security Council, but financial support has not been forthcoming.[52]

Beyond finances lie material difficulties imposed by the context. Rarely can the kind of hard evidence required for courtroom trials be found for the mass violations committed during violent internal conflicts. Ethiopia is an exception. Under Menghistu, violations were documented scrupulously, and volumes of evidence were easily found by the Special Prosecutor instituted to investigate and prosecute abuses. Yet only a few trials have followed in over a decade since Menghistu's overthrow, despite the incoming government's initial zeal in arresting 4,000 suspected violators.[53] More often, as in Cambodia, Mozambique and Sierra Leone, hard evidence for a court trial is difficult to find, as killings are often massive, unplanned and undocumented.[54] Exhumation and post-mortems are unaffordable when hundreds of thousands have been killed. Where witnesses remain alive, they often lack the courage to testify against abusers for fear of reprisal, and witness protection programmes are too expensive for impoverished states.

These examples indicate some of the reasons why prosecution, however morally compelling, is extremely difficult to pursue at the national level in post-conflict countries, for a combination of political, legal, financial and material reasons. Furthermore, if the limited human and financial resources of a weak judicial system, barely recuperating after conflict, are so severely stretched attending to just a few high-level cases, the system can neither provide meaningful rectificatory justice for the past, nor attend to its criminal justice responsibilities of the present.

International trials as an alternative?

The establishment of international tribunals to try war-related crimes in former Yugoslavia and Rwanda and the proposed International Criminal Court suggest that international trials might be a way to compensate for the inadequacies of national trials. Both *ad hoc* tribunals are significant manifestations of the international community's will to defend universal principles and international law, even when violations occur within national borders during internal conflicts. Nevertheless, both tribunals have been beset by problems. Although not a case considered in this study, in the former Yugoslavia the tension between peace and justice has been starkly highlighted by the tribunal's functioning. International forces have been reluctant to apprehend war criminals whose popularity with their citizens and support of the peace agreement is perceived to be crucial for the preservation of peace.[55] There is frustration internally and externally that only relatively minor figures have been tried, while major players retain power, credibility and freedom at home. Milosevic's extradition in July 2001 was obtained after a bitter political tussle and only on the promise of substantial Western aid, but others like Karadzic still remain free.

In Rwanda the substantial discrepancy between international and national trials regarding the treatment of offenders, the legal process and permissible punishments has stoked controversy internationally and led to a backlash nationally within the victim community. Rwandans resent the fact that minor offenders languish and die in insalubrious Rwandan jails, while the arrested masterminds of genocide enjoy the comparative luxury of jails in Arusha built to conform to UN standards. Further, if and when tried, these major perpetrators will face at maximum a life sentence, while those tried nationally face the death penalty under Rwandan law. Rwandan victims feel that perpetrators are being privileged over victims: while the surviving population continues to die of poverty and starvation, international resources are allocated disproportionately to the upkeep of major perpetrators.[56]

The hard-won struggle for the establishment of a permanent International Criminal Court (ICC), achieved in Rome in July 1998, is a further manifestation of the international community's renewed commitment to act against impunity. The ICC is not a focus of this study, as it is not yet established and cannot be treated as a tried measure of rectificatory justice, but significant ramifications for rectificatory justice in post-conflict societies can be anticipated.[57] The USA's stiff resistance to aspects of the Rome Treaty, and Congressional opposition to President Clinton's belated signing of the Treaty at the end of 2000, as well as the low rate of ratification compared to signatories, portend some of the difficulties the ICC will face in establishing its jurisdiction and fulfilling its remit. Even when the ICC is able to overcome potential sources of opposition and address violations in a particular country, it will be able to address at best a few high-profile cases and try a few symbolically important perpetrators, owing to the enormous time and resources required for each trial. It is unlikely that a court with quasi-worldwide jurisdiction will succeed in doing more than the tribunals for Rwanda and former Yugoslavia are able to do with a limited mandate and covering only a single country each.

The ICC recognizes these limits and does not aim to supplant national trials. The Rome Treaty stipulates that primary jurisdiction will still lie with national courts; that is, if prosecution can be conducted at the national level, this will be preferred. This is not unprecedented. The Nuremberg Tribunal tried only twenty-two leading German war criminals and the Tokyo Tribunal tried twenty-eight Japanese,[58] whereas several thousand trials were conducted in national courts under the supervision of the Allied powers.[59] However, this leads back to the enormous obstacles and shortcomings of national trials.

The ICC, when functional, will provide a forum for meting out justice in strict accordance with international law and standards. Owing to pressures of time and resources, its trials will be selective and symbolic rather than comprehensive. Moreover, the ICC will not act retrospectively. The ICC's main objective and function may prove to be <u>deterrent and normative,</u> It will highlight the development and status of international law and opinion on the matter: that no individual is beyond the arm of the law, and that however serious a perpetrator's atrocities, she or he will nevertheless be accorded full rights to a free, fair and impartial trial and humane punishment. Yet it is misleading to believe that the ICC will solve definitively the many problems and dilemmas besetting the pursuit of justice in the transition to peace, or that it will or could offer the main course of action in these cases.

An important consideration today is whether national trials or international trials are the preferable response to past violations. International trials may carry symbolic and legal value. They signal to victims that the international community heeds their sufferings; and to perpetrators that they can no longer act with impunity. However, it is argued that national trials make a greater contribution to reconciliation, healing and peacebuilding. If trials are held far from the home country, they are inaccessible and alien to the local population, who most need to benefit from and follow the process closely; international trials have minimal impact on survivors' personal lives, and provide no palliative for their suffering and loss. National trials, it is contended, may have beneficial ripple effects throughout society. They may help to reinforce the rule of law, build public confidence in law and peace, and strengthen the government's credibility. International trials cannot transmit these national benefits.[60] The ambivalence and even animosity of some Rwandan victims to the international tribunal is related to their estrangement from the Arusha-based trials, and a constant demand of the government has been to relocate the tribunal within Rwanda.

Consequently, a dilemma arises in choosing between national and international trials. As shown above, national trials may not be feasible or desirable in many cases owing to political obstacles, weaknesses of the rule of law, and financial and material constraints. Furthermore, where conducted, national trials may themselves violate legality and human rights if the rule of law is weak, as in Rwanda and Ethiopia. Yet international trials, albeit conducted in strict accordance with universal rights and rule of law, may be incomplete in their coverage; they may be alienating and unsatisfactory for surviving populations.

The yet-undecided fate of a mixed tribunal in Cambodia will be decisive for the future of trials. A UN-assisted trial with a mixture of international and Cambodian judges is proposed and was finally passed into law in August 2001, after years of arduous negotiation led by the UN and the USA. The proposed tribunal is a striking innovation as it combines the features of national and international trials discussed above, thereby reducing the disadvantages of each. Further, it will be convened within Cambodia, allowing for proximity to and engagement with local populations. While ideal in theory, in practice the Cambodian government, and particularly Hun Sen, has been ambivalent about and often resistant to the tribunal. Hun Sen, a Khmer Rouge defector himself, has alternately embraced and chastised Khmer Rouge leaders, sometimes wanting to 'dig a hole and bury the past', and at other times insisting that prosecuting Khmer Rouge leaders could not be avoided. On the other hand, government critics fear that the presence and predominance of Cambodian judges on the tribunal will impair the tribunal's neutrality, given the continued weakness and political manipulation of the rule of law.[61]

In some cases it may not be possible or even desirable to hold trials immediately after conflict terminates. The rule of law may be too weak, resources too few, political risks too high, or political will and capacity too scant. These cases should not be read as failures. Sometimes it may be detrimental to the cause of justice to rush trials in volatile, vulnerable post-conflict situations with weak criminal justice systems. It may be preferable to postpone trials until government is more stable, and the rule of law is better equipped to provide formal justice. A case in point is current attempts to prosecute a former president, dictator and other leaders in Guatemala, who benefited from an amnesty in December 1996 when peace was concluded.[62]

The verdict?   Despite the legal, moral and psychological arguments favouring trials, some scholars hold that 'trials may not be appropriate even in cases where the legal system is intact'.[63] The adversarial and confrontational nature of trials is considered inimical to reconciliation or integration after conflict.[64] Trials tend to harden divisive and hostile feelings between offender and victim, and victims often feel further victimized and humiliated when cross-examined in court. The burden of proof beyond reasonable doubt sometimes lets perpetrators get off free. As noted above, in many post-conflict situations like Cambodia it is difficult to find hard evidence of the quality that will satisfy the requirements of a court of law, but even a publicly recognized criminal cannot be prosecuted without hard evidence, as this violates the rule of law. The rigorous demands of a court of law and the nature of trials may reveal some hard facts, but trials do not lead to a full accounting of the past. They do not elucidate the causes of conflict, patterns of violence, and consequences for victims, which are equally or more important in the aftermath of violent conflict.[65]

These shortcomings, combined with the political, legal, and material difficulties they encounter in low-income post-conflict countries, raise serious doubts about the ability of trials to provide satisfactory rectificatory justice. Even leading human rights lawyers admit to the unfeasibility and undesirability of trials, notwithstanding legal obligations. Mendez concedes that 'certainly there is no guarantee that trials are the best means of redressing past human rights violations, nor are they appropriate in all circumstances'; Zalaquett observes that 'the method of individual trials is futile when we deal with massive past abuses'.[66]

Even in the most promising scenarios, where political will and legal and material resources exist, it needs to be recognized that prosecution by itself can only provide a small measure of rectificatory justice. Trials necessarily reach only a tiny percentage of all violators and consequently provide redress to only a small portion of war victims.[67] Furthermore, structural and systemic injustices suffered by civilians during conflict are rarely taken to task through trials. Fear and intimidation, hunger, disease and death suffered during forced displacement cannot be prosecuted in trial, as individual perpetrators are hard to identify. Attention and resources are focused inevitably on prosecuting individuals responsible for the more spectacular but perhaps less numerous direct physical abuses inflicted on identifiable individual victims. Consequently, prosecution in itself cannot satisfy the varied and multiple needs and demands of rectificatory justice of survivors of conflict.

This is not an argument for discarding the option of prosecution. On the contrary, the hard-won principles of international law must be preserved, not cast away. Rather, this is a call to be realistic about the limitations of prosecution in the aftermath of violent internal conflict in poor countries. It is an argument for making innovative use of and adaptations to existing legal mechanisms, and supplementing them, where necessary, with means beyond the criminal justice system.

From trials to truth commissions: triumph or trade-off?

The case for commissions of enquiry, more popularly called 'truth commissions' (TCs), has gained strength as a viable alternative, if not a preferable choice, to trials. Recent observations suggest that many victims want not trials but simply the truth, exposed and officially acknowledged, as compensation for their loss and suffering.[68] Proponents of TCs contend that they are less adversarial and inimical to reconciliation than trials; that they provide more comprehensive accounts of past facts, patterns, causes and consequences than court trials permit; that they provide an unthreatening platform for victims to be heard; and that they may be therapeutic in giving voice to victims' unspoken suffering.[69]

TCs take many shapes and forms, and their mandates vary significantly between countries. Simply defined, they are 'bodies set up to investigate a past history of violations of human rights in a particular country – which can include violations by the military or other government forces or by armed opposition forces'. Their four defining characteristics are: first, a focus on the past; second, an attempt to depict an overall picture of abuses over a given period of time rather than focus on a specific event; third, a finite and predetermined existence ending with the submission of a report; and fourth, 'some sort of authority, by way of its sponsor, that allows it greater access to information, greater security or protection to dig into sensitive issues and a greater impact with its report'.[70]

Some TCs have been empowered to make recommendations to incumbent governments not only on issues of past violations but also on matters of institutional reform and measures to prevent future injustice. El Salvador's peace agreements specified:

> The mandate of the Commission shall include recommending the legal, political or administrative measures that can be inferred from the results of the investigation. Such recommendations may include measures to prevent the repetition of such acts, and initiatives to promote national reconciliation... The Parties undertake to carry out the Commission's recommendations.[71]

Several observers believe that the Salvadorean TC's most important long-term contribution was its recommendations on rule of law reform and institutional change.[72]

A TC might feel impelled to recommend reforms affecting distributive justice, such as redistribution of resources or opportunities that might alleviate the causes of present conflicts and deter future ones. The Reparation and Reconciliation Committee of the South African TRC, while not intended solely for this purpose, may make a contribution in this direction. Consequently, some TCs may go beyond providing a measure of rectificatory justice, and contribute to legal and distributive justice as well.

A call for caution   In my view, however, the popularity and ubiquity of TCs are a cause for concern. There is often a stated or implicit assumption that truth may be a greater good than justice, or in any case, a worthwhile trade-off. Claims about the relationship between truth and justice have proliferated. It has become axiomatic to claim that the truth is a universal requirement in the search for justice. It is argued that victims have a 'right to truth', which entails both the individual right of victims and the collective obligation of societies to avoid a repetition of violations; it is claimed, furthermore, that governments have a corresponding 'duty of memory' to establish this truth.[73] It is argued that establishing the truth is essential for reconciliation; that truth is a deterrent and that exposing the truth is cathartic for victims who can finally express their untold suffering and redeem their reputations. Zalaquett even asserts that 'truth is almost always an absolute value... Justice in the sense of criminal justice may be an option with certain limitations.'[74] With these assertions proponents of TCs advocate the institution of truth commissions in all post-conflict countries, regardless of the individual needs, capacities and wishes of these diverse societies and their people. Nevertheless, it remains open to question whether TCs are a universal good for all post-conflict societies, and whether truth equates to or supersedes justice for their people.[75]

Despite the popularity and proliferation of TCs, recent evidence is ambivalent about their contribution in the aftermath of conflict. The pioneering researcher on them, Hayner, now entertains some doubts about whether the truth is necessary or desirable in all cases of post-conflict or transitional societies. She agrees that in certain ideal circumstances TCs may serve useful purposes. She identifies the necessary factors as: 'public participation in the crafting of the commission'; 'time and resources for preparation and set-up'; 'flexible but strong mandate for investigation'; 'political backing and operational independence'; 'appropriate funding and staffing'; 'implementation of recommendations'; and last, 'a supportive and cooperative role played by the international community'.[76] Hayner observes that without these conditions TCs may fail. Further, a badly conducted TC may be worse than none at all. The following illustrations corroborate these observations.

El Salvador

The case of El Salvador illustrates that even a TC widely regarded as successful may fall short of responding adequately or conclusively to claims for rectificatory justice. The UN Truth Commission for El Salvador was negotiated into the peace agreements, and enjoyed the nominal backing of both parties, as well as the support and assistance of the international community. Three respected international figures were named to serve as Commissioners: the former President of

Colombia, Belisario Betancur; the former Foreign Minister of Venezuela, Frinaldo Figueredo; and the former president of the Inter-American Court of Human Rights, Thomas Buergenthal of the USA.[77]

The Commission appeared set to succeed. It was sufficiently funded, methodologically sound, and well equipped with an international staff of thirty-six. It had broad powers and full access to all sites and persons under the peace agreement. The Commission, by choice, focused on thirty illustrative and high-profile cases instead of trying to cover all violations during the conflict. Nevertheless, it received over 22,000 complaints of serious violations committed between January 1980 and July 1991, of which 7,000 were received directly from individuals and the rest through the government and NGOs. The Commission released its report on 15 March 1993 with international fanfare and praise.

Notwithstanding the excellent quality of the report, the facts it highlighted and the institutional recommendations it made, it could be questioned how much the Commission contributed to victims' quest for rectificatory justice. First, despite the government's commitment in the peace agreements, the process was hobbled by a lack of co-operation from the government and its institutional allies. Scholars distinguish between establishing the truth and actually acknowledging it publicly. 'It's the difference between knowledge and acquiescence. It's what happens and can only happen to knowledge when it becomes officially sanctioned, when it is made part of the cognitive scene.'[78] Yet in El Salvador, when the report was released amidst international fanfare, the government was dismissive and defensive. Neither the government nor the military acknowledged the report or accepted responsibility for the violations attributed to them. Therefore, despite the report's revelation of facts – often already known or suspected, but now confirmed – victims and survivors never had the moral satisfaction of an official acknowledgement and apology. While a significant section of society had supported trials and backed the FMLN's initial insistence on trials at negotiations, the truth commission itself recommended that the named perpetrators not be tried nationally, impeding this route to judicial remedy.[79]

However impartial a TC may intend to be, its version of facts is not immune to politics in the partisan environment following conflict. One observer noted that testimonies made to the El Salvador Commission were not entirely spontaneous, but highly organized, as political factions organized busloads of victims to testify to the Commission, to ensure that their version of facts was noted.[80]

According to some, the TC's report did not aid reconciliation either. In one view, it 'reinforced the polemic' of the war; in another view, 'some criticized the Truth Commission's Report not because it was not true, but because it should have been put in a way more conducive to reconciliation'.[81]

It is often claimed that TCs provide cathartic release to victims who are finally able to tell their stories. This was not the case of El Salvador where TC hearings were confidential, unlike South Africa's TRC, and the public had limited involvement in both the process and the outcome. Although popular summaries in Spanish were distributed by some NGOs, it is often noted that the report remained unknown and inaccessible to the majority of Salvadoreans.[82] Observers inside and outside El Salvador still acclaim the long-term worth of the Commission's institutional recommendations, which have been implemented gradually, despite early obstacles.[83] What is more contestable is the measure of justice this exercise in truth provided to victims and survivors. Also questionable is the extent to which the TC process combated impunity, in light of the government's defiant response and its hasty amnesty without public consultation or consent.

The Salvadorean experience had ramifications for TCs elsewhere. In Guatemala a 'Commission for Historical Clarification' was agreed as part of the peace accord.[84] However, it was given weak and limited powers, including a strict injunction not to identify violators by name. This contrasted with the government's significant concessions on legal and distributive justice issues. The Guatemalan government presumably had realized the danger of a strong and independent TC like El Salvador's. It sought to avoid a similar loss of credibility by diluting the TC's mandate. The experiences and even the successes of one country can have both positive and unforeseen negative ramifications for the search for justice in other countries.[85]

Haiti

The case of Haiti suggests that a poorly supported, low-profile TC may be worse for the cause of rectificatory justice than none at all. Aristide's reinstalled government formed a National Commission for Truth and Justice in early 1995, with three Haitian and three foreign commissioners serving under the leadership of Haitian sociologist Françoise Boucard. It was mandated to investigate the three years of military rule, and to make a public report including recommendations on reparation, rehabilitation and legal and administrative measures to prevent the recurrence of such violations.[86] Working with scant resources and support, the Commission was hampered by both internal and external factors. Internally, it confronted a constrained political situation, inadequate resources and finances, and lack of co-operation from former military leaders. It also faced pressure to complete its report within a year, before Aristide's term of office ended. Externally, the TC had inadequate international support and backing, and faced obstruction in its enquiries, particularly from the US Administration. MICIVIH had been doing courageous work in monitoring and recording human rights abuses during the coup. It was expected to co-operate with the TC, and share its documentation, but although it provided what modest support it could, little meaningful sharing of information and know-how took place between the two.[87]

The US Administration's alleged role was most pernicious for the TC.[88] The USA, it is claimed, feared that the TC might uncover evidence incriminating American citizens. It was particularly fearful that an enquiry might reveal covert US support via the Central Intelligence Agency (CIA) to the paramilitary force Front pour l'Avancement et le Progrès d'Haiti (FRAPH) that was responsible for much of the mayhem and violations during the military regime. US soldiers illegally confiscated 160,000 pages of documents, videotapes, photographs and other materials from FRAPH and Haitian military headquarters in autumn 1994, which were of vital importance for TC investigations. The US government initially refused to return the materials, despite Haitian requests and pressure from the NGO Human Rights Watch, and insisted on deleting the names of all American citizens from the documents. The US Embassy in Haiti sponsored a press conference for the FRAPH leader Emmanuel Constant, giving legitimacy to a wanted human rights violator. Thereafter Constant, who had entered the USA, was allowed to remain there and avoid Haiti's extradition request.

Despite these obstacles, the Commission succeeded in producing a 1,200-page report which documented 8,652 human rights cases, an impressive feat given its limited mandate and resources. Moreover, the TC kept its deadline and submitted its report just before Aristide stepped down. The report was passed to Aristide's ally and successor, René Préval, but lay shelved for months in the Justice Ministry without being published, distributed or officially acknowledged, purportedly owing to shortage of funds. It eventually received an extremely limited circulation.[89]

The Commissioners deserve credit for their assiduity and competence in completing their work despite considerable obstacles. Yet it remains unclear whether the Commission made a significant contribution to the pursuit of justice, or secured the benefits credited to TCs, owing to the overwhelming constraints it faced and the political inaction following its report. Despite government rhetoric and public demands, there was no follow-up. Manifestly, the report had no beneficial effect on the traumatized population, who had suffered brutal repression and fear under the military regime, on top of a harsh international embargo.[90] Haiti may be a case where, to use Hayner's words, a truth commission badly done may be worse than none at all. Now that the past has been opened and 'dealt with' in the form of a TC, it is difficult to reopen it or start a new process, even though this one bore so little fruit. Consequently, the momentum and opportunity to pursue justice has been lost for the foreseeable future, while victims and survivors continue to clamour for justice.

South Africa

South Africa's ambitious Truth and Reconciliation Commission appeared set to restore confidence in the benefits of TCs for societies emerging from conflict. Extensive consultations were conducted within and outside the country to ensure that the Commission was designed based on the wishes, needs and particularities of the South African situation while fully informed of the experiences of other cases. It particularly drew on the experiences of Latin America, Central and Eastern Europe and Northern Ireland.[91]

The TRC is without doubt the most ambitious and far-reaching TC instituted, as well as the most high-profile, publicized, and extensively researched process of its kind. The seventeen-member commission had at its disposition a substantial budget, adequate staff, and elaborate methodology. It had three separate committees which addressed human rights violations, amnesty, and reparations respectively. The TRC's aims were much broader than past commissions', and imbued with social and theological ideals. As expressed by Commissioner Dumisa Ntsebeza: 'Truth telling is a *sine qua non*, but not for its own sake but for providing, first, comfort for survivors; second, reparation for victims; third, repentance for perpetrators, all of which would lead, lastly, to social reconciliation.'[92]

Despite its aspirations and endowments, the TRC has faced many setbacks, and its benefits have been mixed. At the hearings the lack of contrition displayed by leaders of the National Party's apartheid government has frustrated the black population. However, contrition cannot be forced in the TRC process, and full disclosure even without a word of apology can result in full amnesty. Recent amnesties granted by the TRC to known murderers provoked public outrage.[93] The white minority feels marginalized and even victimized by the TRC's exposure of facts and the implicit suggestion that they may have been silent beneficiaries of the apartheid system, even if they were not direct accomplices.[94] Only 500 of South Africa's 4.5 million whites have signed a recent declaration accepting apartheid's consequences for the black population and white responsibility.[95] Even the

ANC government's attitude has been ambivalent, as indicated. Despite initial support, the ANC's relations with the TRC have soured slightly over time. As the TRC began to take on an identity and conscience of its own and tried to hold the ANC to the same standards as other political actors in the conflict, the ANC's reaction has been indignant and defiant, as Krog reports.

The vaunted cathartic value of the TRC's unique confessional-like atmosphere for victims to share their stories has been seriously questioned. Du Toit observes, 'The Commission emphasizes its role as care-giver... The Christian notion of forgiveness is prominent... the survivors do not relate to this situation... [they] do not necessarily agree with the message of forgiveness.'[96] A psychiatrist attached to the TRC noted:

> People thought that the Truth Commission would be this quick fix...
> and that we would go through the process and fling our arms around
> each other and be blood brothers for ever more. This is nonsense –
> absolute nonsense... there will be no grand release – every individual
> will have to devise his or her own personal method of coming to terms
> with what has happened.[97]

Participants in the TRC process and ANC leaders acknowledge candidly that the Commission embodied not the 'morally ideal but the politically possible' – that the TRC was a political compromise, and the best possible way of achieving some measure of justice in a highly constrained political negotiation.[98] It remains debatable whether the TRC and its recently concluded report will in fact alleviate or exacerbate survivors' demand for justice, and some wonder whether the process has not opened more wounds than it has healed. In Mamdani's words,

> Is it not also possible that the more truth comes to light – and the less
> justice is seen to be done – the more truth may breed outrage among the
> majority and fear in the minority?... While the argument to opt for
> truth-telling as opposed to criminal justice was underscored as a polit-
> ical necessity, the more truth is told the more it may fuel the very
> demand it is supposed to have displaced, that for justice.[99]

The verdict?   In summary, if used in propitious circumstances, backed by the requisite political will and resources, with adequate time and independence, truth commissions may make a useful contribution to the search for justice. However, truth commissions may not be a panacea in all situations, nor may they always be desirable immediately after brutal conflict. As Hayner cautions, 'reliving horrors is not for everyone'.[100]

It was noted that Mozambicans generally expressed no desire to reopen the deep wounds of war in its immediate aftermath.[101] Intriguingly, the Mozambican peace agreements, although led by a church organization and contemporaneous with El Salvador's, did not propose a truth commission or other measures of rectificatory justice.[102] While truth and truth commissions may have their contribution to make to the search for justice in post-conflict societies, their benefits should not be overestimated, and caution is required before advocating commissions indiscriminately in all post-conflict countries. Further, government sponsorship may not always be suitable for TCs to function optimally. As noted in Guatemala, 'Truth really rests within society – it is a political and social need but it has to go at its own pace...The political world needs to recognize the truth but should not supervise it.'[103]

TCs may make a contribution to the search for justice, but it is unrealistic to expect a short-term body of investigation to provide a meaningful measure of justice for years or decades of human suffering. The high expectations TCs generate may be their Achilles' heel. Whatever their benefits, and even in optimal circumstances, they are not a cure-all, and can only form a part of a larger response to rectificatory justice.[104] Truth cannot equate to or replace justice.

Beyond prosecutions and truth commissions: innovation and informal mechanisms

The discussion so far has noted that despite the near-exclusive focus on trials and truth commissions, both are only partial measures that enjoy limited success and face considerable obstacles in post-conflict low-income countries. Trials tend to focus on perpetrators. They are assumed to provide a sense of vindication to victims, but often result in deepening victimization.[105] TCs are sometimes preferred to trials because they balance the focus on offenders and their violations with a focus on victims and their suffering. Yet they too rarely fulfil the expectations placed on them, and are not desirable in all cases. Despite the shortcomings of both mechanisms, most studies restrict themselves primarily to these two mechanisms and debate their relative merits and demerits, instead of looking beyond them in search of other approaches and solutions.[106]

The shortcomings of trials and TCs indicate that it may be judicious and even necessary to adapt and supplement the criminal justice system and officially sanctioned mechanisms. Two suggestions are forwarded. First, existing official and legal mechanisms could be adapted innovatively to suit the specific needs and purposes of post-conflict countries. Second, officially sponsored mechanisms could be supplemented by unofficial, informal, and culturally rooted traditional measures of justice.

Adapting *legal and official mechanisms*

It is necessary to recognize the limits of the criminal justice system in responding adequately to the requirements of rectificatory justice in low-income post-conflict societies, and to adapt them innovatively on a case by case basis. The Organic (Genocide) Law in Rwanda is one example of innovative adaptation of laws to suit the exigencies of a particular society. TCs too could be adapted to suit the purposes and needs of particular societies so that, rather than comply with some predetermined model, they seek to fulfil the requirements of the society in question. A notable example is the TRC which, despite extensive consultation with experts from a range of countries on a range of mechanisms, was designed to suit the particular requirements of the South African political, historical and cultural situation.

A further area where greater flexibility and innovation are required is in the timing of official responses. It is often assumed that the best time to institute formal rectificatory justice measures is immediately after conflict. This may hold true in some cases, but not in all. After brutal conflict has ripped apart families and communities, there may be a vociferous demand for justice in some societies, as in Rwanda, but there may be no immediate desire for rectification in some others, as in Mozambique. Sometimes it may take a long time for these desires to be articulated and demands to be pressed.

Namibia is a case in point. Whereas in 1989 there was no strong opposition to the SWAPO government's neglect of past atrocities, in 1995 the 'wall of silence' was shattered with the publication of a book on the SWAPO detainees by a priest who had been sympathetic to SWAPO during the liberation struggle.[107] Launched with popular support in Namibia in March 1996, the book rekindled the debate about the government's truculent treatment of past violations. Although incensed by the publicity surrounding the book, the SWAPO government responded in August 1996 by finally releasing a long-withheld list of 7,792 names of Namibians who lost their lives while in exile in SWAPO's custody.[108] This is recognized as a significant concession on the part of the government. However, the book's release also reawakened public demands for remedial measures, perhaps in the form of a TC. In September 2000 Major-General Solomon Hawala, the 'butcher of Lubango' responsible for the arrest and torture of detainees, was appointed chief of Namibian Defence Force.[109] The government may have intended this as an act of defiance, but may have strengthened, inadvertently, public determination to obtain rectificatory justice.

Crafting amnesties One little-researched way of adapting legal mechanisms to suit the needs of post-conflict societies is to make innovative use of amnesty provisions to attain a measure of justice despite political compromises required to attain negative peace. Amnesties are unpopular and maligned by human rights activists, as they have a well-earned reputation of bolstering impunity.[110] This is true of blanket amnesties of the type resorted to by Latin American dictatorships in the 1980s. The ARENA government's hasty amnesty after the release of the TC's report in El Salvador falls into this category. Although the amnesty did not violate its recommendations *strictu sensu*, the manner in which it was rushed through Congress made it 'incompatible with the spirit of the Peace Accords'.[111]

In countries like Guatemala, Haiti and South Africa, however, conditional amnesties have challenged entrenched impunity, while permitting a degree of justice to be carried out against violators. In Guatemala the so-called Law of National Reconciliation violated anti-impunity provisions of the Comprehensive Accord on Human Rights, and was vehemently protested by citizens' groups who organized themselves into an 'Alliance against Amnesty'. The alliance aimed to propose legislation to facilitate reinsertion and reintegration of guerrillas without recourse to a general military amnesty. The amnesty provoked deep disappointment because the rebel Guatemalan National Revolutionary Unity (URNG) had steadfastly opposed amnesty throughout negotiations, but underwent a sudden change of heart and negotiated an amnesty with the government in late 1996.[112]

What is less often noted is that the amnesty is strictly conditional. It does not protect abusers from criminal prosecution, and it must be proven that violations were politically linked to the war and not common crimes.[113] There are obstacles to prosecution: offenders have been able to choose compliant judges; there is no appeals procedure; and victims' families bear full responsibility for contesting amnesty applications.[114] However, these problems stem not from the amnesty law itself but from a corrupt judiciary and weak rule of law. Significantly, the conditionality of the amnesty has not saved Guatemala's worst abusers from the prospect of prosecution. In May 2000 the Nobel laureate Rigoberta Menchu lodged accusations in Spain against the former military dictator and current house speaker General Rios Montt, while formal charges have been made by activists in Guatemala against former president Romeo Lucas Garcia, his chief of staff and defence minister. Montt is likely to be prosecuted for genocide in Guatemala itself in a case brought forward by twelve Mayan communities.[115]

In Haiti Aristide stood firm in insisting on a conditional amnesty despite strong pressure from the US Administration to accept a blanket amnesty for coup leaders.[116] Aristide stated that the 1986 Constitution disallowed blanket amnesties for common crimes, but he conceded amnesty for political crimes. When Jimmy Carter, in his eleventh-hour mission to forestall a forced multinational invasion, offered General Raoul Cédras and his henchmen a blanket amnesty, the Haitian legislature refused to comply. The legislature passed an amnesty which only covered crimes against the state, but not human rights abuses against individuals. Although many senior coup leaders including Cédras were able to flee safely into exile, this conditional amnesty opened up the possibility of arresting and trying other abusive military leaders. Unfortunately, it has been difficult to conduct many trials not only due to the escape of key perpetrators, but also due to political paralysis and the inadequacies of the rule of law, discussed earlier and in chapter 3. However, the partial amnesty, secured despite US pressure, represents an important symbolic gain in a country where impunity has reigned for generations.

South Africa's amnesty has been criticized by detractors within and without the country as a sell-out to apartheid's criminals. Yet this amnesty is unique and represents a significant achievement in light of the political constraints at the time. Amnesty is individual rather than of the blanket kind covering entire institutions, and the conditions surrounding amnesty applications and grants are stringent. Each individual must file a separate application, and amnesty is conditional on full disclosure and on the Amnesty Committee's satisfaction that the crimes were political in nature. If the Amnesty Committee – which works in relative autonomy from its parent body, the TRC – is not satisfied with full disclosure, or if the acts are deemed to be criminal rather than political, it may reject amnesty and recommend prosecution. Furthermore, if an individual who has not made an amnesty application is incriminated in TRC proceedings, he or she can be charged. While the Amnesty Committee expected only about 200 applications, and initially very few were filed, it received 7,700 by the deadline for applications on 10 May 1997.[117]

In practice, public outrage has often greeted the TRC's amnesties to notorious apartheid agents. Nonetheless, it is to be recalled that during negotiations the National Party government had insisted initially on full amnesty as a precondition for a peaceful transition. It was an achievement that this could be negotiated skilfully by the ANC into a conditional amnesty without precluding eventual prosecution. As amnesty is individual and only follows full disclosure – itself tantamount to an admission and establishment of guilt – it is more akin to clemency.

Zalaquett points out that despite international laws urging prosecution of certain egregious violations, the Geneva Conventions call for the party in office or both sides to conflict to allow the widest amnesty possible when hostilities cease.[118] Admittedly, caution must be exercised to ensure that amnesty is not abused, as it so frequently is. The cases here illustrate that even in the face of political opposition, if used creatively and strategically, the very tool long identified with impunity can also be deployed to counter impunity and pursue accountability.

Social reparations, informal and unofficial mechanisms

Sometimes when a government is unwilling to do much to address the past, either for fear of revealing its own complicity or hesitation to reopen past wounds, spontaneous, unofficial measures undertaken by independent civil society groups outside the authority of governments assume importance. They may serve the role and functions of official mechanisms, or even outdo them in providing a measure of justice to citizens. Sometimes they may accompany official mechanisms. These informal, unofficial or semi-official, and traditional mechanisms include various forms of reparation, including monetary compensation, and restitution, apologies, symbolic measures like commemorations and memorials, and education.

Although several of these measures have been attempted in previous transitional situations and subjected to some scrutiny, they receive only limited attention in post-conflict societies today.[119] This may be partly because they are less public, dramatic and comprehensive than trials and TCs tend to be. It may also be partly because many of them are not officially sponsored by the state or international bodies, as trials and TCs tend to be. Rather, several are spontaneous and informal. Some are culturally rooted, drawing on local traditions, as examined in the following section. Consequently, they may be considered less effective and less meriting of political attention than the more familiar, tried and tested means of trials and TCs.

Reparation has often been understood narrowly to mean monetary compensation. If this were the case, it might be seldom applicable in low-income post-conflict countries which often lack the financial means for this purpose. The term is actually much broader and includes several measures, both legal and social (as discussed again in chapter 6). In South Africa, for example, the Reparations Committee of the TRC envisages a combination of monetary and non-monetary reparation. In international legal practice, several forms of reparation are acknowledged: indemnity, compensation, restitution, satisfaction, and declaratory judgment, although there is some overlap.

Indemnity and compensation are the monetary forms of reparation. Indemnity aims to 'compensate for all the damage which results from the unlawful act, including a profit which would have been possible in the ordinary course of events, but not prospective gains'.[120] Compensation is defined as 'reparation in the narrow sense of the payment of money as a "valuation" of the wrong done'.[121] Other forms of legal reparation are non-monetary. 'Restitution in kind is designed to re-establish the situation which would have existed if the wrongful act or omission had not taken place, by performance of the obligation which the State failed to discharge: revocation of the unlawful act, return of property wrongfully removed or abstention from further wrongful conduct.'[122] Satisfaction is 'any measure which the author of a breach of duty is bound to take under customary law or under an agreement by parties to a dispute, apart from restitution or compensation'. A declaratory judgement is a declaration by a court regarding the illegality of the act of the defendant state, and can constitute a measure of satisfaction.[123]

Several other measures employed formally or informally in transitional contexts could also be described as social reparation, in that they are not ordered by courts but, like legal reparation, seek to undo or mitigate the consequences of harmful acts.

Symbolic redress may take a variety of forms such as public statements or apologies, publicly restoring the name or reputation of victims, or special measures for particular groups who suffered injustice. When a head of state or government extends an official apology for state-sponsored crimes, whether or not the leader was in charge during the period in question, it can carry powerful symbolic value. The democratically elected presidents of Chile and Argentina, although not personally responsible for the violations committed by prior military regimes, extended a personal apology to citizens and assumed responsibility for state crimes. President Alwyn of Chile sent a copy of the Truth Commission's report to each victim's family with a personal letter of apology.[124] By contrast, in South Africa the lack of acknowledgement and apology on the part of NP leaders for apartheid's injustices has been a sore point in the reconciliation process. However, apologies cannot be forced, and must be volitional to have meaning.

Commemoration is described evocatively as 'a shared context, shared mourning, shared memory', meeting victims' needs as much as society's. Commemoration helps victims 'heal the rupture not only internally but also the rupture the victimization created between survivors and their society'.[125] It could take various forms, such as erecting memorials or monuments, dedicating a day of remembering to pay respect to victims, and creating museums. The Hiroshima museum commemorating the site of the atomic bombing of that city in 1945 is an example. In Rwanda 200,000 genocide victims were reburied symbolically on 7 April 2000, the seventh anniversary of the genocide.[126] In Cambodia and Rwanda several massacre sites have been preserved as monuments to honour and remember the dead. In South Africa a Book of Reconciliation was opened by the Reparation Committee of the TRC for ordinary citizens to express their feelings of compassion or their contrition for the past,[127] and was somewhat better received by whites than the attempted declaration acknowledging white guilt. Several independent, non-governmental or state-sponsored centres have been set up in post-conflict countries to deal with the post-traumatic stress of victims and offenders. UNICEF, for example, has set up workshops in Mozambique to provide counselling to child soldiers, while UNESCO has a programme on the culture of peace that addresses human consequences of conflict.[128] Sometimes education, through measures such as committing events to history, rewriting textbooks, and changing academic syllabuses, aims to ensure that the events are committed to public memory. Such education acknowledges and pays homage to victims' experiences, and may also play a deterrent role.

Purges among the leadership are a semi-official mechanism which has received little attention in post-conflict countries, although they were popular in some Central and Eastern Europe transitions under the name of lustrations.[129] A successful example was the work of the Ad Hoc Commission in El Salvador. This three-person Commission was separate from the more publicized Truth Commission, and was mandated to vet the 232 most senior military officers. The Commission's confidential report listed those they believed should be retired from military service for their human rights abuses. After much delay and backtracking, the ARENA government did eventually remove from service all named officers, albeit often with full honours.[130] Nonetheless, this was a considerable achievement considering the military's close ties to government and the latter's efforts to shield military leaders from blame and prosecution.

Culturally rooted responses

Responses to rectificatory justice sometimes arise from within a society and do not conform to any of the tried and tested measures described above. Rather, they are shaped by that society's particular context, history, culture and needs. For example, after extensive worldwide consultation, South Africans grounded the TRC in the indigenous concept of *Ubuntu*, as it was more evocative for a majority – though not the totality – of the South African population than any imported concept could be. *Ubuntu* is derived from a Xhosa expression and means 'people are people through other people'. In this view, 'An environment of right relationships is one in which people are able to recognize that their humanity is inextricably bound up in others' humanity.'[131]

Two evocative examples of spontaneous culturally-specific responses to claims for rectificatory justice are Guatemala, where an innovative response was shaped independently by civil society, and Mozambique, where the response drew on age-old cultural practices and traditional healers.

In Guatemala the government's only concession in the peace negotiations on past violations was to establish a Commission of Historical Clarification with a circumscribed mandate.[132] Faced with this inadequate measure in a country where war had caused lasting wounds and where the popular demand for justice ran deep, the Church set up an alternative – the Recovery of Historical Memory or REMHI project.[133] While entirely independent of the government, REMHI functioned in many ways like official commissions do, using professional techniques and skilled staff. It trained 800 *animadores* ('animators') to work throughout the country, using indigenous languages, as the majority of victims were of indigenous origin. REMHI documented the cases of 55,000 victims, although this still represented only 25 per cent of the total. It also recovered 500 massacre sites.[134]

Beyond documentation, REMHI also attempted to respond to claims of rectificatory justice. Like the TRC, REMHI provided a forum for victims to narrate their stories and express their loss. It conducted mass exhumations leading to the identification of many disappeared persons. It also performed symbolic burials and cremations that had deep symbolic value in indigenous cultures, and provided relief to survivors and victims who had lost their beloved.

REMHI worked with poor and predominantly indigenous victims and their communities, and had to be sensitive and flexible in its approach. As REMHI's director Ramirez explains, 'Sometimes our human rights approach and tools did not work. People talked about human rights violations for which human rights language had no typology. So we realized our tools had to be more flexible and open to be able to capture the truths of people.' REMHI did not seek to compete with the official Commission, but to complement it in recognition of the latter's restricted mandate and powers. It assisted the Commission by using its own deep knowledge of the culture and access to people. As planned, it handed its final report to the Commission, providing much valuable information. Its success in providing a sense of justice – in greater measure than some elements in Guatemalan society desired or could tolerate – was tragically proven by the assassination of its leader, Bishop Ghirardi, just two days after the report was released.[135]

REMHI's achievement is notable, as it achieved independently through communities what an official process could not have achieved in the prevalent political conditions. It uncovered and dealt with hidden truths in a culturally sensitive and responsive way that understood and sought to meet survivors' needs.

The government acknowledged its contribution indirectly. In August 2000 President Portillo officially recognized state responsibility for human rights abuses during war. Nevertheless, his attempt to institute a national day to commemorate victims was overruled by his own right-wing party led by the former president, General Efrain Rios Montt, the war's worst abuser. The case to prosecute Montt for genocide takes on particular relevance here. Further, Bishop Ghirardi's assassins, three military officers, were convicted in July 2001, although the chief prosecutor then fled the country for safety.[136]

In Mozambique, by contrast, the decision to take no official measure to deal with the past was based primarily on a mutual agreement between the two parties to 'forgive but not forget'. After a generation of war, the population, according to some observers, appeared to concur with the government's approach. Ordinary Mozambicans seemed to share a desire to move beyond the suffering of the war, and did not demand any official reckoning with past injustice.[137] However, many Mozambicans turned to informal, traditional mechanisms to come to terms with their trauma.

Although Christianity has gained ground in Mozambique, a majority of the population, particularly rural, still practises animism, and traditional purification rituals have a powerful hold on them. Although the phenomenon has not been extensively researched yet, it has been observed that traditional healers have played a significant role in dealing with victims and perpetrators by conducting a variety of purification rituals according to the nature of trauma experienced.[138] These rituals are conducted mostly in rural areas, where hostilities and violations were centred during the conflict. Many combatants returned to their villages after the war, and faced the prospect of reintegration with those they violated, often their own neighbours or family members. The traditional belief is that harm is done not just to the individual involved – victim or perpetrator – but to the entire family or community. Consequently, reconciliation and reintegration require that entire communities participate in the ritual to rid themselves of the harm. The rituals generally involve cleansing the violation or effacing the trauma, and are designed to erase the act and its impact from collective memory. With the ceremony, the violator is forgiven and the victim is healed, and each can be reconciled and reintegrated with the community as before.

The scope and impact of traditional remedies as witnessed in Mozambique are significant but should not be embellished or overestimated. These measures have provided some measure of solace or 'justice' to victims, perpetrators and survivors in the absence of official responses. They have operated in special and specific sets of circumstances, and carried meaning due to deeply ingrained traditional beliefs. They are unlikely to be replicable elsewhere. Some scholars urge caution in turning to traditional figures to dispense justice after conflict, as this may legitimize sources of authority which are not necessarily benign.[139] The difficulties of contending with customary law in volatile post-conflict situations, noted in chapter 3, are also relevant here. Admittedly, caution is required to ensure that such measures do more good than harm, and are not imposed by traditional leaders on unwilling subjects. Furthermore, the risk in overemphasizing and idealizing traditionally based responses is that it may shift responsibility from governments, political leaders and international donors. It may lead them to substitute formal mechanisms backed by official commitment and resources with informal, inexpensive and politically convenient ones. These traditional measures are potentially important, but should be seen primarily as interim measures and/or necessary complements to official responses, and not as comprehensive and self-sufficient responses to rectificatory justice.

Caution notwithstanding, in countries like Mozambique which have undergone brutal conflict, informal measures rooted in local culture may offer a lifeline for traumatized citizens, and provide an important stopgap measure when political will or capacity to resort to official measures and the criminal justice system are lacking.

Unofficial and traditional measures may provide only a small part of the overall response to a society's needs and demands for rectificatory justice, as in South Africa, or a major part of it, as in Mozambique and Guatemala. Nevertheless, they represent an important part of the rectificatory response to the multidimensional needs of war-scarred survivors in post-conflict societies.

From 'perpetrators' and 'victims' to 'survivors' of conflict

Trials are defended by their proponents as a vindication of victims' needs and rights, although they focus predominantly on perpetrators. Truth commissions are defended as a better response to victims' needs than trials, although they provide *de facto* exoneration to perpetrators. The problem is that typical responses to rectificatory justice, centring on trials and TCs, are caught in the dialectic between perpetrators and victims; they reify the homogeneity of each group and the insurmountable difference between the two groups. This is an unhelpful approach either for dealing effectively with rectificatory justice claims or for laying the foundations for lasting peace.

Responses to rectificatory justice have tended to stereotype victims' needs and portray them as homogeneous, inflexible and unchanging over time, as illustrated by the studies of procedural justice noted earlier. Recent testimonies gathered by TCs from El Salvador to South Africa have demonstrated that victims' needs, and their wishes and capacities for justice, are variable. It is now recognized that victims 'differ remarkably in their desires for revenge, for granting forgiveness, for remembering, and for moving on'.[140] It is facility rather than veracity that reinforces arguments favouring one mechanism over another – trials or TCs – as the best responses to victims' needs. More seriously, as observed in South Africa, 'we become complicit in silencing the voices of victims by speaking on behalf of victims and making them appear uniform'.[141]

An important distinction glossed over by most treatments of rectificatory or transitional justice is between the terms 'victim' and 'survivor'. There are many reasons why this distinction is crucial. Those who suffered during conflict, whether they lost a life, a limb or a family member, are referred to ubiquitously as victims. This term makes them appear ill and in need of treatment, or impotent and in need of help. Many arguments for truth commissions are based on their imputed therapeutic value in contributing to healing victims.[142]

However, some survivors, for example in South Africa, say, 'We have had these experiences, but we do not want to present ourselves as victims in need of healing.'[143] While use of the term victim might open recourse to 'victims' rights' which are intended to empower, in practice this appellation disempowers victims by emphasizing their denial of and need for rights. It strips victims of choice and reduces their capacity for regaining agency. As one woman testified to the TRC, 'I resent being called a victim. I have a choice in the matter. I am a survivor. Lindy was a victim, she had no choice.'[144] (The term victim defines individuals in terms of their past, and ignores the desire many might have to move beyond the past, inhabit the present and look to the future.) The anti-apartheid activist Father Michael Lapsley, who was gravely injured by a letter bomb, captures this: 'I do not see myself as a victim but as a survivor of Apartheid. This is part of my triumph of returning to South Africa and living my life as meaningfully and joyfully as possible. I am not captured by hatred, because then they would not only have destroyed my body, but also my soul.'[145]

Trials and TCs tend to define 'victim' narrowly using strict criteria in order to delimit their task of vindicating victims. Generally, victims are defined as those who directly suffered certain enumerated physical or familial losses. However, this definition becomes meaningless when applied in conditions of internal political conflicts. Violence is so random and civilian-focused in most contemporary conflicts that all inhabitants of a society, regardless of their affiliation, may suffer chronic fear and insecurity during conflict, even if they manage to escape with their lives. In South Africa, Mamdani notes, 'gross violations of human rights involve mainly (not peripherally) the victimization of communities (and not individuals)'.[146]

Furthermore, in many conflicts physical violence is compounded and underpinned by structural violence and systemic injustice which affects a much larger part of the population. Apartheid provides a graphic example where, in addition to the large numbers of those targeted for political reasons by the apartheid regime, the entire non-white population suffered the systemic consequences of apartheid's injustice. These included pass laws, forced removals, constant insecurity, lack of access to opportunities, and even prescriptions on who they could or could not marry, through the prohibition of interracial marriages. Much the same applied to Namibia, where, although the main hostilities were concentrated in the Ovambo region above the 'red line', the entire non-white population was subject to the apartheid system. As Albie Sachs commented: 'If you want to ask anybody for forgiveness ... as a white person ... do it to a community that has been historically oppressed, not just to an individual that has suffered from oppression... They didn't choose to be oppressed.'[147]

Structural and systemic injustice is prevalent and entrenched in many if not most countries undergoing conflict. In Guatemala, in addition to being the targets of military and paramilitary violence, indigenous peoples were also the targets of systemic injustice, and were politically and economically marginalized for generations. In Rwanda the economic and political marginalization of Hutus during the Belgian colonial period was replaced by the political exclusion and discrimination of Tutsis by Hutus after the 1959 revolution in the long and bloody prelude to the genocide. In such cases, it is inadequate to describe only those who were physically impaired by conflict as victims. Minow acknowledges the need to 'redefine victims as the entire society'.[148]

If an entire society is made up of victims, however, who, if anyone, is a perpetrator? For Marie Smyth, a Northern Ireland peace activist, these are the two crucial questions: first, is everyone a victim, and second, is everyone a perpetrator? The standard approach to rectificatory justice, whether through trials, truth commissions or both, overemphasizes the distinction between perpetrators and victims. The two categories are treated as mutually exclusive, rigid and unchanging. The intransigence in the retributive justice model on punishing perpetrators to vindicate victims' suffering implies that the former are entirely culpable and the latter wholly blameless. Yet it is sometimes observed – though rarely discussed – that in many conflicts the distinction between victim and perpetrator may not be so sharp. 'Victims and perpetrators are never purely marked and radically distinct in... extreme circumstances.'[149]

People find it more comfortable to accept that they might all be victims, for, as Smyth points out, there are politics behind the claim to victimhood. Reiterating the passivity, suffering and helplessness implicit in the term victim, Smyth also notes 'victims are never guilty, never responsible or strong. That is they don't have to take responsibility for their actions.' Most crucially, 'Victims never harm others.'

It is more discomfiting for members of a society to acknowledge ways in which, by action or inaction, by benefiting from an unjust system or being a passive bystander, they might have contributed to perpetrating or permitting injustice. Smyth notes: 'We've all dehumanized humans... There are many ways to commit violence bar physical force. The spectrum between violence and non-violence is not twosided if we raise the question of who benefited from the violence.'[150]

The distinction between perpetrators and victims breaks down in South Africa, and the category of beneficiaries becomes important.[151]

Only a limited number of persons were engaged by the apartheid state directly to carry out the harsher aspects of its policies and its war against anti-apartheid activists. Nevertheless, many more people participated in implementing apartheid's far-reaching administrative laws and regulations which affected most aspects of life, even if they did not directly torture or assassinate anti-apartheid activists. An even larger number benefited from the gains of the apartheid system which ensured that the wealth of a well-endowed nation was enjoyed by only a tiny fraction of its population to the exclusion of the majority. These dynamics were particularly acute under apartheid, but are identifiable elsewhere as well, as in Guatemala and Haiti. Ignoring structural injustice allows one to focus only on the narrow category of direct perpetrators and ignore the beneficiaries of the system who allowed or enabled injustice to be perpetuated, just as it allows one to overlook the victimization of a much larger proportion of society.

Acknowledging that everyone is a perpetrator in some way requires an acceptance that 'wrongs have been committed on all sides'.[152] The German philosopher and Holocaust survivor Karl Jaspers identifies four types of guilt – criminal, political, moral and metaphysical.[153] Criminal guilt belongs to the perpetrator narrowly defined, while moral, metaphysical and political guilt belong to bystanders as well. Metaphysical guilt emanates from solidarity between people: 'If I fail to do whatever I can to prevent [injustice] then I too am guilty.' Describing moral guilt, Jaspers says, 'passivity knows itself morally guilty of every failure, every neglect to act whenever possible, to shield the imperilled, to relieve wrong'. Political guilt is collective, and stems from the fact that 'a people answers for its polity', because of every citizen's responsibility to participate in governance. In the context of Nazism, Jaspers noted for this reason, 'Every German is made to share the blame for the crimes committed in the name of the Reich. We are collectively liable.'[154] Post-genocide Rwanda gives new meaning to Jaspers's categories. The sheer struggle for survival in a killing field led everyone, Hutu or Tutsi, extremist or moderate, to share a burden of guilt – criminal, political, moral or metaphysical – making everyone in some sense a perpetrator.

There may be a legitimate fear that treating an entire society as one of perpetrators will do exactly what current attempts at rectificatory justice try to avoid – create collective guilt instead of individualizing criminal accountability for violations. Collective guilt is unhelpful as it leads to perpetuating stereotypes of perpetrators and victims – holding all Hutus, rather than identified individuals, guilty of genocide and considering all Tutsis to be victims is counterproductive and recharges cycles of revenge and violence.[155]

However, an exclusive focus on individual accountability, and on the individual identification of perpetrators and victims, is not helpful either, as it denies both the guilt and the victimization of the vast majority of society. Moreover, it ignores what all citizens in society share in common: that they are all survivors, whatever their past role, and that they now have a common stake in building a future together.

Minow observed the need to define the entire society as one of victims. While this is an advance as it acknowledges the real impact of conflict on an entire society rather than a targeted few, to do so would only entrench the notion of victimhood, and concomitant helplessness. Rather, it is more useful to recognize that in such circumstances, to emerge alive, regardless of one's role and affiliation during conflict, is to be a survivor. More useful than Minow's notion of collective victimhood is a redefinition of the entire society as *survivors*. While everyone is a victim, everyone is also a perpetrator, making the distinction pointless. It is necessary to go beyond a simplistic dichotomy between perpetrator and victim and adopt the discourse of survivor, whatever one's individual past.

The term 'survivor' has positive etymological connotations. The prefix 'sur' connotes moving beyond, overcoming, as in 'surmount' or 'surpass'. It is empowering. It is prospective while not foreclosing retrospection. This identification does not excuse or efface the individual guilt of perpetrators or the individual suffering of victims, but provides an avenue for moving beyond it. Adopting this common identification that embraces all members of society may render more feasible the task of (re)building a new political community that overcomes divisiveness between perceived perpetrators and victims. And this is the most decisive challenge facing post-conflict societies that will determine whether peacebuilding achieves its twin objectives.

Conclusion

I have argued in this chapter why the current approach to rectificatory justice in low-income societies emerging from political violence is unsatisfactory, and neglects the complexities and specificities of these situations. The focus on two principal mechanisms is inappropriate; a more comprehensive, sensitive and innovative approach is required. The first element of this approach is a recognition of the shared identity of all members of society as survivors with a common stake in rebuilding community and a shared future. This requires going beyond the focus on the individual that underpins trials and truth commissions, and engaging all members of society. The two main components of this approach are, first, adapting innovatively the existing legal and official mechanisms to suit the needs and exigencies of individual societies; and second, supplementing these official and legal mechanisms with appropriate unofficial, informal and culturally rooted measures. This is elucidated further in chapter 6.

It is equally important to recognize that rectificatory justice, as understood and attempted until now, lacks a firm grounding since it is divorced from legal justice on the one hand and distributive justice on the other. To provide a real sense of justice to survivors, rectificatory justice must acknowledge its close relationship with both legal and distributive justice.

Rectificatory justice and legal justice / rule of law are mutually interdependent, as this chapter has underlined. Insofar as prosecution is pursued as a means of rectificatory justice, it is necessary to restore and strengthen the rule of law simultaneously to arrest, incarcerate and provide fair trial to perpetrators. In the interim, however, given the prevalent weakness and corruptibility of the rule of law and the limitations of criminal justice systems in meeting the claims of rectificatory justice, a case was made for adapting, innovating and supplementing existing laws.

The interdependence between rectificatory justice and the rule of law goes deeper, however. The observations here reinforce the argument in chapter 2 that it is not only the institutions of the rule of law but its underlying ethos that matters. Minimalist rule of law does not offer a sufficient response to the claims of rectificatory justice: even if its institutions were restored to perfection after conflict, minimalist rule of law would fall short. Only maximalist rule of law – where laws, legal institutions and law enforcement agencies are underpinned by a commitment to justice and human integrity – will be able to provide the comprehensive, sensitive and flexible responses to rectificatory justice claims argued for in this chapter. This response, we saw, may not lie within the given letter of the law, but may need recourse to its underlying ethos to find innovative, context-specific expression.

The functional dependence of rectificatory justice on distributive justice was also underscored in our discussions here. Narrowly targeted measures of rectificatory justice may not be adequate or effective in post-conflict societies where everyone is both a victim and a perpetrator, if they are not accompanied by measures of distributive justice which address wider structural and systemic injustice. It is for this reason that the discussion of distributive justice in the following chapter is crucial not just for itself but also to validate rectificatory justice.

Survivors in Guatemala express willingness to forgive their individual perpetrators, but ask, 'Can we forgive a system which is continuing to marginalize us?' Their answer: 'There is no reconciliation possible between a marginalized society and a system which brings about marginalization.'[156] As Villa-Vicencio recognized in South Africa, unless the TRC 'unleashed a process to deal with the economic consequences' of apartheid, it would fail its mandate of reconciliation, for rectificatory justice for survivors is not just about criminal justice but about social justice. In ten years, the TRC and the transition will be judged on the basis not of who went to jail but whether the quality of life is better.'[157] Without social and institutional change addressing systemic injustice and bringing about distributive justice, the reconciliation that rectificatory measures strive to achieve will remain elusive. Positive and negative peace will not find their harmonious balance.

In place of the current approach, I have advocated here a survivor-oriented approach to rectificatory justice that seeks to rebuild fractured community and recognizes its nexus with legal and distributive justice. This approach finds an eloquent reaffirmation in the words of anti-apartheid activist Albie Sachs: 'The final aspect will be the true honouring of everybody. It will be street lights, education, the health system, the sense of dignity, participation and true equality.'[158]

5

Distributive Justice:

Alleviating the Effects of Conflict or Targeting Causes?

Introduction: addressing causes or effects?

Since 1960 more than half the countries in the world classified as low-income have experienced armed conflict.[1] Already poor, these countries are more impoverished by violent conflict or political crisis, their economies set further back, their infrastructure destroyed, the livelihoods of families and productive capacities of individuals wiped out. Over the past decade, a plethora of international agencies have rushed to assist affected countries, particularly in stabilizing the economy, stimulating stalled economic growth, rehabilitating infrastructure and restoring productive capacity.

The influx of attention and assistance to war-torn societies is welcome. Nevertheless, I argue in this chapter that international actors and national governments have been preoccupied with the material effects of conflict while neglecting its underlying causes. Their concern with meeting the material and economic demands of post-conflict reconstruction excludes the reasons why people were incited to violent conflict in the first place. Despite their rhetorical claims to address underlying causes of conflict in peacebuilding, in practice international and national peacebuilders have given scant attention to distributive justice claims underlying political conflict.

In this chapter, beginning with an examination of underlying causes of conflict, I argue that peacebuilders have been misguided in their economic approach to countries emerging from war.[2] <u>They have</u> <u>prioritized economic growth over equity, ignoring the grievances of</u> <u>war-torn populations about distributive inequities</u>. They have treated countries emerging from violent conflict like ordinary peaceful countries in their economic policy prescriptions, overlooking the potential social and political ramifications in this volatile environment. This chapter describes some of the reasons for and the deleterious effects of this approach.

While chapters 3 and 4 addressed legal and political aspects of peacebuilding, the analysis here concentrates on economic aspects. It focuses on international financial institutions (IFIs), particularly the Bretton Woods Institutions (BWI), namely the World Bank Group (WB) and the International Monetary Fund (IMF), because of their influence on economic reconstruction and policy, as well as national policy makers.

Identifying the 'causes' of internal conflicts

Many scholars have sought to investigate the causes of recent violent conflicts – variously referred to as internal conflicts, political crises, 'complex political emergencies' (CPEs) or 'complex humanitarian emergencies' (CHEs).[3] These studies confirm that identifying the definitive causes of contemporary internal conflicts is no simple matter. The causes of violent political conflicts are multiple, complex and diverse, and may sometimes evolve and change even during the course of conflict.[4] It is facile and even dangerous to generalize and oversimplify the complex and unique causes and courses of contemporary political conflicts.

Notwithstanding complex causality, one set of commonly identified causes of conflict is related to experiences or perceptions of distributive injustice. Often, although by no means always, underlying or proximate causes of conflicts appear to centre on contentions about distributive justice: unequal access to, distribution of, and opportunities for political power and socio-economic resources. Recent studies indicate that, although various 'trigger factors' may set off conflicts, distributive inequities and structural or systemic injustice are key underlying features. In general, in societies engaged in or emerging from conflict, demands for distributive justice tend to centre on gross or unjustifiable inequalities in the distribution of, access to, and/or opportunities for socio-economic and/or political power and their accruing benefits.

Inequality takes multiple forms. Stewart identifies four categories of inequality: in political participation; in economic assets; in income and employment; and in social aspects. She stresses that it is 'horizontal' inequality in political, social or economic dimensions – that is, inequality among groups – rather than vertical inequality between individuals that is 'the fundamental source of organized conflict'.[5] When inequality is shared by a group identified along a variety of lines that distinguishes it from others – for example, class, race, religion, or ethnicity – it may be used by group leaders to create a sense of group identity. This is used to mobilize groups by emphasizing their social exclusion. Unassuaged grievances about real or perceived socio-economic and cultural inequalities may translate into attempts to seize political power or win autonomy from the state, in order to control the allocation of resources and opportunities. It is not only disadvantaged groups that take up arms to demand more; privileged groups or institutions also resort to violence to resist having less. In Haiti, for example, the overthrow of President Aristide only seven months after he took office was motivated by the fear of the military and economic elite of losing their entrenched privileges, given Aristide's public commitment to social justice.[6]

Political and economic exclusion or inequality are closely linked and may be contemporaneous in many societies. Conflicts often arise where there are 'sharp economic differences between conflicting groups associated (or believed to be associated) with differences in political control'.[7] The analysis in this chapter focuses on socio-economic inequalities, but recognizes the importance of and overlap with political inequalities.

The manifestation of such conflicts along cultural, ethnic or racial lines led to theories of bio-cultural determination or so-called ethnic conflicts. While still popular in some circles, these theories have been soundly criticized, especially for their racist undertones.[8]

One scholar observes that in the 1990s – when the ethnic thesis gained popularity – the most war-prone states were not the most (ethnically) diverse. He notes, however, that ethnic differences provide 'easy material for group mobilisation by political leaders ...[and] the sense of ethnic identity coheres around resentment and claimed grievance'.[9] And this is easiest done when horizontal inequalities stratify societies.

Resource scarcity is often posited as a cause of conflict. Nevertheless, it is observed: 'The cause [of conflict] is not so much lack of resources per se, as injustice: social, economic and political structures that maintain the dominance of an in-group at the centre of power, over an out-group at the periphery, to the extent of denying the most basic economic, social and political rights.'[10] Indeed, one recent study posits that countries with abundant mineral resources are more likely to suffer rebellion than resource-poor countries.[11]

Scholars have studied the economic functions of violence in war. In prolonged conflict, warlords make profit and ordinary people earn their livelihoods by perpetuating 'top–down' and 'bottom–up' violence respectively.[12] Studies of war economies that sustain war, including illegal trade in minerals, gems, drugs and arms, provide valuable insights into war's dynamics and the search for solutions.[13] If ignored, war economies can complicate conflict resolution and undermine post-conflict reconstruction. The existence and persistence of war economies make it more rather than less urgent to redress grievances about inequalities in order to reduce incentives to seek gain through perpetuating violence. Furthermore, war economies can explain why conflicts persist but not why they start.

A thesis that has gained currency, nevertheless, is that it is 'greed' more than 'grievance' that drives current wars. The World Bank's Paul Collier most vehemently defends this.[14] It is important to factor in the economic motivations of leaders who incite and sustain war. Nonetheless, as Keen, a leading expert on war economies, observes, 'Though Collier is right to suggest that rebels may be reluctant to admit the degree to which they are driven by greed, there are equal dangers in suggesting that the expression of grievances tells us nothing about their real motivation.' Keen echoes the argument made here: 'Indeed, if we do not ask people why they are resorting to violence or listen to their own accounts of why this may be, we are lost.'[15] Greed could foster violent crime but, without widespread societal grievances to exploit, could not incite violent political conflict.

It is not claimed here that economic, political, ethnic, religious or other factors play no role in causing or triggering conflict, and that distributive factors are the main causation. The argument here is subtler: distributive inequalities are not always a sufficient cause, but are very often a predisposing factor for conflict. Although many other factors may be involved, 'the other factors are all permissive, but would not succeed in bringing about a conflict in the absence of these inequalities'.[16]

This argument about inequality is distinct from the thesis linking poverty and conflict. As Duffield observes, 'the association of underdevelopment with a high risk of conflict is now a core assumption within development discourse', leading to the inclusion of conflict prevention within development strategies and a view that development *per se* reduces conflict.[17] I refute this view that poverty or underdevelopment *per se* cause conflict, as evident from the number of deeply impoverished but relatively peaceful countries.

Several economic factors often coalesce with greed and grievance to trigger war. Pastor and Boyce identify a combination of five economic factors underlying CHEs, including in El Salvador, Nicaragua and Guatemala:

> slow or stopped growth, particularly in the context of rising expect-ations; difficulties in apportioning burden-sharing; underlying inequities that are fundamentally responsible for the burden-sharing challenge and for the CHE itself; external actors who negatively complicate the scen-ario; and the cumulative and mutually reinforcing effects of a downward spiral of social conflict and economic downturn.[18]

Rwanda, as discussed later, demonstrated most of these conditions in 1994. The distributive impact of structural adjustment programmes (SAP) designed by the Bretton Woods Institutions has also sometimes been held responsible for stoking conflict, not least in Rwanda.[19] UN Secretary-General Kofi Annan observed that SAP have led to reduced social spending and diminished provision of basic services, and that 'when this is coupled with a perception that certain groups are not receiving a fair share of diminishing resources, the potential for conflict is evident'.[20] Some scholars contend, however, that SAP have both positive and negative effects, and that IFIs cannot be held responsible for violent conflicts.[21] It is noteworthy that the *distributive* effects of SAP on societies, rather than SAP *per se*, are considered likely to cause conflict.

It is well beyond the purview of this chapter to identify exhaustively all the causes of contemporary violent political conflicts or crises. Rather, this section has underlined the salience of inequality and claims for distributive justice as one critical set of causal factors for violent internal conflicts, and, consequently, as an important issue for consideration in the aftermath of conflict.

Inequalities and distributive injustices underlying recent conflicts

Inequality as an underlying causal factor appears in almost all the conflicts treated in this book, and several other conflicts not addressed here.

In Rwanda all the features discussed above coexisted and coalesced in 1994. Whereas the 1994 genocide is commonly attributed to either ethnic hatred, a culture of obedience in a strictly hierarchical society, or external factors, the deep underlying socio-economic and political inequalities that caused the genocide are overlooked, as Hintjens analyses. In the 1950s Hutus and Tutsis were 'identical in the language they spoke, religious beliefs, education and income level and in the acres they farmed and the number of children they bore'. However, after independence in 1962, Hutus took political power and 'Batutsi were subjected to strict quotas in secondary and higher education and in public employment' and 'made to feel disadvantaged'.[22] Batutsi continued to exercise power in the private sector and liberal professions, while political and administrative office and the military were dominated by Bahutus. When unfavourable external conditions and falling coffee prices in the mid to late 1980s triggered an economic crisis in Rwanda with rising debt and trade deficits, the Hutu President Habyarimana began scapegoating traders, merchants and intellectuals – exclusively Tutsi vocations – as responsible. The invasion of the Tutsi-led RPF from Uganda in 1990 coincided with harsh SAP imposed as conditionality for loans from the World Bank and International Monetary Fund, leading to severe food shortages and a two-thirds devaluation of the currency. The democratization process and political conditionality required by the Arusha Accord, amidst continuing economic crisis, also coincided with rising opposition within Hutu ranks and southern Hutu resentment of northern Hutu political domination. Rather than accommodate opposition, the Hutu leadership turned instead to ethnic politics, blaming Tutsis rather than the globalizing economy, IFIs or themselves for their predicament, and planned the genocide as the final solution. Andersen corroborates Hintjen's analysis on external factors. Andersen notes that the three strategies pursued by multilateral development assistance, namely, economic structural adjustment, multiparty democratization and peace implementation, had contrary and mutually negating effects that ultimately weakened the regime and precipitated conflict.[23]

A brief appraisal of the other countries referred to in this study also reveals grievances in the causation of conflict. In Guatemala the top 20 per cent of households earn 63 per cent of household income, while the bottom 20 per cent earn a mere 2 per cent of it. Moreover, poverty affects the indigenous population disproportionately. While the indigenous comprise 60 per cent of Guatemala's population, 90 per cent of them live below the poverty line (with 81 per cent living in extreme poverty) compared to 66 per cent below the poverty line among non-indigenous Guatemalans. The life expectancy of the indigenous population is eighteen years lower than that of the *ladino* population.[24]

In El Salvador productive land was concentrated from the 1900s in the hands of an oligarchy of a few families. Contentions about land redistribution were a major factor leading to the outbreak of conflict.[25] In El Salvador and Guatemala war was triggered, among other reasons, by the impossibility of changing these socio-economic injustices through non-violent political channels within repressive regimes.[26]

In Haiti about 4 per cent of the population owns 66 per cent of the country's resources, while 70 per cent of the population owns 20 per cent, and 10 per cent of the population are estimated to be entirely destitute.[27] Aristide's meteoric rise to power in 1991 was fuelled by the popular demand for greater distributive justice after the Duvalier era. Aristide's campaign slogan summed up the simple demand for social justice of poor Haitians: 'from misery to poverty with dignity'.[28] The violent military coup was also motivated by concern for distributive justice, that is, the desire of the military and economic elite to keep it unchanged.

According to the World Bank's most recent estimates, South Africa's bottom 20 per cent has a 3 per cent share of income, compared to 63 per cent for the top 20 per cent.[29] South Africa under apartheid was estimated to be the second most unequal country in the world after Brazil, by all economic, social and political indicators. In South Africa, as in Namibia, this inequality was racially based, as apartheid was 'specifically designed (and largely successful) in preventing poverty among whites'. In South Africa, whereas poverty among whites is close to zero, poverty among Africans stands at 64 per cent, among coloureds at 33 per cent and among Indians at 3 per cent.[30] The violent struggle in both South Africa and Namibia aimed to overturn the unjust apartheid regime and its discriminatory policies.

In Cambodia, although reliable income distribution figures do not exist, distributive justice claims underlay the conflict. The Khmer Rouge was the product of a class struggle rooted largely in the country's deep historical inequalities, although their uprising in the 1970s was also triggered by the devastating US bombardment of Cambodia during the Vietnam War. Pol Pot and his comrades tried to mobilize impoverished and illiterate rural peasants against the urban, educated elite. Under Khmer Rouge rule from 1975 to 1979 anyone seen to be 'modern' was killed, including 'doctors, technicians, Buddhist monks, teachers, intellectuals, or students', as well as anyone 'having studied abroad, speaking French or English or any of the Vietnamese dialects, having a fair skin or wearing glasses'.[31]

Interestingly, in Mozambique the long, brutal conflict between the FRELIMO government and RENAMO rebels was not caused directly by contentions about distributive justice. Rather, as acknowledged by many Mozambicans today, the war was instigated externally by Rhodesia and later sustained by South Africa, which created, funded and trained RENAMO for strategic reasons of their own.[32] Nevertheless, the skewed pattern of investment and development resulting from international reconstruction assistance, favouring the southern Maputo region over the north, has fuelled RENAMO's increasingly violent rhetoric about distributive injustice. Ironically, the generous donor response to recent floods in southern Mozambique has exacerbated RENAMO hostility: 'As they send visible support to flood victims, donors risk increasing the North–South gap and Mozambique's political tensions.'[33]

Distributive justice claims are rarely uniform, and are articulated in different forms from one case to another. In El Salvador and Guatemala the demand was primarily for a more equitable distribution of assets, particularly land. In Namibia and South Africa demand for land, concentrated in white hands, has been prominent, and Zimbabwe's controversial land seizures have stoked these demands further. In Haiti, by contrast, the claim for social justice was expressed in simpler terms as the fulfilment of basic needs and the reduction of poverty, rather than specific redistribution of assets.

To clarify once again, we are not claiming that all contemporary conflicts centre on grievances regarding distributive injustice. Yet they emerge as salient in all the cases considered here. Given this frequent salience, there is a strong rationale for addressing distributive justice as a priority issue in the aftermath of conflict. Some of the literature on peacebuilding and post-conflict reconstruction does speak of the need to identify and remedy causes of conflict at least in theory, as noted in chapter 1. However, these causes are rarely identified and addressed as issues of *justice*. The human *consequences* of conflict – human rights abuses, war crimes, and crimes against humanity – analysed in chapter 4 are readily and rightly regarded as justice issues. Yet international and national actors hesitate to treat *causes* of conflict as justice issues, although they stem largely from distributive injustices. Despite vociferous public demands in some countries, until recently international actors and national governments have paid scant attention to redressing distributive injustice and promoting equity after conflict.

International factors and actors

Since the vast majority of countries emerging from conflict are low-income and severely debilitated by conflict, they are deeply dependent on IFIs, particularly the World Bank and the IMF, for their rehabili-tation. Not only do the Bank and Fund extend substantial assistance and sponsor several post-conflict projects, they also act as catalysts and guarantees for other sources of financing. As such, the Bretton Woods Institutions bear significant responsibility for the economic fate of low-income countries emerging from conflict. Yet, despite their considerable efforts to address the effects of conflict and reconstruct war-torn societies, the Bank and Fund have ignored largely underlying causes of conflict and distributive justice issues. As Boyce notes, IFIs have been willing to rebuild economies and finance peacebuilding activities, but have neglected to 'secure a distribution of economic benefits which will... redress the social tensions which fuelled the war'.[34]

The economic paradigm and the policy prescriptions of the Bank and Fund have hampered rather than fostered greater distributive justice and equity in war-torn countries.

The 'Washington Consensus'

The understandable preoccupation of post-conflict governments is to catch up quickly with years of lost economic development, while simultaneously undertaking the monumental and costly task of recon-structing society. The prevailing economic consensus on the 'right policies' believed to assure economic growth and development has a powerful hold on national governments as they plan their post-con-flict economic policies, whether independently or in conjunction with IFIs and other major donors. This consensus view has been referred to as the 'Washington Consensus', as it is presumed to reflect the com-bined wisdom of the IMF, the World Bank, and US policy makers in Washington, DC.

The term 'Washington Consensus' was coined by the economist John Williamson in 1989 in the aftermath of Soviet collapse. At a time of economic volatility, it summarized ten prescriptions for policy reform in ten principal economic areas, including fiscal discipline; tax, interest, and exchange rates; liberalization; and privatization. The seeming simplicity and beguiling infallibility of the consensus gave it a popularity and life of its own.[35]

Soon the IMF and World Bank began to insist that their loans were conditional on acceptance of consensus-oriented policy reforms. In terms of economic policy the consensus translates to liberalization and export-orientation; privatization; fiscal and budgetary discipline with an emphasis on low inflation; and structural adjustment, consisting mainly of a downsizing of government's administration, responsibilities and budget. A former World Bank Chief Economist, Joseph Stiglitz, describes the basic logic of the consensus: 'Good economic performance required liberalised trade, macroeconomic stability, and getting prices right. Once the government dealt with these issues – essentially, once the government "got out of the way" – private markets would allocate resources efficiently and generate robust growth.'[36]

This consensus underpinned SAP and associated policy conditionalities put forward by the World Bank and IMF to developing countries requiring their assistance since the 1980s. The extensive literature on the impact of SAP on developing countries is not explored here, as the specific concern is with the impact of the Washington Consensus on societies emerging from conflict.

The consensus is broadly based on neo-liberal economics. However, neo-liberal economic theory has faced mounting challenges from political economists through the 1990s.[37] Classical neo-liberal economists typically presume that social planners choose optimal economic policy instruments to maximize welfare, within given resource constraints. As Alesina notes, although such models are important tools of analysis, 'they cannot explain the occurrence of frequent and large departures from first-best policies'. The discipline of political economy tries to remedy this. 'A political-economic approach takes into account the institutional constraints and rigidities in which policymaking occurs by emphasizing the role of distributive conflicts, ideological and opportunistic incentives of the politicians and other factors.'[38]

A basic flaw with the neo-liberal economic model is that it is predicated on assumptions of perfect market conditions.[39] 'Contemporary economic theory typically takes for granted the basic underpinnings of an economy', such as well-defined and accepted social distribution, a legal system, and a state providing public goods. However, 'all of these preconditions are compromised or shattered by most CHEs, especially civil war'.[40] Carbonnier notes that 'some of the basic assumptions underlying traditional economic theory (e.g. rational economic behaviour of individuals) are starkly contradicted by the reality of war-torn societies'. Yet rather than accounting specifically for these major 'market imperfections' and correcting and adapting the model accordingly, the neo-liberal approach regards these 'imperfections' as incidental, exogenous circumstances. It does not treat conflict and war as significant factors which might affect quite considerably the model's functioning and outcomes. Carbonnier concludes that *'fundamental aspects of post-conflict rebuilding have been overlooked*, mainly because they do not fit into the prevailing paradigm'.[41]

The consensus did not bring the success expected in reforming countries through the 1990s, and its requirements kept changing in response to economic crises and developments, resembling a 'confusion' more than a 'consensus'. As Naim observes trenchantly, 'Throughout the decade, policy makers in reforming countries saw how the bar defining success kept being lifted, and how the changes they were expected to make became increasingly complex and, sometimes, politically impossible.'

The failure of the Washington Consensus to account for variable and highly volatile political conditions and its adoption of a context-neutral rather than a context-specific political economy approach have made it unsuitable and even harmful in war-torn societies.

The growth–equity trade-off

As Stiglitz states, 'The goal of the Washington Consensus was to provide a formula for creating a vibrant private sector and *stimulating economic growth*.'[42] The emphasis on economic growth in contemporary economic theory has sidelined and even overshadowed the necessary and parallel concern with the distributive impact of growth.

The focus on growth predates the Washington Consensus. Since the 1960s the popular economic belief is that growth is the only way both to achieve economic progress and to alleviate inequalities, since richer countries seem to display lower inequality. As observed in 1969, 'faith in the equalising effect of economic growth is shared alike by adherents of socialism and capitalism', and growth was powerfully believed by developing country leaders to 'create the necessary conditions for an equalitarian society'.[43] The initial belief was that growth in and of itself, without any regard to its distributive impact, would reduce inequality in the long run.[44] This was gradually replaced by the now orthodox belief that actively promoting equity was, in fact, detrimental to growth.[45]

Recently this thesis has been contested and disproved by a range of economists. Several economists have established that, both theoretically and empirically, greater equity promotes growth, rather than the contrary.[46] By way of example, Alesina and Rodrik examine the relation between political conflict and economic growth using a simple endogenous growth model. They demonstrate that 'more concentrated wealth distributions are conducive to lower rates of economic growth'. Their study concludes that 'equality is conducive to growth', primarily in democratic regimes, and that 'it is easier to avoid damaging conflict over redistributive policies when the economy's assets are widely shared'.[47] Persson and Tabellini demonstrate through a series of studies that more inequality brings about slower growth. Their study concludes: 'A more unequal size distribution of income is bad for growth in democracies. While more land concentration is bad for growth everywhere.'[48] The relationship between inequality and growth has been studied from many perspectives. One set of studies shows that 'if wealthy voters have relatively more capital...income inequality is bad for growth because it leads to more capital taxation'.[49] Another study demonstrates that more equality is good for growth because a large middle class is needed to generate demand for manufacturing products and facilitate a growth takeoff.[50]

The cumulative evidence supports the view that political stability, equity and growth are all positively correlated in what Pastor and Boyce would call a 'virtuous cycle'.[51] Despite this evidence, none of these findings influenced significantly the shape of post-conflict economic policies and the treatment of equity.

We are not arguing that growth should be sacrificed for the pursuit of equity. The argument is that the interdependence of the two should be recognized and both should be pursued simultaneously. Admittedly, rapid growth is needed in countries debilitated by war. However, this growth has to be equitable, not simply for humane reasons but for economic and political ones. As Pastor and Boyce state, 'Both peace and growth can benefit from an improved balance in the distribution of income and wealth.'[52] Instead, with its continued emphasis on economic growth, the Washington Consensus has neglected equity, overlooked existing grievances, and been detrimental rather than beneficial to the cause of distributive justice in societies that have emerged from war.

The impact of World Bank/IMF policies

The application of World Bank/IMF orthodox economic policies without suitable adaptation to the disruptions in and special needs of individual war-afflicted societies has often aggravated inequities experienced or perceived by the population.[53] In extreme cases, these policies have undermined the goals of peacebuilding itself.[54]

It should be noticed that the World Bank's role in post-conflict societies is more far-reaching than the Fund's and includes rebuilding infrastructure, demining, and supporting demobilization, and reintegration.[55] We are not critiquing this panoply of tasks, but more specifically their economic policy prescriptions. Here, the Bank has supported and complemented the IMF's task of re-establishing macroeconomic stability through stabilization measures and structural adjustment programmes to promote growth and revitalize the economy.

Today the Bank acknowledges that its approach to post-conflict societies so far was not 'politically realistic'.[56] Until very recently IFIs were not sufficiently mindful either of the special needs and circumstances of developing societies ravaged by conflict, or of their political vulnerability and volatility after conflict, which risked affecting the outcome of policies applied. In effect, a political economy approach was lacking, and societies emerging from violent conflict were treated like any other (stable) economy.[57] In 1995 the Bank and Fund developed special facilities to respond to the particular needs of post-conflict countries. Although this signals an improvement, even with its new facility, the IMF clearly acknowledges that its 'key role in post-conflict countries is to help re-establish macroeconomic stability'. The IMF also concedes that it prefers countries to use its regular lending channels if they are eligible, or to demonstrate their intention to graduate rapidly from special arrangements to regular ones. Moreover, it insists on a 'demonstrated commitment on the part of the authorities, to provide confidence that the IMF's resources will be adequately safeguarded', although it recognizes that post-conflict countries face special circumstances.[58]

In El Salvador, Haiti, Mozambique and Cambodia, among others, it has been documented that the IMF and World Bank handed down essentially the same economic package that countries not debilitated by prolonged political conflict and concomitant destruction and human suffering would have received. In all four cases the detrimental results of this approach have been documented.[59] While it is not possible, for reasons of space, to explore the impact of IFI policies in detail in all four countries, some illustrative examples are discussed here, with a focus on Haiti. Two elements of the typical adjustment package which often run counter to demands for distributive justice and exacerbate popular perceptions of injustice are examined: privatization and liberalization.

Privatization

In theory, privatization makes eminent economic sense as a means to turn around sick, unproductive state enterprises, cut government waste and corruption, and raise efficiency and profits. However, what is less appreciated by IFIs is that privatization may also widen economic disparities – and perceptions of inequality – in deeply unequal post-conflict societies. In many countries the only nationals in a position to purchase privatized enterprises are the same elite whose control and exploitation of economic and political power fed the grievances that led to conflict. In many cases, 'privatization would be impossible or merely involve the enrichment of senior government officials'.[60]

In Haiti Aristide returned to resume his interrupted presidency in 1994, bearing in hand a 'Strategy of Social and Economic Reconstruction', and US$1.2bn in promised funding from the US, IFIs and other donors. The BWI condition for disbursing the funds was the privatization of major state-owned enterprises (SOEs) and public utilities. This included the telephone and electricity companies, the cement factory and flour mills, airports and naval ports, and the central bank. The only Haitians who could afford to bid for these companies were the handful of richest families in the country. Most of them allegedly had been closely linked to the Duvaliers and / or the abusive military regime that overthrew Aristide. The name that appeared on almost all bids was that of Mev, one of the country's richest families, who had supported the previous military regime. Popular resentment arose among ordinary Haitians that the very families who had abetted oppressive regimes, exploited the poor, and contributed so little to the nation's coffers should be the beneficiaries of privatization. Resentment led to mass mobilization and violent protests.[61]

The poor strongly opposed privatization for two reasons. First, they argued, private ownership (whether by nationals or foreigners) and the profit motive would further increase the price of basic goods and public services on which all ordinary Haitians were dependent. Meanwhile, poor Haitians were already crippled by the cost of living, which had skyrocketed since the UN embargo imposed during the military regime. Second, they argued, if state-owned enterprises were privatized, the government would have less revenue for social spending on education and health. They feared that these sectors too would pass into private hands and lead to higher prices for consumers. Popular organizations argued: 'Since the rich traditionally avoided taxes, the state needed revenues generated from the SOEs to pay for desperately needed social services.'[62]

The World Bank counters that privatizing SOEs reduces government deficit and debt by saving resources squandered on subsidizing inefficient enterprises. The Bank argues that even if prices are temporarily raised, citizens are better off in the long run because this saves government debt whose burden ordinary people would otherwise have to bear. The Bank also notes that as domestic expertise and capacity often may be lacking in poor war-ravaged countries, privatization may require foreign ownership. The Bank does not see this as detrimental to the country's interests, as competitive international bidding is thought to yield the most cost-effective option for consumers.[63]

The Bank's argument is valid from the perspective of economic efficiency, but it overlooks the reality of domestic sentiment, particularly in post-conflict contexts. Haiti had already experimented with privatization in 1986, at BWI urging. The same Mev family had purchased the sugar mill, but promptly shut it down and opened a sugar importing plant in its place. This move had a deleterious effect on domestic sugar production and refining capacity, which were well-established Haitian activities. It also destroyed the livelihoods of peasants dependent on growing sugarcane.[64] Burnt by this experience, poor urban consumers as well as rural producers and peasants feared and resisted privatization.

State employees who argued that most SOEs could be made profitable again also resisted privatization. Haiti's SOEs had suffered severe neglect, corruption and inefficiency under the Duvaliers, and were severely weakened during the Cédras regime. However, during Aristide's brief rule in 1991, his prime minister, René Préval, had turned around the SOEs significantly and, allegedly, most or all SOEs went from deficit to surplus. The telephone company, Teleco, continued to generate sufficient profits to sustain Aristide's government in exile for three years.[65] Labour union leaders believed that it would be possible for several SOEs – particularly the telephone and electricity companies and the cement factory – to make profits again, as in 1991.

Admittedly, the IFIs' case for privatization rested on the inability of Haiti's government to manage state-owned industries and services without damaging the economy and indebting itself further. Despite the economic rationale, the Bank and Fund neglected the sentiments and legitimate fears of an impoverished population, and the hostility generated by their policies and their (perhaps unintended) consequences.

This experience is not unique to Haiti, as similar effects have been observed in other post-conflict countries. In Sierra Leone privatization 'ended up putting much of the economy in a few oligopolistic hands and deepening a popular sense of grievance'.[66] The logic of privatization is not coherent with the logic of aggrieved post-conflict populations who wish to gain, not lose further from peace.

Liberalization

Liberalization has two aspects: first, the liberalization of foreign investment, and second, the liberalization of foreign trade, through reduced trade barriers.

A strong economic case can be made for liberalizing foreign investment: impoverished countries, usually deeply indebted, urgently require the stimulus of foreign investment, its boost to local production, and the jobs it generates. In low-income countries especially in Central America, the recent influx of foreign investment facilitated by liberalization has focused on *maquila* or assembly industries producing for foreign markets. Following the logic of classical economic theory that the comparative advantage of low-income countries is cheap labour, these industries do not produce goods in-country but bring in goods produced elsewhere for cheap assembly, then resell them outside the country. In some post-conflict countries such industries have had positive effects. In Cambodia, over the last few years, *maquila*-style garment factories have expanded rapidly. They are reckoned to be 'probably the only private enterprises where minimum wage laws are observed, and are also the site of the first efforts to form trade unions in the country'.[67]

However, such positive effects do not always ensue, and foreign investment may sometimes exacerbate perceptions of social injustice. In Haiti assembly industries may have provided much-needed employment, but attracted more criticism than praise from Haitian workers. Assembly plants allegedly pay low wages, often violate minimum wage law, and are frequently accused of exploiting and mistreating workers. Reportedly, 'More than half of the approximately 50 assembly plants producing in Haiti for US markets are paying less than the legal minimum wage.'[68] Many urban workers are peasants who were pushed off their subsistence farms and into towns by rural impoverishment, stemming from neglect of the rural sector. These peasants believe that liberalization is part of a 'US-imposed' plan to push peasants off the land and into low-paid labour in towns to destroy Haitian agriculture, while assuring a supply of cheap goods to the USA.[69]

This popular perception was reinforced by the battle over the minimum wage. As part of his social justice platform, Aristide had promised on his election in 1991 to raise the legal minimum wage. In 1994–5 there was a compelling need to raise the minimum wage, unchanged at 15 Gourdes/day (about US$1/day) since 1985. The embargo imposed during the coup years had been accompanied by high inflation that reached 50 per cent in 1993–4 and eroded much of the minimum wage's real value, leaving waged labour destitute. Even the IMF noted that 'the legal minimum wage has declined significantly in real terms in recent years'.[70] However, when Aristide tried to implement the wage rise in 1995, he faced bitter opposition from several sources: from his neo-liberal prime minister, Smarck Michel, who was bent on following the World Bank/IMF stricture of fiscal discipline; from *maquila* industries which feared an erosion of their profits; and from certain external donors, led by USAID, which claimed that this risked 'jeopardizing' Haiti's comparative advantage in cheap labour.[71]

Although Haiti's labour code requires the minimum wage to be raised whenever inflation exceeds 10 per cent, USAID's administrator is reported to have said in 1994, 'I don't think the [Haitian] economy is ready... for such measures.'[72] After a bitter struggle, Aristide was forced to accept only a minimal increase to 36 Gourdes (about US$2.40), although this was worth less in real terms than the old wage of 15 Gourdes in 1990. After paying for transport and the day's meal, a minimum-wage worker can barely meet 25 per cent of the basic minimum needs of a family of five. Wage labourers are largely dependent on 'loan sharks' – moneylenders charging excessive interest – as they lack access to banks.[73] This is despite the IMF's vaunted achievements in stimulating the commercial banking sector in Haiti, which, it acknowledges, as yet caters mainly to business customers in big cities, and not to poor people needing micro-credit. The perception among workers that liberalization is a deliberate 'US' ploy to hurt their interests may be misplaced, but it cannot be disregarded, as it shapes popular acceptance of economic policies, and influences their outcomes.

It could be questioned whether assembly industries – foreign-owned through foreign investment liberalization or domestically owned for export promotion – contribute anything beyond their foreign exchange earnings to the development process. They do not stimulate industrialization, as they are based on imports, nor do they contribute to consumption, as goods are re-exported. In Haiti, for example, light manufactures comprised 81.5 per cent of exports in 1997, but of US$159.4m earned, US$135.4m consisted of imported inputs. By comparison, that year, agricultural exports that were domestically produced comprised only 8.9 per cent or US$17.5m of total exports.[74] Assembly industries, with their low start-up costs and quick turnover, may provide the kick-start to the economy that is urgently needed after the disruption of conflict. However, it must be questioned whether they are a productive use of foreign investment for post-conflict countries that need to rebuild their economic capacities and develop sustainably.

The economic logic behind the second element, liberalization of ✸ trade, is that imports stimulate competition and heighten domestic productivity and efficiency, while exports earn much-needed foreign exchange. The liberalization of imports may run counter to the post-conflict priority of restoring the labour force's productive capacity. Although intended to stimulate local production by enhancing competition, imports introduced into markets shortly after disruptive political conflict may further debilitate or destroy domestic production. Imports may also disrupt local markets, as tastes turn towards imported goods.

In Haiti Aristide's government was required to comply with the IFIs' stricture to lower import tariffs on several goods including rice, which was produced locally by Haitian peasants. Imported rice and other food articles quickly swamped Haiti's markets, and were preferred by middle- and upper-class urban consumers to local rice. In 1997 food accounted for 45.1 per cent of Haiti's imports, contributing to a huge trade deficit: US$706.6m spent on imports (of which US$318.4m was spent on food articles) far outweighed the meagre US$195.5m in export earnings.[75] The impact was crippling. Rice producers and sellers lost their domestic market to imports, costing them their livelihoods. Domestic capacity to produce rice was devastated, as rice fields and irrigation systems became unviable and were abandoned, particularly in Haiti's fertile Artibonite valley.[76] Urban poverty was exacerbated as displaced and pauperized peasants swarmed to cities for work, aggravating unemployment.

Liberalization also exacerbated political instability, as peasants organized mass demonstrations to protest against import and other structural adjustment policies, and to demand explanations from government.[77] The Haitian experience corroborates Fitzgerald's observation: 'These assumptions ... [underlying] liberalization as a means of correcting fundamental imbalances ... do not hold in wartime economies, and the application of "peacetime policy" can easily undermine production and increase poverty.'[78]

The logic of export-led growth for unstable post-conflict societies in a volatile global economy with falling primary commodity prices is questionable. Some political economists question whether the Bank and Fund would emphasize export-led growth as much if their strategy were not motivated by their insistence on debt-servicing in hard currency, which requires export earnings.[79] The Bank sympathizes with the difficulties imposed on post-conflict countries by debt-servicing, but holds that debt-forgiveness might be interpreted by belligerent governments as IFIs' willingness to underwrite the cost of wars. Even supporters of debt-reduction within the Bank cite Rwanda, Zimbabwe, Ethiopia and Eritrea as illustrative cases to reinforce this point.[80] This argument notwithstanding, the question remains whether countries emerging from debilitating conflict can be expected to continue servicing their debts and impose this additional hardship on their vulnerable populations, at a time when scant resources are so desperately needed for other aspects of peacebuilding and reconstruction. Often post-conflict countries are obliged to undertake new loans not for rehabilitation, but simply to service their old or inherited debts.

The vaunted enhanced Heavily Indebted Poor Countries Initiative was proposed as an answer to this crisis. However, a report published in the wake of the IMF/World Bank Prague meeting in September 2000 noted that even with the enhanced HIPC, nine out of twelve countries reviewed 'will continue to spend far more on debt servicing than on health and primary education *after* they have received debt relief'.[81] Despite global pressure from Jubilee 2000, a popular campaign for debt-forgiveness, third world debt was not cancelled by creditors, but HIPC's coverage was extended. Several post-conflict countries, including Mozambique and Rwanda, are covered. Whether this will make a real difference to their debt burdens, and whether this will change the attitude of the IMF and World Bank towards export-led growth in post-conflict countries remains to be seen.

Economic versus political stabilization

The BWI policies emphasize economic stabilization but do so often to the detriment of political stabilization and peacebuilding. This argument is made in different ways in the works of Boyce, Carbonnier, Weinberg and Paris cited here. Economic stabilization requires low inflation, tight fiscal and budgetary discipline and a small government, all of which are difficult conditions to fulfil in post-conflict situations. To undertake the process of reconstruction and to fulfil the requirements of peace agreements where such accords exist, post-conflict governments are required to take on more rather than fewer activities, to enlarge both their budget and their staff, and to risk inflation due to rapid economic expansion and activity after economic slowdown or stagnation during conflict.[82] The BWI insistence on macroeconomic stabilization and budgetary and fiscal discipline at the time of transition to peace may contradict and undermine the objectives of the peace process, whatever sense they might make in economic theory.

In Cambodia the World Bank itself acknowledges that it 'continued to push for downsizing the civil service when the political coalition arrangement under the peace accord was based in part on raising the size of the civil service to absorb large numbers of the incoming parties' functionaries'. The Bank's evaluation concludes: 'The Bank's position was not politically realistic from the outset.'[83]

In Haiti, too, the BWI insisted on the need to downsize government, although the state was already 'a phantom where government services were concerned'.[84] Ordinary Haitians' common complaint was that after generations of being treated as *moun an deyors* ('people on the outside' or 'the excluded') by irresponsible regimes, they now wanted more – not less – government services to fulfil their demands for social justice.[85]

In El Salvador the Fund and Bank demanded that the government reduce its budget deficit, without consideration for how this reduction was to be achieved or what the appropriate magnitude of government revenue and spending should be. This lack of direction from IFIs led the government to opt for reducing social spending on essential services such as health and education which affected the poor, rather than the less popular alternatives of raising taxes or cutting military spending as means to reduce the deficit and raise revenues. The IFIs' insistence on budgetary constraint also provided a ready excuse for the government to claim it did not have enough money to finance the terms of the peace agreement, such as the reform of the police and judiciary and the limited land redistribution policy. Simultaneously, it was observed that IFIs did not put enough pressure on the government to reduce military expenditures, as this was considered an inappropriate interference in political affairs by the Bank and Fund at that time.[86] The lax attitude of IFIs, combined with the dramatic rise in crime following the end of conflict, provided justification to the government to maintain high levels of military expenditure, contradicting the spirit of the peace accords. Critics observed:

> Both justice and prudence dictate that the World Bank not throw its considerable weight against the hard-won gains of the Accords. It should be the role of the Bank to devise a program of structural adjustment that reinforces the attainment of social peace. The recent strategy of the Bank in El Salvador, on the contrary, has worked against the peace process.[87]

This observation should be noted by all IFIs operating in countries exiting from war.

Another area where the BWI have shown their inclination to prioritize economic over political stabilization is in their neglect of the rural sector and agricultural economy. The BWI focus on the urban industrial economy stems from their belief that the future is not in agriculture and that 'land is not the solution to rural poverty'.[88] The harmful – albeit perhaps unintended – effects of the BWI policies on the rural agricultural sector in Haiti was noted earlier. In El Salvador, while the Bank generally neglected the rural sector, the policies it did advocate hurt the interests of the poor and of the economy. For example, despite compelling rationales, it opposed price supports for basic grains on the weak argument that such protections might be difficult to dismantle once introduced.[89] More serious, the Bank's agricultural policy contradicted the spirit and text of the peace agreement. According to observers, the Bank unravelled the measures aimed at addressing the social and economic causes of the conflict, which centred largely on claims for land redistribution, but ignored critics. 'Perhaps the most alarming sign of the Bank's indifference to the objective of consolidating the peace embodied in the Peace Accords is their response to this criticism... In the Bank's view... what is needed is not more land distribution, but more and more diverse sources of income.'[90]

The BWI neglect of the rural sector is misplaced in most low-income countries emerging from conflict, as a significant majority of poor people are rural, and land redistribution is often a central demand underlying conflict – as in Guatemala, El Salvador and Namibia. There is an unmet need for BWI to prioritize the rural economy and attend to distributive justice claims in this area.

Sharing responsibility

The arguments so far suggest that the Bank and Fund were solely responsible for disregarding claims for distributive justice, and neglecting underlying causes of conflict in the post-conflict stage, sometimes undermining peacebuilding in the process. However, IFIs have often been abetted actively by other influential donors.

In Haiti the US Administration and USAID were largely responsible for the shape of the policies imposed on Haiti when Aristide returned to power in 1994.[91] The Bank and Fund had been supportive of Aristide when he assumed his presidency in 1991. When Aristide took exile in Washington, DC, the US Administration put great financial and political pressure on him. US policy makers and USAID officials, along with the World Bank and IMF, pressured Aristide to accept the terms of a neo-liberal economic package on his return to office. Consequently, Aristide, who had swept to democratic victory on a bold platform of social justice, returned sheepishly to Haiti in 1994 bearing what was seen by ordinary Haitians as a US-imposed structural adjustment package designed to further cripple and increase the dependency of the poor.[92] Unsurprisingly, Aristide's credibility with his own electorate was tarnished. The USA was also allegedly prescriptive in its choice of Aristide's Prime Minister, who wields more executive power than the President in Haitian politics. The choice was a neo-liberal economist favourable to the IMF/World Bank plan, Smarck Michel. Due to their sharply differing ideologies, Michel and Aristide came into conflict as reform went ahead, resulting in serious delays in implementation, the alienation of Aristide, and ultimately Michel's resignation. Subsequent US insistence that Aristide should not seek to extend his presidential term, although he had spent three years of his term in exile, added to political turmoil. In the Haitian case, therefore, it is more accurate to hold the US Administration and USAID, rather than IFIs, responsible for the shape and content of economic policies adopted after transition, and for their deleterious political and economic ramifications. The extent to which the USA presumed to control Haiti's fate was revealed in a comment made by the US Deputy Secretary of State in March 1995 amidst the handover of responsibilities from the US-led Multinational Force to the UN: 'I assure you, even after our exit in February 1996, we will remain in charge by means of the Agency for International Development and the private sector.'[93] This specific example illustrates a general point. IFIs cannot be held solely responsible for shaping post-conflict policies that neglect distributive justice, as they are often encouraged to do so by other actors, in this case, the USA.

National factors and actors

The discussion so far has focused on the role and responsibilities of international actors in shaping post-conflict economic priorities; it has not yet addressed the crucial role of national actors. Admittedly, post-conflict governments are beholden to IFIs and donors for aid, and susceptible to their strictures. The Washington Consensus, and unquestioned trust in the growth formula, has influenced deeply economic policies and attitudes adopted by post-conflict governments, and sidelined, if not ruled out, the possibility of responding positively to popular demands for distributive justice in the aftermath of conflict. However, often post-conflict governments have acted autonomously in determining their economic priorities and marginalizing social justice.

El Salvador is usually portrayed as a case where IFIs dictated policies that had a pernicious impact on equity and peacebuilding, and this is how it was depicted above. Yet a more complex picture emerges from discussions with insiders to the economic negotiations. Some observers suggest that the ARENA government's agenda in opting for peace was principally to get access to international capital and finance which was suspended when the war intensified, and to implement SAP in order to reshape the flagging economy.[94] Observers also suggest that it was not the IMF and World Bank which twisted the ARENA government's arm to implement SAP, but that the package actually reflected the policy preferences of the ARENA government itself. It has been observed – and not only by WB/IMF staff but also by independent critics of the Fund and Bank – that the IFIs might have been willing to be more flexible with El Salvador if that is what the ARENA government had said it wanted. However, it was convenient for the government to use the Bank and Fund as an excuse to put in place policies that would otherwise have diminished the popularity of ARENA.[95]

In Haiti, too, internal politics are largely responsible for the collapse of economic reforms and the economic downturn. Haitian law requires that parliament approve economic programmes, and that the Prime Minister as head of government sign them, before they can be implemented. Haiti had no prime minister from 1997 to early 1999, and no parliament from January 1999 till late 2000. The delayed legislative elections did not resolve the crisis, as results giving Lavalas victory were disputed. Consequently, for that long hiatus, necessary parliamentary and prime ministerial approval could not be obtained for critical economic programmes proposed by the Bank and Fund, which, therefore, could not be implemented. Political infighting and government paralysis and neglect have deepened the economic crisis.

BWI indeed have adjusted and made efforts in this unstable climate. Following their early inflexibility in Haiti, the Bank and Fund subsequently became willing to make concessions. Aristide's successor, President René Préval, proposed a halfway measure to accommodate both the IFIs' insistence on privatization on the one hand, and popular opposition to it on the other. Préval offered to retain state ownership of certain key enterprises while having them privately run by a professional competent firm, and the Bank was poised to accept.

However, the ensuing domestic political impasse held up progress on this front. Despite continuing political uncertainty in Haiti, the Fund and Bank remain engaged in the country. They still disburse funds approved before the collapse of government, monitor the situation, and collaborate with the government where invited to do so.[96] Further action on distributive justice now depends more crucially on the recovery of the political process in Haiti than on external actors.

In Namibia as well, the shape of the response to demands for distributive justice was largely internally determined, although the IMF played a significant role in helping with the transition.[97] Despite its initial commitment to a redistributive socialist agenda during its long struggle against apartheid and colonial rule by South Africa, SWAPO changed its economic posture well before independence, and began courting the white business sector. SWAPO had adopted a conciliatory attitude towards white Namibians (and South Africans) as early as 1980.[98] SWAPO toned down its socialist leanings during its liberation struggle to placate international supporters, and adopted a market-friendly capitalist approach on independence to dissipate anxiety among foreign donors and investors.[99] After independence SWAPO diluted its rhetoric of distributive justice and adopted a policy of national reconciliation at both the political level (mentioned in chapter 4) and the economic level. Economically, its motivation was to placate white Namibians who controlled business and capital, and to discourage out-migration and consequent capital flight by whites. The SWAPO government was also keen to generate confidence in foreign investors that Namibia was business-friendly and safe for investment.

Admittedly, the external influence of global market considerations on SWAPO's posture cannot be disregarded. As observed, this reconciliatory, market-friendly posture might have been 'the only realistic strategy for the SWAPO government in the global conditions of the 1990s'.[100] Also significant were the Constitutional Principles, framed in 1982 primarily by the Western Contact Group within the UN Security Council, which forbade SWAPO from expropriating private property without market price compensation, and required it to retain whites in the civil service until the end of their terms.[101] These arrangements cut off two primary avenues for providing distributive justice to aggrieved and impoverished blacks, access to assets via land distribution, and employment via government jobs, both of which had long been denied to them.

Furthermore, despite attempts, scant progress was made on the crucial issue of land distribution which SWAPO recognized as 'arguably the single most important reason that led to the liberation war'.[102]

In mid-1991, two years after independence, the government convened a long-awaited 'National Conference on Land Reform and the Land Question'.[103] Although not binding on the government, the conference, according to President Sam Nujoma, was intended to achieve the greatest possible national consensus on this critical issue, and provide 'the opportunity for Namibians to come forward with their problems and to suggest solutions to the question'. The nature and proceedings of the conference were all the more noteworthy as they represented 'an exceptional display of openness and democratic practice on the part of a government grown out of a movement not previously noted for either'.[104] The conference produced a 24-point consensus, cemented broad agreement that significant land reform was necessary to correct deep inequities, and even won the concession on the part of some rich white farmers that some redistribution of resources was called for. Yet the government has made scant progress in translating this consensus into practice, and no major land redistribution has yet taken place. Long government inaction amidst persistent demands for land redistribution deeply alienated and angered the population.

The government belatedly undertook an official resettlement target of 243,000 Namibians on 686 million hectares. That the plan was ill-conceived is evident in the discrepancy between the 83 per cent of total land surface this resettlement would entail and the 44 per cent of national land already set aside for national parks and diamond concessions. By mid-2000, only 461,000 hectares, less than 1 per cent of the requirement, had been purchased, and 27,000 Namibians had been resettled on communal land. Further, much of the land redistributed is of marginal quality. There is an ominous likelihood that the government might seek a more drastic solution. Nujoma has publicly supported Zimbabwe's land expropriation. SWAPO's two-thirds majority in parliament makes it possible for them to change the constitutional requirement of just compensation for land appropriation. Amid rising demands from communal farmers, the Namibian National Farmers' Union warned in August 2001 of Zimbabwe-style land takeovers.[105] The land issue may finally be addressed in Namibia – but perhaps not in the consultative, consensual, non-confrontational manner initially intended.

The discussion so far elucidates that despite strident demands from sections of the public for redistribution, in numerous countries fragile post-conflict governments face considerable political, moral and economic constraints which mute, diminish or delay their response to distributive justice.

Politically, the opposition of established elites to any redistribution that threatens to reduce their political and economic privileges often hamstrings post-conflict governments. This may be a self-serving threat maintained or fabricated by governments to preserve their own interests and power base. For instance, the ARENA government's stubborn resistance to any socio-economic redistribution during peace negotiations may be more related to the fact that its power base is the private business sector, than to any real fear of a violent backlash being provoked by redistribution. But sometimes this threat may be very real, as manifested by the military's overthrow of Aristide in Haiti. Both SWAPO and the ANC, once in power, opted for diluted policies of redistribution in order to placate the rich white community and avoid antagonizing them.

Morally, post-conflict governments may be faced by an apparent dilemma between liberty and equality, as outlined in chapter 2. While the marginalized or powerless may demand greater equality in the name of justice, the rich and powerful may stridently protect their interests in the name of liberty. Whatever their own leanings, national governments also have to contend with an international climate where the prevalent liberal-democratic ideal in the Western-dominated international community tends to favour freedom and liberty over equality; the priority it accords to personal freedom, private property and individual initiative tends to temper its concern with promoting equality. The adoption of neo-liberal, free-market policies by erstwhile left-wing rebel movements or governments – ANC, SWAPO, and FRELIMO – is partly a manifestation of the priority accorded to liberty over equality.

The hesitation of national governments to promote equity after conflict stems, then, from a complex mix of factors. They include: the risk of a backlash from elite groups and powerful institutions opposed to redistribution; the fear of alienating the business community and scaring off foreign investment; the desire to safeguard individual liberty even at the expense of equity; the lack of resources to finance redistribution of assets or opportunities; and binding conditions against redistribution of assets or employment signed into peace accords. Rather than serving as the bulwark of peacebuilding, distributive justice has been its largely neglected appendage.

Progress? a way forward?

International and national actors, IFIs and bilateral donors, share joint responsibility for the scant attention accorded to distributive justice in post-conflict societies so far. All actors – national and international, as well as bilateral, regional and non-governmental – need to change their attitude and accord greater attention to equity and distributive justice after conflict. Nevertheless, it would be expedient for BWI to take the lead in light of their dominant role in post-conflict reconstruction, as their posture may serve to induce change in other actors.

Three changes in the paradigm and policies of the BWI would be required for equity to be promoted in societies emerging from conflict, according to our analysis so far. First, the Washington Consensus must be adjusted; second, growth and equity must be pursued in tandem; and third, political and economic stabilization must be balanced. There are incipient signs that BWI are undergoing change in all three areas, as their experience with post-conflict countries grows and as they learn from at least some of their own past mistakes.

The Washington Consensus is no longer as unchallenged as it once appeared, not least owing to the repetitive battering it has received from unexpected economic crises and developments that confounded predictions. Joseph Stiglitz, the World Bank's senior economist, himself candidly confessed in early 1998 that the Washington Consensus was flawed and incomplete. He suggested that a 'Post-Washington Consensus' was emerging, which placed greater emphasis on equitable, environmentally sustainable, human-oriented development. It should be noted that, despite this assertion, Stiglitz retains in his framework the basic premises of growth, competition, private ownership and smaller government.[106]

James Wolfensohn, World Bank President, states that the Washington Consensus, 'if ever it existed', is now extinct, at least in Bank practice. Wolfensohn avers that the Bank has undergone a complete overhaul in its approach to developing countries, and proposes a 'Comprehensive Development Framework' that goes beyond the traditional concerns of the Washington Consensus and emphasizes instead the 'structural, social and human aspects' that must underpin development.[107] While encouraging, sceptics foresee no imminent change, as the Bank is not monolithic, views diverge, and neo-liberal Bank economists still disagree.

The IMF is some way behind the Bank in opening itself to scrutiny, and the two have sometimes clashed over their divergent approaches. There is also frequent divergence between financial institutions and development agencies like UNDP, as the latter are more directly oriented towards human development and social justice. However, the BWI economic approach clearly is undergoing some adjustment to current realities.[108]

Regarding the balance between growth and equity, both Bank and Fund have recently changed their public postures and softened their emphasis on growth. Wolfensohn has prioritized 'inclusion' and equity during his term, stating publicly, 'Without equity we will not have global stability. Without a better sense of social justice our cities will not be safe and our societies will not be stable. Without inclusion, too many of us will be condemned to live separate, armed and frightened lives.'[109]

The IMF, although usually considered more conservative and homogeneous than the Bank, has expanded its traditional focus on growth, and now talks in terms of 'quality growth'. This slogan has been quickly picked up within the organization, particularly by those working on the newer cases of post-conflict peacebuilding such as Guatemala.[110] A significant change is perceptible in the attitude and approach of IMF senior officials, particularly those dealing with post-conflict African and Central American countries. The senior official responsible for Guatemala remarked, 'If El Salvador had happened today, it would have been treated very differently [by the IMF].' He added, 'we can't talk about economic progress without talking of social issues. The IMF now talks more and more about equity and redistribution.'[111]

These attitudinal changes have begun to impact the IFIs' treatment of war-torn countries. After their self-acknowledged lapses, the Bank and the Fund seem to have learned some lessons from their past errors of omission and commission. The Bank's self-evaluation alludes to 'the folly of some conventional wisdoms', and indicates that some of the deleterious effects of its standard policies on post-conflict countries have been recognized.[112]

In 1996 the Bank identified post-conflict reconstruction as one of six immediate priorities.[113] The Bank's 'Emergency Recovery Assistance' covers countries affected by wars, civil disturbances or natural disasters. Its emergency recovery loans are intended to be 'adapted in form and scope to the emergency's particular circumstances and retain flexibility'.[114] A small Post-Conflict Unit was created at the Bank in 1997, with a team comprising experts in economics, human rights, conflict resolution, indigenous issues, judicial reform and rule of law.[115] Although the Unit as yet has little clout and has often clashed with the post-conflict units of competing organizations like the UNDP, its composition would seem to reflect an emerging acknowledgement in the Bank that post-conflict reconstruction requires more than an economic or technical approach.

The IMF's recently adopted post-conflict arrangements, despite the limitations alluded to earlier, do reflect an increased sensitivity to the volatility and vulnerabilities of war-torn societies, and to their diversity. A senior official clarified that the IMF did not impose uniform policies without adaptation in different countries, as was often charged, and protested that 'This "one-size-fits-all" [critique] is highly overstated'. Another senior staff member involved in drafting the IMF's post-conflict facility said, 'Each programme is very much based on the specific circumstances of the country in question.'[116]

This emerging attitude change reveals a new concern for both economic and political stabilization, with potentially significant ramifications for post-conflict peacebuilding. The IMF's earlier concentration on fiscal and budgetary discipline is turning to a concern not simply with the size of the overall budget – for which it was much criticized in El Salvador – but with its composition, and with an emphasis on higher social spending. IMF officials responsible for Guatemala lauded the provisions in the peace accords to stipulate a fixed minimum amount of social spending. They described these provisions as fulfilling the IMF's own concern with maintaining high levels of social spending – a significant change from past practice.[117] Boyce and Pastor propose that in order to promote peace IFIs should actively use 'peace conditionality' rather than economic conditionality, that is, that they should make disbursement of funds contingent on governments' fulfilment of peace agreements.[118] Boyce reports that in Guatemala: 'In contrast to the Salvadoran experience, the World Bank has explicitly linked its aid to implementation of the peace accords, as have several bilateral donors and the European Union.' The Bank was even willing to reduce its promised funding by one-third if the government did not make progress, particularly on the socio-economic accord.[119]

The Bank has also begun to adopt the language of peacebuilding and conflict prevention. In 1998 Wolfensohn noted that the Bank's post-conflict reconstruction efforts must 'integrate a concern for conflict prevention'. He stated: 'We must also support member governments' attempts to ameliorate the conditions that may lead to conflict, through distributive policies and the participation of excluded groups in development.'[120] These words are still more apparent in rhetoric than reality. However, they are not negligible. They attest to a new willingness on the part of IFIs to accept at least in principle that peacebuilding and conflict prevention are directly within their remit, and that distributive justice issues are central to both. This may be only the beginning of a long process of needed change, but I believe it is quite a promising one.[121]

Conclusion

This chapter argued for addressing the grievances that underlie conflict and promoting distributive justice in the aftermath of conflict. For many peacebuilders, the pressing concern after conflict is simply keeping people alive by providing basic physical security, food, water and shelter, all the more so when conflict is accompanied by drought or famine, as in Mozambique.[122] This preoccupation leads agencies and IFIs like the Bank and Fund to justify adopting what they believe is the most efficient and inexpensive way to save and sustain lives: through rapid economic growth, privatization, liberalization, economic stabilization, budgetary constraint and government downsizing.[123]

Despite economic rationales, the consequences of this approach must be envisaged for a population that fought or suffered bitterly to achieve greater distributive justice, and who dreamt that the end of conflict would restore equal dignity between them and their erstwhile foes. After conflict, there is, indubitably, a need to feed the hungry and rebuild their shattered lives – to attend to the socio-economic consequences of conflict. It is risky, nevertheless, to ignore the systemic injustices and structural inequalities (real or perceived) that preceded war, to ignore the reasons why aggrieved people were mobilized by leaders to take up arms against their own neighbours. The striving for rapid economic growth and stabilization purportedly to feed conflict's survivors has to be balanced with a striving for greater equity between these survivors, so that they regain human dignity and are not lured back to violence to express unassuaged grievances. This is not an easy balance to achieve within the constraints of post-conflict environments. Yet to pursue the former while neglecting the latter may imply pursuing an illusory negative peace through preserving lives, without the necessary underpinning of positive peace, to give those lives equal dignity.

National and international actors have often appeared to be driven in their post-conflict reconstruction efforts by a myopic vision, which is frequently accompanied by a deficit of commitment.[124] The policies of national political actors are often demarcated by a specific time horizon – that of the electoral calendar. Peacebuilding strategies undulate to please the electorate before the next election. The policies of international actors often reflect the pressure to demonstrate quick and visible results and to plan a rapid exit strategy. The focus on 'kick-starting' the economy and the penchant for 'quick-impact micro-projects' is no coincidence. Neither is the haste to organize elections the moment guns are laid down. However, economic growth is no substitute for equity and genuine economic participation, and 'free and fair' elections do not equate with political equality or authentic political participation. Hun Sen's little-anticipated coup in Cambodia illustrates how easy it is to unravel costly but short-sighted post-conflict reconstruction strategies that look only to effects but evade underlying causes, strategies that attempt to cling to negative peace but ignore its dependence on positive peace.

Peacebuilders might believe that the economic strategies they adopted were perhaps flawed, but not erroneous. They might congratulate themselves that Mozambique has emerged from its gruelling conflict to become the darling of the donor community. They might observe that El Salvador, notwithstanding mounting crime, has weathered peacefully the electoral successes of the FMLN rebel-movement-turned-political party. Even Cambodia, which seemed to lurch towards anarchy when Hun Sen grabbed power, has made an awkward return to electoral democracy.

There is not much room for complacency. Once-peaceable Mozambicans are paying heed to RENAMO's vitriolic rhetoric of the inequality bred by skewed neo-liberal reconstruction policies that have enriched the south but ignored the north. In South Africa and Namibia increasing restiveness and frustration within the black community over continuing racial inequality stand uneasily in the shadow of Zimbabwe's violent land expropriations. Guatemala saw the most far-reaching measures of distributive justice, as will be examined in chapter 6. Yet the palpable disappointment of ordinary people is eloquently summed up in the reaction of one Guatemalan on the socio-economic accord: 'I try to accept this, but then I think of all the pain, all the death, and I ask myself – *is this all?*'[125]

As noted by Keen, 'Creating a peace that takes account of grievances is a political endeavour. It means going beyond the mere reconstruction of the peacetime political economy that *generated* war. It also means guarding against the processes of highly uneven development and inequitable growth.'[126] Until recently, international and national actors have shied away from this political undertaking. They have overlooked the crucial distinction between alleviating the material effects of conflict and addressing underlying causes of conflict. In the process, they also overlooked the interdependence between the negative peace objective underlying the former, and the positive peace objective implicit in the latter.

In chapter 4 it was suggested that the most appropriate role for international actors might be to facilitate rather than impose rectificatory justice. For distributive justice I would argue that international actors, headed by the Bretton Woods Institutions, should play a leading role. The World Bank and IMF in particular need to act as catalysts for other donors and for post-conflict governments,(by demonstrating an equal commitment to equity and to growth, to political stabilization and economic stabilization, to positive peace and negative peace.)

With longer-term vision and commitment, and prompted by mobilized civil society movements, international actors and post-conflict governments may finally begin to put distributive justice squarely on the agenda of post-conflict reconstruction. By doing so they would ensure that the structural injustices underlying and exacerbated by conflicts are not suffered in vain by their survivors.

Section III
Synthesis and Recommendations

6
Recapturing Justice from the Shadows of War

Introduction: assessment, diagnosis, prognosis

This book set out to demonstrate that peacebuilders largely have failed to build peace with justice in the aftermath of conflict. I argued that they have failed to address justice in an integrated multidimensional manner, and to understand and respond adequately to the complexities of each dimension of justice in low-income war-torn societies. I also argued that there is a gap today between philosophical theories about justice and the practice of restoring justice in societies emerging from violent conflict or crisis. It is time now to take stock of the collected evidence presented so far in this book, and to assess the past, diagnose the present, and make a prognosis for the future.

In this closing chapter, we first assess the progress made by peacebuilders in the period covered in this book, that is, peacebuilding's maiden decade from 1989 to 1999. Then, based on a diagnosis of where we stand at present and of the needs for the future, a new conceptualization is proposed for addressing each dimension of justice. This new conceptualization seeks to narrow the wedge between theory and reality, and offer practical recommendations to peacebuilders to enhance their ability to restore justice after political conflict and crisis.

Assessing the past

What overall assessment could we make of the performance of peace-builders in addressing justice in the period covered in this book? I argued that international peacebuilders have erred in addressing each of the three dimensions of justice, in chapters 3, 4 and 5. Nonetheless, in each chapter I also identified hopeful signs of improvement. My overall assessment is cautiously positive: I believe that international peacebuilders, led by the UN, did improve their ability to understand and address all three dimensions of justice in the decade between 1989 and 1999. A non-linear but nevertheless incremental trajectory of learning and performance on the part of peacebuilders is discernible from Namibia to Guatemala. Indeed, a comparison of the treatment of the three dimensions of justice in the peace negotiation process in El Salvador towards the beginning of the decade and in neighbouring Guatemala some years thereafter illustrates the non-negligible progress made by the international community and particularly the UN and BWI.

In terms of legal justice and the rule of law, the Guatemalan peace agreement built upon the substantial precedents in El Salvador for legal reform, but went further in an important and so far little-regarded area. For the first time in a peace settlement, the marginalized indigenous population was given recognition within the law, with provisions for their customary laws to be incorporated alongside formal law, as noted in chapter 3.

In terms of rectificatory justice, there were both advances and setbacks as compared to El Salvador during peace negotiations. On the negative side, to avoid the humiliation caused to El Salvador's ARENA government by the Truth Commission's report, the Guatemalan government allowed only a diluted Commission of Historical Clarification to investigate past atrocities, to the great disappointment of much of its population, as noted in chapter 4. However, civil society took matters into its own hands and mobilized the Campaign against Amnesty to demonstrate its discontent. Furthermore, civic and church actors organized the REMHI project, described in chapter 4, which proved an innovative, ambitious and largely successful independent, non-official experiment in reparative justice. More significant is what transpired thereafter within Guatemala. The government publicly accepted state responsibility for abuses perpetrated during war. More strikingly, despite the amnesty law, the former military dictator Rios Montt is to be prosecuted for genocide in

Guatemala itself, in a case brought forward by the very Mayan communities he abused.

The most significant progress on the part of both international and national actors is in the treatment of distributive justice issues during peace negotiations, which I had argued was the most neglected dimension of justice thus far. The comparison between El Salvador and Guatemala demonstrates this. In the Salvadorean case, key UN negotiator, de Soto, is the first to avow that the UN Secretariat responsible for the political settlement and the IFIs responsible for economic policy and planning worked in disharmony and often at cross-purposes. In effect, the UN pursued political stabilization and the BWI pursued economic stabilization, each with little regard for the other.[1] In El Salvador the economic agreements were left to be addressed at the tail-end of the negotiations. This was partly because national and international negotiators recognized that it would be difficult to reach consensus between the parties on economic issues which constituted the contentious underbelly of the war, and that progress in other areas might be easier to achieve.

At the national level, too, circumstances were not conducive. Although the FMLN had fought its twelve-year war primarily on the basis of socio-economic grievances, it soon realized it would achieve little in terms of real concessions on economic grounds from the business-backed ARENA government. FMLN was also poorly informed and less adroit in its treatment of socio-economic matters than on human rights issues. The ARENA government was lax on legal and human rights issues to gain political mileage with international backers. However, it was intransigent on socio-economic issues, granting the most minimal concessions, unsurprisingly, given its private sector constituency and neo-liberal leanings. Finally, the economic negotiations had to be rushed through owing to the impending end-of-year deadline when UN Secretary-General Perez de Cuellar's term in office ended. Although the land transfer agreement was proclaimed as a historic gain for social justice, in effect it was merely a measure of 'negative peace' to allay serious grievances. The limited land transfers targeted only ex-combatants and returning refugees, and cannot be counted as veritable measures of distributive justice.[2]

By contrast, the Guatemalan peace negotiations were marked at international level by deeper collaboration, co-operation and understanding between the political and economic arms of the UN and Bretton Woods system. UN peace negotiators had learned the consequences in El Salvador of spending inadequate time and attention on the socio-economic aspects of the peace agreement. In the Guatemalan negotiations socio-economic issues were given more time and addressed earlier in the process. The agenda went well beyond palliative measures for limited groups of ex-combatants and repatriated refugees, as in El Salvador. Instead, it addressed entrenched structural and historical inequities, such as the economic exclusion and deprivation of indigenous populations.

In an unprecedented advance on prior experiences, the UN negotiator Jean Arnault invited the IFIs and development banks to read early drafts of the socio-economic accord, and to lend their expertise and advice to the process and final product. This included the World Bank, the IMF, UNDP, the Inter-American Development Bank, and the UN Economic Commission for Latin America. IFIs came out of this experience with a much broader and deeper understanding of the political ramifications and repercussions of socio-economic issues, while on the political side the UN became more sensitive to the economic costs of post-conflict reconstruction, which they had been criticized for neglecting in El Salvador. After the peace deal, IFIs tempered their aid disbursement to the pace of the government's implementation of the peace accord. The Bank even spoke of reducing funding when the government delayed on implementation. That is, in Boyce's and Pastor's terms, IFIs practised a degree of peace conditionality in Guatemala, as noted in chapter 5.

At national level as well, Guatemala's socio-economic negotiation process demonstrated an unprecedented degree of openness and a willingness on the part of internal actors to seek and build consensus. This is particularly noteworthy for a society divided by thirty-five years of brutal conflict and by a much longer history of discrimination and exclusion of the poor and the indigenous majority. For their part, indigenous groups had become increasingly mobilized during the conflict, and were better able to articulate and press their demands.

At the negotiating table for the socio-economic accord, alongside the parties to the conflict, sat the Assembly for Civil Society representing the views of the non-governmental and civic sector, as well as the apex organization of Guatemalan business, the Comité Coordinador de Associaciones Agrícolas, Comerciales, Industriales y Financieras. Consequently, the civil society sector and the private business sector were made partners and stakeholders alongside political parties in the negotiations, an exercise never before attempted at this level. Although ASC and CACIF were not official parties to the agreements and did not have a voting position in the negotiations, their presence on the same table, exchanging views alongside the parties, represented a breakthrough, and their influence on the outcome was significant.[3]

When asked whether Guatemala had secured 'a just peace or just peace', Jean Arnault, the UN's key peace negotiator in Guatemala and subsequently head of the UN Verification Mission in Guatemala (MINUGUA), responded:

> If a just peace means criminal accountability for past leaders, then Guatemala doesn't meet the criteria. But if the test is the transformation of society and a comprehensive blueprint, including not just the end of war but also institutional, socio-economic provisions and bridging the gap between the indigenous, the rich and the poor, then Guatemala is the strongest example of what can emerge from a peace process.[4]

Peacebuilding in Guatemala is far from secure, and observers note that the country and government are again in 'turmoil'.[5] Lynchings, land conflict and mass protests against tax rises have paralleled advances like the Montt prosecution. It is premature to pass judgement on the consolidation of peace in Guatemala, and that is not the point here. The point rather is to underline the progress made in the treatment of justice issues within peace processes, between the early and later 1990s, particularly by the UN and BWI. In terms of the arguments in this book, Guatemala would seem to signal a broadened understanding of justice, beyond the primacy of rectificatory justice, on the part of peacemakers and peacebuilders. The Guatemala agreements are a tacit acknowledgement that however egregious the violations of war, rectificatory justice cannot be pursued to the exclusion of legal and distributive justice – the three dimensions of justice coexist and must be addressed together.

Returning to the necessary elements we identified in our proposed definition of peacebuilding in chapter 1, we can note parallel progress from Namibia through to Guatemala. These elements were: first, pursuing the parallel objectives of negative and positive peace; second, addressing the underlying causes of conflict; third, recognizing the political nature of the undertaking; fourth, engaging local populations and strengthening indigenous structures.

Regarding the balance between negative and positive peace, leading UN peace negotiators post-Guatemala note with pride that a ceasefire agreement – that is, securing negative peace – is treated as the last item on the negotiating agenda, whereas in cases like Namibia, Mozambique and Cambodia, it was a priority issue. Rather, attention is now focused first on judicial reform, human rights provisions, and structural and institutional change (mirroring the three areas of justice) to vouchsafe the building of positive peace (while preserving negative peace). The earlier approach of peacemakers to negotiating peace and planning for peacebuilding was to 'limit the agenda even though the people who will ultimately have to implement the settlement...will face difficulties because not every question has been answered'.[6] By the late 1990s UN negotiators' avowed aim was to make the negotiating agenda broad and comprehensive, and answer as many questions as possible in advance to simplify the task of peacebuilders and ensure that it goes beyond the maintenance of negative peace.

On addressing underlying causes of conflict, the chief UN negotiator in El Salvador notes that the main lesson peacemakers learned in the 1990s was: 'Look into causes of conflict and address questions of putting into place avenues and mechanisms so that combatants don't rise again.'[7] This is not only an advance on the part of the UN. As noted in chapter 5, the rhetoric and, gradually, the practice of the World Bank and IMF seem to be changing, with talk of equity, quality growth, and recognition of their responsibility to integrate issues of conflict prevention in post-conflict strategies and to address distributive issues underlying conflict.

Regarding the political nature of peacebuilding, the statements of UN and the UN Department of Political Affairs (DPA) officials suggest the growing recognition within the system that peacebuilding is essentially a political undertaking and not merely a checklist of technical tasks. The Bretton Woods Institutions too, as noted in chapter 5, have broadened their earlier treatment of post-conflict reconstruction to ensure it is not only addressed by economists but also by social and political scientists.

On the indigenous aspect and associative nature of peacebuilding, de Soto notes another major lesson learned by the UN from past experiences: 'Build constituencies. Work with people in the country – not only with those at the negotiating table.' He adds, '[the UN] believes in beginning from the bottom up'.[8]

In the previous chapters I demonstrated serious shortcomings of peacebuilders in each dimension of justice. Much of the progress noted in all three dimensions is still rhetorical and potential more than effective. Yet overall our study would indicate that the attitude and actions of UN and BWI peacemakers and peacebuilders began to undergo a gradual but discernible evolution between 1989 and the late 1990s, in terms of their approach to peacebuilding generally and the treatment of justice issues particularly. But has this change persisted, and can we be optimistic about the building of just peace in the future?

Miall, Ramsbotham and Woodhouse suggest that the era of UN-led 'post-settlement peacebuilding' has ended, after a ten-year career.[9]

Indeed, the UN's pre-eminent role in peacemaking and peacebuilding seems to be in recession in conflicts since 2000. A host of new regional and sometimes national actors have assumed pride of place in peacemaking, peacekeeping and peacebuilding – the OAU, the Economic Community of West African States (ECOWAS), NATO, the UK and Australia. It is as yet premature to evaluate their performance, but I would confess that so far this new panoply of actors elicits none of the cautious optimism I believe UN and BWI actors were beginning to merit. The recent peacemaking attempts of the erstwhile OAU in Ethiopia-Eritrea, the ECOWAS peacekeeping operation in Sierra Leone, and the 'peacebuilding' missions of NATO in Kosovo and Macedonia are not entirely reassuring. Their apparent preoccupation with order and negative peace is as worrying as their relative lack of interest in justice and positive peace.

Diagnosing the present, predicting the future

On 28 July 2001 former Yugoslav President Slobodan Milosevic was extradited and handed over to the *ad hoc* Tribunal for Former Yugoslavia in The Hague. At first glance this appears an unambiguous triumph for universal justice, a testimony of the price the international community is willing to pay for a just peace. Who could fail to rejoice that a war criminal finally will be judged? But can this be called 'justice'? The high-profile extradition revealed primarily the financial bribe the West is willing to pay to taste long-denied victor's justice; and it revealed that countries with limited means eventually will succumb to such bribes. Captivity has not quietened Milosevic's vitriol on the illegality of the Hague tribunal and the 'truth' of his cause, souring the sweetness of victor's justice.[10]

Behind this symbolic triumph, I see the confirmation of my fears expressed in chapter 1 and a substantiation of the arguments I put forward there. The enormous if belated efforts to capture Milosevic confirm a continuing international obsession with a single dimension of justice – rectificatory justice for war crimes and crimes against humanity. They confirm the international community's preoccupation with the human consequences (war crimes) and material effects (economic destruction) of war to the neglect of its underlying causes and symptoms. They indicate, even, a sinister if unspoken attempt to barter one dimension, rectificatory justice, with another, distributive justice. They are a tacit attempt to cancel out the human consequences of war – war crimes – by underwriting the cost of reversing the material effects – the socio-economic destruction – of war. The contribution of Milosevic's extradition to the restoration of 'justice' is questionable; to the consolidation of peace in that troubled region, dubious.

The Milosevic case does nothing to allay my fears for the cause of justice in low-income societies emerging from conflict and crisis. Nor does the massive deployment of NATO troops in mid-2001 for a 'peacebuilding' mission to collect rebel guns in Macedonia. The populations inured to war and injustice in poor countries will have to wait long and perhaps in vain to taste justice, given current international trends. International peacebuilding now depends on the whims and vagaries of a clutch of rich countries. Given their narrow geo-strategic and economic interests, it is unlikely that these rich countries will underwrite and support endeavours to restore justice in its plenitude in low-income countries devastated by war. The lack of financial support for the proposed Sierra Leone Tribunal, despite the international outcry over the atrocities, is a telling example. Genuine international commitment to building peace and justice in post-Taliban Afghanistan will be seen as a test case.

The reality of injustice and the elusiveness of justice for the majority of poor people emerging from violent conflict and confrontation is borne out not by the Yugoslav or Macedonian cases, but by the fate of embattled countries like the DRC. Since 1998 alone, an estimated 2.3 million people have died in that country, yet the international response has been abysmal. The UN has been hobbled by the reluctance of member states to contribute sufficiently to the peacekeeping/peacebuilding force, with a mere 5,000 soldiers deployed in a country many times the size of Kosovo, not to protect traumatized Congolese but their own installations. There is little talk of justice for the decades of legal, political and socio-economic injustice Congolese have suffered. There is little talk of reparation for the economic injustices and crimes that have proliferated alongside war crimes. Neighbouring countries and foreign commercial interests have colluded with warring factions and government forces to strip the DRC of its natural and mineral wealth without any benefit to their Congolese owners. The international community's rapid embrace of the DRC's new leader, Joseph Kabila, with little attention to his legitimacy or his past, is not so much a sign of concern for the Congolese but another signal of the international community's obsession with order and the cessation of hostilities, or negative peace.[11]

This should not be read as an attempt to undermine the importance of order or of negative peace, as they are essential prerequisites.

However, it is necessary to underline the unsustainability of order in the absence of justice, and the necessity of balancing negative with positive peace.

Facing the future: reconceptualizing the three dimensions of justice

If there was reason for cautious optimism in 1999, as I indicated above, it has dissipated considerably today. The lessons learned by the UN and BWI are disappearing amidst the competing agendas of a diversity of actors. I would argue that there is a burning and unprecedented imperative today to return justice to centre-stage. There is a need to reiterate that simply ending hostilities is no guarantee of peace. Peacebuilders need to recognize that a uni-dimensional approach to justice is inadequate. They need to address simultaneously all three dimensions of justice, linked to the underlying causes, the symptoms and the consequences of conflict, and to recognize the dynamic linkages between them. They also need to be more cognizant of the complexities within each dimension of justice, and to eschew simplistic solutions. This requires a new conceptualization of the three dimensions of justice with practical recommendations on how to apply them in practice to marry justice with peace in the aftermath of war. This is what I propose below.

Reconceiving the rule of law in post-conflict societies

In chapters 2 and 3 it was suggested that the minimalist conception of the rule of law, despite its advantages of being clear and bounded, might not be appropriate in post-conflict settings, and that a maximalist conception might be more fitting. Yet the examination of practice on the ground in chapter 3 revealed that international actors seemed to be adopting what was described as 'programmatic minimalism': that is, an approach which is minimalist in its conception and programmatic rather than sustained in its implementation. They adopt a standardized, technical, apolitical, 'one-size-fits-all' approach to rule of law reform, which sidelines the substance of the rule of law in favour of its form, and which seeks minimal engagement with local legal traditions and populations. It was argued that this approach favoured order and sidelined the population's demand for legal justice after conflict.

Conceptualizing 'incremental maximalism'

I propose here a conceptual and practical framework for rule of law restoration in post-conflict societies described as 'incremental maximalism', to replace programmatic minimalism. Incremental maximalism implies a framework which embeds the rule of law in justice, human rights and values, and which concerns itself with both its form and its substance, with both its institutions and its ethos. This conceptual framework would be accompanied by an incremental programme for its realization, which sets realistic, long-term targets for the gradual achievement of its more ambitious goals. Most importantly, it would consciously build on the fourth and so far missing leg of the rule of law identified in chapter 3, by engaging throughout the full participation and involvement of local populations, and seeking to build their confidence.

Incremental maximalism would seek to integrate and balance customary law and local legal traditions with modern law and universal principles of legality. This does not mean ceding to what are claimed to be local practices without due consideration for their content, impact and ramifications. Rather, this approach would aim to achieve the balance described in chapter 3 of accommodating accepted and acceptable local practices with universal standards, rather than simply imposing the latter. I do not advocate an unmitigated 'communitarian' approach to the rule of law, but rather a pragmatic union of 'communitarian' and 'liberal cosmopolitan' visions.

This is not an argument against a minimalist conception of the rule of law *per se*. It is entirely conceivable that in societies where respect for human rights, participatory democracy, and an articulate and empowered civil society are firmly rooted, it will be both legitimate and adequate to have a minimalist rule of law. In such cases, parallel political and civic processes in societies will ensure that justice and human dignity are respected. However, in societies emerging painfully from systematic and sustained violations of justice, dignity and rights, a minimalist rule of law will rarely suffice. This is because minimalist rule of law is more readily susceptible to manipulation in vulnerable political situations, and is more easily infused with the intent and content that suit ruling regimes. This was exactly the problem with the rule of law in South Africa, where, under apartheid, 'Law, which should have been a pillar of justice and social stability and a wall against violence and chaos, became instead an agent of injustice and social instability and a catalyst for violence and chaos. Law was systematically reduced...to a continuation of violence by other means.'[12]

Despite the end of conflict, there often remains a large vested interest for political and institutional actors to maintain control over the legislature, the judiciary, and law enforcement – over both the making and the dispensing of law and justice. Political actors often try to undermine attempts to put in place a genuinely maximalist rule of law that would inhibit predatory executive behaviour. In this context, it is particularly necessary to take justice out of the political sphere, where it is vulnerable to manipulation, and to put it at the centre of the rule of law, to make it inviolable.

Unless the goal of a maximalist rule of law underpinned by justice and rights is adopted by consensus between national and international actors at the outset, even if this goal is to be achieved incrementally, it is improbable that a minimalist approach will spontaneously give birth to a maximalist outcome. And a minimalist outcome may not suffice either to sustain negative peace, or to deliver positive peace.

Practical implications of incremental maximalism: creating a social compact

Incremental maximalism calls for a change in the *modus operandi* of both international and national actors involved in rule of law restoration. It will not suffice for international actors to 'fix' the technical bits of the rule of law and depart, without involving themselves deeply in its political and cultural ramifications. Nor can governments and civil societies relinquish their responsibility and investment in the rule of law to external actors.

So far, as noted in chapter 3, rule of law programmes have shied away from engaging local populations substantively for a range of reasons. Yet 'a crucial element of justice in post-conflict societies is to create a sense of ownership' and 'responsibility'.[13] People cannot feel such ownership and responsibility unless they have played a part in shaping the face of justice in their societies. This is what incremental maximalism aims to do.

It is observed that the aim of a justice package is 'to create a social compact, whereby the people of a country recently in conflict voluntarily agree to a system of law and order'.[14] Creating such a social compact requires the substantive input of both the political apparatus – government and opposition parties – and the civil apparatus – individuals, groups and social movements in society. The two, political and civil societies, are necessary complements of – and checks on – each other, and it is their combined will and capacity that is required for giving cultural meaning to and generating confidence in the rule of law.

The process of writing a new constitution has provided many societies with an avenue to create such a social compact, and articulate a shared political and civic commitment to justice and rights, in terms that are both embedded in local culture / s and imbued with universal norms. The progressive constitution adopted rapidly by consensus in Namibia, and the lengthy consultative process resulting in a culturally inclusive constitution in South Africa are two diverse illustrations.[15] As laws are required to conform to and respect the constitution, the commitments expressed in maximalist constitutions can be actualized and perpetuated in future legislation.

Incremental maximalism also requires a social compact between national and international actors. As noted in chapter 3, although national engagement is critical for success, rule of law reform in weak post-conflict societies is significantly dependent on international assistance and expertise. Some international actors are increasingly aware of their limitations – their tight budgets, their dependence on proving tangible achievements, their short-term interests and timeframes. They recognize the operational necessity for local communities and governments to be fully invested in the process, and to take their place when external resources and interest dry up, in order to ensure that the achievements made in securing the rule of law, however limited, are not squandered. International actors have a responsibility to obtain national engagement to anchor their achievements, and ensure that national authorities act representatively and responsibly. On the national side, there must be sufficient will and capacity on the part of both the political leadership and civil society to balance out the short-term programmatic minimalism of international actors.

After chaotic and violent conflict, national and international actors may view negative peace – avoiding a relapse into conflict – as the more pressing strategic objective, and they may favour it over positive peace – the strengthening of structures to underpin and consolidate peace. It is tempting for them to treat the rule of law as a tool to secure the former rather than the latter objective. However, although programmatic minimalism may succeed temporarily in providing short-term stability and a degree of negative peace, it is likely to fail in consolidating positive peace, for the reasons presented in chapter 3. It is for this reason that incremental maximalism is proposed here as a sounder basis for restoring the rule of law in post-conflict societies and for balancing the objectives of negative and positive peace.

Reconceiving rectificatory justice in post-conflict societies

In chapter 2 it was noted that none of the current philosophical approaches to rectificatory justice responded adequately to the needs of post-conflict societies to rectify past violations. All three alternative philosophical approaches to punishment, the current-day substitute for rectificatory justice, utilitarian, retributive and informal, face serious challenges within the field. Utilitarian punishment has been discarded as inappropriate because it treats humans as means to an end. Retributive justice, despite its renewed popularity, leaves troubling questions unanswered. Informal justice seeks to fill the gaps left by formal legal mechanisms, but is dismissed as unsatisfactory and even dangerous.

In chapter 4 it was observed that international actors tend to oversimplify rectificatory justice claims in the search for simple universal solutions, and sometimes impose, rather than facilitate, a society's response to violations committed during conflict. Renewed retributivism manifested itself in the growing support for trials and custodial punishment as responses to conflict's violations. Truth commissions could be seen as partly a response of informal justice.[16] It was argued that what was required in post-conflict societies was an approach that goes beyond individual offenders and victims and addresses the whole society of survivors.

Conceptualizing 'reparative justice'
In the aftermath of conflict it is necessary to formulate a conception of rectificatory justice which goes beyond traditional notions of punishment – utilitarian, retributive or informal – in seeking to respond to violations committed during conflict. A conception is required which comprehends and responds to the needs of all 'survivors' of conflict – victims, offenders and society at large – and which strives to balance the sometimes contradictory imperatives of positive and negative peace. In this context, a new concept of 'reparative justice' is proposed as a more appropriate response to the claims and demands of rectificatory justice in post-conflict societies.

As conceived here, reparative justice would emanate from the concept of reparation which is long established in law and social psychology, but would go beyond it. Psychologists describe reparation as follows:

> The term *reparation* has a double meaning. First, it is a psychoanalytical concept, developed by Melanie Klein (Klein & Riviere, 1937/1987),

that is used to explain the intrapsychic process of repair. But it is also a legal term used, for example, in connection with economic compensation after a war. This double meaning is significant because repair in the psychoanalytic sense must occur at both the individual and social levels, but it can only take place fully if it is linked to reparation in the legal sense – that is with truth and justice for the victim and compensation when it is helpful.[17]

In law the objective of reparation is defined as follows: 'Reparation must, as far as possible, wipe out all the consequences of the illegal act and re-establish the situation which would, in all probability, have existed if that act had not been committed.'[18]

The legal and psychological definitions of reparation offer the starting point for the construction of reparative justice, which seeks to provide an integrated response to claims for rectificatory justice in post-conflict societies. Reparation already has its manifestations in concrete legal and social practices, as discussed in chapter 4. As noted, the main forms of legal reparation are restitution, compensation, indemnity, satisfaction and declaratory judgment, and combine monetary and non-material means; the common forms of social reparation undertaken in transitional societies include commemoration, symbolic redress, official acknowledgement, apology, education, and establishing the truth. Reparative justice would make use of combinations of these legal and social means of reparation, while providing an overarching framework to understand and respond to the various claims for justice for past violations arising in the aftermath of conflict.

Reparative justice as conceptualized here comprehends and seeks to redress the *two* principal kinds of injustice suffered by the victim: first, the legal injustice, such as injury, loss of life, employment or property; second, the moral or psychological injustice, that is, victimization, trauma, and loss of dignity. Further, and as a consequence, reparative justice envisages the possibility of both material and non-material remedies, including formal legal measures as well as informal or symbolic ones. Material damages may be paid back in cash, but may also include reclaiming or restitution of property, education, housing, health care and employment. Non-material reparation may include several measures such as the social reparation measures noted earlier of disclosure of truth and public recognition of wrongdoing.[19]

Reparative justice is more victim-oriented than traditional approaches like retributive justice as it does not focus only on meting out just deserts to offenders. However, reparative justice is more than just a victim-oriented approach. It is explicitly 'survivor-centred'. It encompasses the differential and overlapping needs of all people within a given society who have survived conflict and are now required to build a political community together, regardless of their divergent pasts. The central aim of reparation is to overcome the alienation caused by the offence and to rebuild the basis of trust for renewed co-operation.[20] Based on this understanding of reparation, reparative justice encompasses and responds to the concerns of all the diverse actors in society who are the necessary beneficiaries of rectificatory justice – not only offenders and victims but also governmental authorities and the public.

From the point of view of the authorities, reparations represent an acknowledgement on the part of the offender that he or she is not above the law. From the point of view of the public (and victim), reparations imply a desire and willingness to live within the law, by accepting responsibility for wrongdoing and undertaking to correct it. And from the point of view of the offender, reparations provide a basis for rebuilding trust that may have been undermined by the offence, thereby creating the conditions for reassuming a normal place in society.[21]

Reparative justice is both *sensitive* to the nature of offences and their impact on victims, offenders and societies, and *flexible* in devising a suitable combination of responses to them. Importantly, as suggested in the legal definition of reparation cited above, reparative justice does not exclude punishment or prosecution. Indeed, formal legal redress and punishment are likely to remain important parts of the response to past abuses in several post-conflict cases, not least due to the stipulations of international law, and the symbolic and political goal of combating impunity. The imminent establishment of the International Criminal Court will be an important contribution in this direction. Nevertheless, how a society adapts its criminal laws to conduct fair trials, and how it decides to determine appropriate punishment may vary according to its individual needs, possibilities and constraints. The means chosen may not always be individual prosecution and incarceration; for example, sometimes collective trials may replace the former and community work may replace the latter, as Rwanda is experimenting in its national and traditional *gacaca* trials. Reparative justice offers the possibility of combining available measures or innovating new ones to address the varied requirements of each post-conflict situation. In fact, reparative justice requires and demands such combinations.

Rectificatory justice, it was seen earlier, was discarded from philosophical discourse centuries ago, and only retains a thin meaning today. The concept of reparative justice seeks to rejuvenate the concept of rectificatory justice, but to give it a form and shape that caters to the specific, albeit varied, requirements of post-conflict rectificatory justice.[22] Reparative justice offers a broader framework that is more suited to the kinds of violations committed during conflict and the suffering they cause. The starting premise of the concept is that after devastating conflict has torn society apart the need is to accommodate and harmonize the various functions of justice vis-à-vis offender, victim and survivor, within the available means, resources and human requirements of a given post-conflict society and its population. Reparative justice is informed by, but not subjugated to, the sometimes antagonistic claims of peace and justice, while cognizant of the constrained possibilities of response in an impoverished post-conflict setting.

Practical implications of reparative justice

How would the conceptualization of reparative justice proposed here translate to the pursuit of rectificatory justice claims in post-conflict society? Reparative justice makes a threefold contribution to the understanding and pursuit of justice claims for past violations in low-income war-torn countries.

First, the conception of and response to reparative justice as depicted above seeks to eschew the narrow understanding that a single mechanism might suffice within a society and across societies to respond to the varied and contending claims of surviving populations emerging from conflict. Reparative justice reflects the understanding that in order to respond to the various needs of victims, perpetrators and entire societies of survivors, a variety of responses – combining official and non-official, formal and informal, material and non-material or symbolic measures – rather than a single response will be required.

Second, reparative justice as described here would not seek uniform responses across countries, but instead would strive to find responses that are nationally specific and decided nationally. It would be mindful of international legal standards and universal ethics, but not apply them blindly without adaptation to local needs.

Third, and in order to fulfil the previous condition, reparative justice would seek to include the local population meaningfully in order to frame responses that are based on consultation and reflect popular wishes. Further, it would seek to include the population both in the decision of responses to reparative justice and also in the process of its implementation, however difficult this may appear to be in a post-conflict situation where intimidation and insecurity are widespread.

Perhaps the reason why South Africa's TRC had such appeal, despite its critics, is that it tried to fulfil many of the goals which are described here as reparative justice under its own singular aegis. It tried to balance negative and positive peace by proposing amnesty while insisting on conditional amnesty. It sought to ensure formal justice by leaving open the option of prosecution. It tried to provide material and non-material reparation and compensation. It attempted to generate history lessons and a faithful accounting of the truth. It offered a safe yet public forum for the expression of both the suffering of victims and the guilt of perpetrators. It sought to proffer some measure of cathartic psychosocial healing to some of those who testified within its confessional-like ambience. It attempted to extend a measure of symbolic redress with its book of reconciliation for survivors to sign as an expression of their compassion or contrition. It even sought to adopt a survivor-oriented approach, while focusing on victims and perpetrators. The survivor-oriented ethos of reparative justice is captured in the concept of *Ubuntu* which underlay the TRC: 'an environment of right relationships is one in which people are able to recognize that their humanity is inextricably bound up in others' humanity'.[23]

Indeed it was the ambitiousness of the TRC that made it both remarkable and disillusioning, for it generated unrealistically high expectations, which a single short-term commission could not possibly fulfil. The TRC experience reinforces the rationale of reparative justice: it is important not to overload a single mechanism with responsibility for fulfilling all the varied and complex demands of reparative justice vis-à-vis offenders, victims, survivors, and society at large. While it is necessary to be aware of these many demands and seek to respond to them all, it may be judicious and necessary to divide this responsibility between different measures, informal and formal, official and traditional. This has been recognized in South Africa itself:

> The South African Truth Commission is only one of the structures through which we should hope to dismantle the old regime of truth in order to replace it with new and multiple narratives... As we construct new historical narratives, it will be in the currency of heterotopias, multiple idealisms, rather than the singlemindedness of utopia... Our state-sponsored Commission has no monopoly on processes of historical rectification.[24]

These evocative words provide a powerful vindication for reparative justice. The former Prosecutor of the *ad hoc* International Tribunal for former Yugoslavia and Rwanda, Justice Richard Goldstone, and the Vice-Chairperson of the TRC, Alex Boraine, in light of their own experiences with rectificatory justice, echoed enthusiasm for the reparative justice approach portrayed here as a bold and promising alternative to current approaches.[25]

The conceptualization of reparative justice proposed here is preliminary. Rigorous theoretical consideration will be required to elaborate the concept and make it applicable to post-conflict settings, both theoretically and empirically. Even so, its application in practice in post-conflict societies will raise some difficulties. A first difficulty in applying reparative justice might stem from the central principle underlying legal reparation, that of 'wiping out all consequences' of the acts perpetrated. While the principle may be legally sound, it is difficult to apply in the kinds of cases faced in post-conflict societies. It is hard to devise remedies that might 'wipe out all the consequences' of genocide, systematic rape, or mass violation of human rights, which are the heritage of today's internal conflicts. Nor is it easy to estimate an appropriate monetary or non-material compensation for the deep emotional damage and trauma of victims which defy measurement. The problem of calculating appropriate reparation is compounded when victims are entire groups or society at large, as is often the case.[26] The measures of legal and social reparation mentioned above suggest some of the available options for reparative justice in these cases. These measures need to be subjected to philosophical, legal and political scrutiny to evaluate whether they fulfil the requirements of justice in ethical, legal, political and practical terms.

Reparative justice, notwithstanding teething and conceptual difficulties, offers a more promising, encompassing, flexible and sensitive approach to comprehend and accommodate the concurrent and different needs of all survivors in society and to cement the parallel processes of building negative and positive peace. It merits deeper reflection and further development conceptually; and practically it requires greater experimentation by practitioners to test its viability in societies emerging from violent conflict.

Reconceiving distributive justice

In chapter 2 it was noted that the three main distributive questions affecting developing countries – meeting basic needs, fulfilling socio-economic (and political) rights, and reducing inequality – were inadequately addressed in philosophical theories. Chapter 5 demonstrated some of the reasons why, despite strident public demands, international and national actors have given short shrift to distributive justice in the aftermath of conflict. It was observed that while external and internal actors paid attention to the human and material consequences of conflict, they largely overlooked the causes of conflict emanating from grievances about distributive injustices, whether real or perceived. They attended to economic reconstruction and rehabilitation but sidelined demands for socio-economic equity and overlooked the distributive impact of their post-conflict policies.

Conceiving a two-stage response to distributive justice
It is proposed here that in place of current approaches, a two-stage response to distributive justice claims should be adopted in post-conflict societies. The initial response to distributive justice issues in post-conflict societies would be a backward-looking response, and the second and subsequent response would be forward-looking.

In the initial backward-looking stage, the demand for distributive justice in post-conflict societies has a distinctly rectificatory flavour – a demand for rectification for a pattern of past injustices and inequities in distribution. Consequently, so must the response to it. The approach to distributive justice at this stage must start by first looking back: at the country's history and the particular structure and impact of inequalities that directly or indirectly instigated its conflict. This implies that it must look farther back than the traditional concerns of rectificatory justice, characterized earlier as the consequences of – that is, the abuses perpetrated during – conflict, to the actual causes underlying conflict itself. In doing so, it must not be distracted by the considerable material effects of conflict, the physical destruction of economies and infrastructure (as noted in chapter 5), which are an important but distinct concern. That is, distributive justice in post-conflict societies must consist, first and fundamentally, in examining the past. It must seek to redress deep-rooted historical injustices stemming from structural and systemic inequalities between groups in the actual possession of, access to and opportunities for economic and political power which, in some way, contributed to conflict.

As noted in chapter 5, political and economic inequality are usually linked in complex and mutually reinforcing ways. The distributive justice response must seek to address these inequalities directly, identify their diverse sources, and attempt to reduce them, both in reality and in popular perception, to manageable, non-conflictual levels. This would require the development of philosophical and conceptual approaches to distributive justice that are unselfconsciously egalitarian. Some of the egalitarian theories noted in chapter 2 may provide a grounding for this stage; Nussbaum's and Sen's approach to inequality, based on their concepts of capabilities and functionings, might provide the most promising avenue. These and other egalitarian approaches need to be developed further and applied to the specific realities and deep inequities prevalent in most post-conflict societies. This initial stage, then, aims to mitigate or eliminate grievances that stoked conflict in the first place and could rekindle violence if ignored. Although backward-looking, it is the first step both to preserve negative peace – by avoiding a resurgence of violent grievances – and to sow positive peace by replacing conflict-producing inequities with equity.

Once the deepest and potentially conflict-producing inequalities underlying conflict have been addressed in the first stage, the second and subsequent forward-looking stage would concern itself with the traditional priorities of distributive or social justice. This stage would begin, now more plausibly, from the hypothetical assumption of rough equality and rational free choice implicit in most contemporary approaches in Western political philosophy. It would then undertake the daily business of social justice, based on conceptions of fairness and justice that are acceptable to the various parts of the society in question. Nevertheless, as this discussion here centres on low-income societies, the main criteria for distributive justice would still need to be centred in the three categories of needs, rights and equality, which, as discussed in chapter 2, have been inadequately addressed by contemporary philosophers.

As these are the primary concerns in the second stage, philosophers should give greater attention to addressing the neglected categories of needs and socio-economic rights particularly in post-conflict settings. As mentioned above, Nussbaum's and Sen's capabilities are perhaps the most useful way to reintegrate needs criteria into philosophical and practical perspectives, and to build a needs-based approach to distributive justice in developing countries. In light of the weaknesses of both rights and duties at present, as argued in chapter 2, rights approaches should be integrated with duty-based approaches to provide a stronger deontological framework for action. However, utilitarian considerations should not be ignored entirely, for the reasons presented in chapter 2. In low-income societies, with many demands and few resources, it is imperative to consider how to maximize social utility when taking policy decisions.

In practical terms, in developing societies, where the question is not that of dispensing of the surplus but of meeting basic human needs, the approach proposed here for the second stage may translate to the human development and human security agenda proposed by development economists and sponsored by the UNDP.[27] It would emphasize poverty alleviation and the provision of basic needs, greater social spending on health, education and other public services that benefit the poor, and progressive rather than regressive taxation. A genuinely 'post' Washington Consensus approach that pursues equity in tandem with growth and prioritizes social spending could also be accommodated here. That is, the second stage would look to the welfare of the whole society in a forward-looking or prospective way, while taking particular care of the interests of the most needy and disadvantaged, as, for example, Rawls's theory of justice as fairness sought to do. Rawls's 'difference principle' – which may be inappropriate for the first stage, as it does not account for extant distributions and inequalities – might be usefully applied in the second stage, as it insists that all future distributions should be 'to the greatest benefit of the least advantaged'.[28]

Without the first stage, however, the second stage will be rudderless. Unless people believe that their lot has been addressed directly rather than evaded, their grievances alleviated rather than marginalized or aggravated, and their standing or agency raised to comparable levels with other individuals in society, regardless of their group identity, the presumption of equality characterizing the forward-looking stage may provoke a violent reaction at worst or deep frustration at best.

Nevertheless, it is the first stage that is the more difficult, as it is the less travelled and more contentious path, for it is not so much the *end* – equality – but the *means* to achieve it – redistribution – that evokes fear and resistance. In some cases what is needed at the first stage might be evident enough. More often, it is difficult to ascertain the appropriate course of action that responds to legitimate claims for justice without evoking a backlash from those opposed to such measures that could derail incipient peace – as in pre-genocide Rwanda and more recently in the aborted peace in Sierra Leone. The course of distributive justice, steering the balance between positive and negative peace, may be difficult to identify.

In South Africa an obvious first step was to abolish all apartheid laws and thus eliminate the framework on which the pervasive system of structural violence had been based. Yet the growing resentment and frustration of the black majority at the cosmetic change in sociopolitical inequality since 1994 demonstrates that merely dismantling the legal structure of apartheid was an insufficient response to the much more pervasive impact of the systemic inequality imposed by apartheid on the black majority.

Ideally, the strategy for the rectificatory stage might be arrived at by undertaking some form of consensus-building dialogue on the issue of contention between the various actors concerned in society. It may be perilous in divided post-conflict societies to impose a decision that is adopted unilaterally by government, dictated by an external body, or even arrived at by a simple majority decision. A majority decision, albeit 'democratic', might neglect the needs and threaten the security of less vocal minorities and disadvantaged groups. Nevertheless, as illustrated by the consensus-building exercise over the land issue in Namibia, noted in chapter 5, the difficulty of forming a consensus may sometimes be overshadowed by the greater obstacles faced in implementing that consensus.

Practical implications
In chapter 5 it was noted that peacebuilders focused on the effects rather than the causes of conflict. Approached from a 'two-stage' perspective, the conduct of peacebuilders could be described as a jump to the second, forward-looking egalitarian stage of distributive justice without addressing the first, backward-looking rectificatory one. That is, post-conflict reconstruction programmes have taken the simplified approach of presuming the equality of all members of society, instead of first recognizing and responding to their inherent inequality. These programmes have tended to treat all 'survivors' of conflict similarly and aimed to confer equal treatment on all, by addressing societal needs as a whole rather than first addressing the needs of the worst-affected survivors within society. This approach ignores the reality that the impact of conflict on individuals and groups in society is rarely equal; conflict, like any other natural or manmade disaster, disproportionately affects the most vulnerable.[29]

Further, their approach ignores the deep inequalities that preceded and underlay conflict. In orthodox economic theory, there is a tendency to treat a dollar's-worth of growth as having equal value and impact for the rich or the poor. In reality a dollar has much greater value for the poor – who have fewer dollars at their disposal – than for the rich.[30] Peacebuilders too assume that all members of society have equal standing and that all goods accrued through post-conflict reconstruction will be equally shared and equally beneficial to all – that growth in gross terms will be beneficial regardless of its distributive impact.

The attitude of peacebuilders has been to presume rather than to consciously promote equality. This is perhaps due to the contentiousness of addressing directly the fundamental demand for redress, and the implicit fear that it may lead directly to demands for redistributing unequal assets and opportunities which is politically unpalatable or risky. In their perhaps understandable eagerness to provide for the population at large, rather than target and rectify the situation of the worst-affected individuals and groups, peacebuilders have ignored the past and focused on the future: on economic regeneration, growth, stabilization and rehabilitation.

Although the analysis of distributive justice concentrated on economic inequalities, a parallel jump to the forward-looking second stage could be plotted on the political level. The preferred mechanism employed by the international community to confer 'political equality' on post-conflict populations is the holding of democratic elections, which have accompanied many internationally sponsored transitions to peace (witness Namibia, Cambodia and Mozambique, to name a few cases). Underlying this strategy may lie a simplistic assumption that all citizens in society have equal standing, and by exercising an equal vote in their country's future their voices are equally heard, and political equality has been secured. However, if the deep political inequality and exclusion – which, it was noted, so often parallels economic inequality and exclusion – has not first been addressed, elections may prove a superficial exercise.

Elections by themselves will rarely translate to real access to political power and its privileges, or to political 'equality' in any meaningful sense. In Cambodia and Haiti the impoverished rural peasantry forming the majority of the population are no closer than before to enjoying equal political power for having queued up to vote in internationally sponsored elections, or at least for having been offered the opportunity to do so. In Haiti electoral turnout dwindled from 90 per cent in 1991, when Aristide won a landslide victory, to a dismal 11 per cent in the 1998 elections, although 'democracy' nominally continues. As a Haitian peasant mused: 'For us, elections are like getting the peel of the (sugar)cane.'[31] Yet both the sugar and the taste of hope are beyond reach.

Some scholars argue that electoral democracy and the holding of elections so shortly after a transition to peace may be detrimental to peacebuilding. Paris argues against both legs of the peacebuilding strategy imposed by the international community on fragile post-conflict societies: liberal democracy and market capitalism. He observes that both are inherently competitive and heighten animosities, instead of fostering co-operation, in the tense aftermath of conflict.[32]

The extreme resistance that sometimes meets economic redistribution – despite popular pressures demanding it – may sometimes outweigh resistance to political redistribution, as in El Salvador. Sometimes both national and international peacebuilders have played one off against the other: faced with powerful lobbies resisting economic redistribution, peacebuilders may turn to political 'redistribution' by way of elections as a stopgap measure. The strategy is not always unsuccessful. In El Salvador political redistribution seems to have succeeded partially in assuaging the demands for distributive justice that precipitated the war. From a poor showing in the first post-conflict elections, the FMLN has now replaced the governing ARENA party as the largest Congressional force, and controls town councils in eight of fourteen provincial capitals.[33] This expanding political space has enabled the FMLN to achieve through legal means some of the socio-economic changes it hoped to wrest by waging war. Although FMLN leaders were not able to negotiate these desired changes into the peace agreement, they have now been able to influence economic policies through legislation as recognized political actors.[34] FMLN leaders now in parliament concede that if the political space they now enjoy had existed for them in the 1970s, they might never have taken to arms: it was the impossibility of bringing about socio-economic change through available political channels that forced them to war.[35]

More often, however, the political strategy of holding elections does not further distributive justice. Haiti, South Africa and Namibia are all cases in point where the vote has not procured significantly greater political or economic equality for the disempowered and increasingly disenchanted majority. The apparent opening of political windows via elections, paradoxically, may shut the door more firmly to real political and economic opportunities, by hardening the opposition of vested interests who do not wish to give up more than they already have been forced to concede during negotiations. There is a potential danger in substituting political measures for economic, rather than making the two go hand in hand. Electoral democracy does not in itself lead to political equality, and does not better the prospects for economic equality, unless deliberate parallel measures in this direction are undertaken.

This approach suggests that when a post-conflict reconstruction strategy is drawn up, where possible at the peace negotiation stage itself, the causes of conflict must be emphasized as much as the consequences. Distributive justice strategies should be adopted for both stages: backward-looking measures which aim to rectify past systemic injustices and inequalities which caused deep grievances and divisions in society and underlay conflict; and forward-looking measures which aim to meet basic needs, socio-economic as well as political rights, and to improve overall social utility. Further, both socio-economic and political inequalities should be addressed simultaneously and in conjunction with each other, in recognition of their interdependence. The two-stage approach proposed here and its practical implications are ambitious but not unrealizable, as suggested by the case of Guatemala which is examined above.

With this, we complete the tour of the three dimensions of justice, proposing in each a reconceptualized approach bringing theory and reality nearer one another. This reconceptualization offers, I believe, a more conceptually rigorous and practically coherent way to address justice within the peacebuilding process in the years ahead.

Conclusion

We began this book by noting that restoring justice after political conflict or crisis is as much a social as a political imperative, for conflict touches the lives of everyone in society. Our examination of the three dimensions of justice confirmed this and underlined the necessity of grounding both peace and justice in the interests of all survivors in a community.

In addressing issues of justice peacebuilders often imposed rather than proposed or facilitated solutions. In doing so, they neglected the fulcrum of both peace and justice – the inhabitants of war-torn societies themselves. Returning to the cosmopolitan–communitarian dichotomy referred to in chapter 2, peacebuilders adopted what could be described as a liberal cosmopolitan approach. They presumed that their values had universal validity and that their approach was globally applicable; they assumed that their recommended solutions were in the best interests of the population served. In the process they often failed to integrate communitarian values inherent in local culture. They did not consider sufficiently the ineluctable necessity of grounding their values, approach and solutions in the local population and context, with all its constraints. Above all, they did not realize that the touchstone of success would not be legal prowess, technical expertise or high economic growth rates, but rather inspiring public trust and confidence in a just society.

What is required is an approach based on mutual understanding, a 'social compact' between all stakeholders in war-torn societies: civilians and combatants, citizens and governments, international peacebuilders and national recipients. However, as the philosopher Taylor notes, 'An obstacle in the path of this mutual understanding comes from the inability of many Westerners to see their culture as one among many.'[36] This does not imply that all peacebuilders so far have been Western. They clearly have not, as witnessed by the full range of national, international and regional actors involved and the diversity of UN and BWI staff who dominate peacebuilding endeavours. It is the attitudes rather than the nationalities of peacebuilders that are often perceived as 'Western' in orientation, as the debate around Afghanistan again reveals. Galtung notes, 'Whatever is Western ... tends to be conceived of as universal. The West is so powerful that such ideas as "Western history = universal history" and "Western culture = universal culture" are found not only among Westerners.'[37] This is reinforced by the concentration of financial means in a handful of countries also perceived as 'Western' who determine the fate of peacebuilding.

In chapter 2 I alluded to the predominance of 'Western' philosophical discourse that neglects the realities of injustice in non-Western settings. I noted that a significant impediment to advancing our understanding of the three dimensions of justice in low-income war-torn societies was the paucity of philosophical discourse emerging from developing countries that encounter conflict and injustice. In closing I reiterate the need to reverse this imbalance. We need an approach that bridges the cosmopolitan/communitarian divide. We need to strive for an authentically universal understanding of and response to justice that is enriched by a variety of cultural inputs and philosophical traditions. As Taylor contends: 'World convergence will not come through a loss or denial of traditions all around, but rather by creative reimmersion of different groups each in their own spiritual heritage, travelling different routes to the same goal.'[38]

Justice is at once philosophical and political, public and intensely private, universal in its existence and yet highly individualized and culturally shaped in its expression. The seeming universality of the value of justice reinforces the tendency of scholars and practitioners to treat it without nuance, without reference to its manifold cultural and individual expressions. Peacebuilders did seem to learn some lessons in the treatment of justice over the past decade. And yet the path ahead is murky and uncertain. The need for a clear understanding of justice and a commitment to address it in all its complexity is as urgent as ever. It is essential to pursue justice in the shadows of war. The survivors of war deserve no less.

Notes

Chapter 1   The Three Dimensions of Justice in Post-conflict Peacebuilding

1   Smith, *State of War*, p. 13. For detailed trends, see Wallensteen and Sollenberg, 'Armed Conflicts 1989–98'.
2   Cited in Gunson, 'Guatemala's "Peace without Justice"'.
3   A seminal compilation is found in Kritz, *Transitional Justice*.
4   See especially O'Donnell and Schmitter, *Transitions*; O'Donnell, 'Illusions'; and Linz and Stepan, 'Toward Consolidated Democracies', for long-term comparative perspectives. Also, Ratner and Abrams, *Accountability*, pp. 133–8.
5   Zalaquett, 'Balancing Ethical Imperatives', pp. 203–16.
6   Danieli, 'Preliminary Reflections'; Maynard, 'Rebuilding Community'; Becker et al., 'Therapy with Victims'; Chirwa, 'Collective Memory'; Honwana, 'Sealing the Past'.
7   Extensive coverage in Kritz, *Transitional Justice* and McAdams, *Transitional Justice*.
8   For example, in 'Reckoning with Past Wrongs', David Crocker focuses on democratic transitions. Consequently, he includes post-conflict societies that transit to democracy, but excludes those that don't democratize after conflict, therefore providing incomplete coverage of post-conflict societies. Kritz's edited collection in *Transitional Justice* also focuses on new democracies rather than war-to-peace transitions in low-income societies.
9   Boutros-Ghali, *Agenda for Peace 1995*, p. 43.

10 Smith, *State of War*, pp. 14–15; Stewart, 'Root Causes'. The opposing thesis that economic motive, not distributive injustice, causes war is addressed in ch. 5.

11 Shenon, 'UN Plans'; Mydans, 'Cambodia's Bygones'.

12 Citations in order from Galtung, 'Three Approaches', pp. 297, 298; Galtung, *Peace by Peaceful Means*, pp. 271, 265.

13 UN, 'Agenda for Peace', para. 21. NB: Prof. Andy Knight contends that peacebuilding was always the UN's implicit aim, and is tacitly expressed in the UN Charter (personal correspondence, 13.05.1999).

14 Miall et al., *Contemporary Conflict Resolution*, pp. 185–215 (p. 188).

15 Lederach, *Building Peace*, pp. 20, 63–72, 14–15.

16 Boutros-Ghali, *Agenda for Peace*, p. 61. Socio-economic aspects discussed in Goodhand and Hulme, 'From Wars to Complex Political Emergencies', pp. 13–26.

17 This inventory approach is exemplified in: UN, 'Inventory of Post-Conflict Peacebuilding Activities'; UNDP, *Building Bridges*. In 'Peacebuilding and Human Security' Cockell ostensibly aims to eschew the inventory approach, but succumbs to it. He identifies four sectoral components of peacebuilding, providing for each an exhaustive task list (p. 11).

18 My analysis of peacebuilding and the UN was assisted by interviews with officials in UN Department of Political Affairs (DPA) in New York, who all underlined this point: Assistant Secretary-General Alvaro de Soto (09.09.1997), DPA Director Francesc Vendrell (29.10.1998), Theresa Whitfield (30.10.1998), Tapio Kanninen (30.10.1998).

19 Cousens and Kumar, *Peacebuilding as Politics*, introduction, p. 4.

20 Lederach, *Building Peace*, p. 95; Cockell, 'Peacebuilding and Human Security', p. 9.

21 However, results are ambiguous, as discussed by writers in Griffiths, *Building Peace*.

22 Lederach, *Building Peace*, p. 75.

23 Ibid., p. 95.

24 Boutros-Ghali, *Agenda for Peace 1995*, p. 93.

25 Paris, 'Peacebuilding and the Limits' (p. 56). For other trenchant critiques of international peacebuilding see: Bertram, 'Reinventing Governments'; Pugh, *Regeneration of War-torn Societies*, where Pugh describes the 'urge to engineer' (pp. 3–4); David, 'Does Peacebuilding Build Peace?'

26 Cockell, 'Peacebuilding and Human Security', p. 8.

27 Evans, *Cooperating for Peace*, p. 39.

28 See both in Boutros-Ghali, *Agenda for Peace 1995*.

29 See UN, 'Renewing the United Nations'. Cockell discusses the UN's equivocation on the concept's scope in 'Peacebuilding and Human Security', pp. 15–16.

30 See e.g. Carnegie Commission, *Preventing Deadly Conflict*; Evans, *Cooperating for Peace*, pp. 61–80.

31 Agencies listed in Anstee, *International Colloquium*; World Bank, *Conflict Prevention*.
32 De Soto and del Castillo, 'Obstacles to Peacebuilding'; Bertram; David; Paris; Pugh.
33 See Kreimer et al., *World Bank's Experience*; Moore, *UN and Complex Emergencies*; UNRISD, *Rebuilding War-torn Societies*.
34 Ratner, *New UN Peacekeeping*.
35 Discussed in Chopra, *Peace Maintenance* and *Politics of Peace Maintenance*.
36 Ramsbotham, 'Clausewitz in Reverse', pp. 9–10; conceptual framework on p. 22.
37 Mamdani, in 'Reconciliation without Justice', links rectificatory and social/distributive justice. In Henkin, *From Peace to Justice*, human rights (i.e. rectificatory justice in part) and legal reform or rule of law are linked but not described as justice issues. However, such linkages are piecemeal, and I have so far not found any study or interviewed any practitioner who has identified or addressed justice holistically.
38 However, in 'Peace Over Justice', Bratt contradicts arguments for pursuing justice *with* peace.
39 World Bank, *Social Indicators 1996*, pp. 104–5, 316–17. NB: South Africa's Gini index of income inequality is a steep 54.8 per cent.
40 Klasen, *Poverty and Inequality*, p. 8.
41 BBC, 'Opposition Candidate Shot'.
42 Bowcott, 'Aristide Bid'; Associated Press, 'Haiti Raids'.
43 *Africa Confidential*, 'Kagame under Siege'; 'Bizimungu Bust-up', p. 3.
44 McNeil, 'Tangled War'; *Africa Confidential*, 'After Sam, Maybe'; 'SWAPO Steamroller'.
45 *Africa Confidential*, 'Talks Break Down'.
46 World Bank, 'Concepts'.
47 UNDP, 'Working for Solutions', p. 4.

Chapter 2 Concepts of Justice in Contemporary Philosophy

1 Mani, 'Restoring Justice', presents a preliminary version of this analysis, originally presented at the 25th Annual Conference on Legal and Social Philosophy, Reading University, April 1998. My analysis benefited from discussions with and feedback from eminent philosophers present, including Duff, Barry, and Campbell, whom I thank.
2 Aristotle, *Nicomachean Ethics*, pp. 111–45. Translations of Aristotle's terms vary. Ostwald's translation used here employs 'complete' and 'partial' justice. Discussion in Finnis, *Natural Law*, pp. 161–97.
3 Aristotle, *Nicomachean Ethics*, pp. 116–17.
4 Ibid., p. 117.
5 Ibid.
6 Finnis, *Natural Law*, p. 185, citing Merkelbach, *Summa theologiae moralis*, p. 253. 'Commutative justice' refers to rectificatory justice.

7 Varied opinions presented in Hutchinson and Monahan, *Rule of Law*. Hutchinson and Monahan describe the rule of law as inimical to democracy; Raz describes it as an aspired ideal in *Authority of Law*, pp. 211–29; Fuller considers rule of law's principles essential for law's existence, in *Morality of Law*, pp. 33–93.

8 Aristotle, *Politics*, book III, xv–xvi.

9 This precise definitional confusion was addressed by a small group of eminent scholars, human rights lawyers and UN practitioners in a seminar entitled 'Promoting the Rule of Law in Post-Conflict Societies' on 26.09.1997 at Harvard University. The Common Security Forum (CSF) sponsored the seminar, and I organized and rapporteured it. I have drawn substantially on the seminar findings for my analysis in this book. See CSF, 'Seminar Report', pp. 1–2. I thank all participants for helping clarify issues.

10 Aquinas, *Summa Theologica*, p. 157. Aquinas is an Aristotelian.

11 Dworkin, *Matter of Principle*; Golding, *Philosophy of Law*, esp. pp. 24–51.

12 Golding, *Philosophy of Law*, p. 25, citing Austin, *Province of Jurisprudence*. NB: Positivism derives from utilitarianism, and naturalism from deontology, which are discussed below.

13 See Hart, 'Positivism' and *Concept of Law*.

14 'Minimalist' and 'maximalist' are my own terms. Dworkin, 'Political Judges'; Prempeh, 'New Jurisprudence'.

15 CSF, 'Seminar Report', pp. 4–5. I thank Prof. Henry Steiner particularly for expressing this view (personal discussion, Harvard University, MA, 27.09.1997).

16 Flathman, 'Liberalism'.

17 Hayek, *Road to Serfdom*, as cited in Raz, *Authority of Law*, p. 210.

18 Neumann, *Rule of Law*, pp. 31–5 (p. 32).

19 See Neumann, *Rule of Law*; Flathman, 'Liberalism'; Gaus, 'Public Reason'.

20 Raz, *Authority of Law*, p. 221.

21 Hart, *Concept of Law*, pp. 17–37; 'maximalist'-leaning Dworkin concedes this point in *Taking Rights Seriously*, p. 11.

22 CSF, 'Seminar Report', pp. 5–6. I thank Neil Kritz in particular for his articulation of this view (personal discussion at US Institute for Peace, Washington, DC, on 10.09.1997).

23 Dicey, *Law of the Constitution*, pp. 202–3.

24 Walker, *Rule of Law*, pp. 1–3, 336–8.

25 CSCE, 'Copenhagen Meeting', point 2, p. 3. NB: OSCE was then called Conference on Security and Cooperation in Europe – CSCE.

26 Dworkin, 'Political Judges', pp. 12–13.

27 Fuller, *Morality of Law*, pp. 33–94.

28 Raz, *Authority of Law*, pp. 216–18; Rawls, *Theory of Justice*, pp. 238–9. Both start from Fuller's eight principles.

29 The CSCE document categorically states that democracy and the rule of law are prerequisites for progress in participating states. This reference

does not imply that I myself believe rule of law and democracy must always be linked, as I don't.

30 NB: Contemporary legal theories like sociological jurisprudence, legal realism and critical legal studies have contributed a third radically different perspective on the rule of law. They observe that judicial discretion and uncertainty are prevalent even in the most sophisticated legal systems, and that the rule of law doesn't necessarily guarantee predictability and certainty in practice, as claimed in theory. Consequently, these approaches prefer realistic and elastic rather than formal definitions of the rule of law. CSF, 'Seminar Report', p. 4, and discussion with Steiner.

31 CSF, 'Seminar Report', pp. 6–8.

32 ICJ, *Development*, p. 25.

33 UN, *Human Rights*, vol. 1, p. 1.

34 CSF, 'Seminar Report', pp. 7–8. Rwanda is an example.

35 Finnis, *Natural Law*, p. 179.

36 The lawyer Roht-Arriaza, for example, also turns to punishment theories in her search for 'normative bases for combating impunity' in *Impunity*, p. 13.

37 Duff, 'Alternatives to Punishment', p. 43.

38 Discussed in Lacey, *State Punishment*, ch. 2; Duff, *Trials and Punishments*, chs 6–7; Cragg, *Practice of Punishment*, chs 1–3.

39 Hart identifies these three questions in 'Prolegomenon'.

40 Bentham, *Introduction to Principles*. Discussion in Tunick, *Punishment*, pp. 67–84.

41 Sen and Williams, *Utilitarianism and Beyond*, pp. 3–4.

42 Bentham is cited by Tunick, *Punishment*, p. 73.

43 Murphy, *Retribution*, pp. 147–201; Cragg, *Practice of Punishment*, pp. 44–6, 198–203. Cragg notes that studies show that 'judges whose goal was rehabilitation or incapacitation generated longer and harsher sentences on average than did retribution-oriented judges' (p. 54).

44 Hampton, 'Expressive Theory', pp. 8–9.

45 Duff, 'Penal Communications', p. 11.

46 See Hayry, 'Defence of Utilitarian Theory'.

47 Kant, *Perpetual Peace*, p. 58.

48 Hampton, 'Expressive Theory', pp. 1–26.

49 Reiss, *Kant*, pp. 154–5.

50 Hegel, *Elements of Philosophy*, section 100, p. 126. Italics in original.

51 Reiss, *Kant*, p. 156.

52 Hampton, 'Expressive Theory', p. 1.

53 Jacoby, *Wild Justice*, p. 4.

54 Argued in Murphy and Hampton, *Forgiveness and Mercy*, pp. 108, 6.

55 Duff, 'Penal Communications', p. 25.

56 Hampton, 'Expressive Theory', p. 1.

57 Jacoby, *Wild Justice*, p. 298.

58 Hampton, 'Expressive Theory', p. 8.

59 See Neier, *War Crimes*; Minow, *Vengeance and Forgiveness*. Discussed in ch. 4.

60 Duff, 'Penal Communications', pp. 32–3; 'Alternatives to Punishment', pp. 51–2.
61 Duff, 'Alternatives to Punishment', pp. 53–4.
62 Lacey, *State Punishment*, pp. 198–9.
63 Duff, *Trials and Punishment*, p. 295.
64 Murphy, *Retribution*, pp. 93–115.
65 Hampton, 'Expressive Theory', pp. 24–5.
66 Hart, *Punishment and Responsibility*, pp. 1–27.
67 Matthews, 'Reassessing Informal Justice'.
68 Abel, *Politics*, vol. 2, introduction, p. 2. See also Auerbach, *Justice without Law?*
69 Duff, 'Penal Communications', pp. 80–3; Cragg, *Practice of Punishment*, pp. 169–203; Wright, *Justice for Victims*.
70 See Wright and Galaway, *Mediation and Criminal Justice*, for varied experiments and assessments. VORPs are principally used for minor, non-violent offences, but their use in violent crimes is examined in Umbreit, 'Violent Offenders'.
71 See 'Sentencing as Conflict Resolution' in Cragg, *Practice of Punishment*, pp. 178–86.
72 Marshall, 'Out of Court', p. 49.
73 Duff, 'Penal Communications', pp. 67–87.
74 Both quotes ibid., p. 85.
75 Auerbach, *Justice without Law?*, p. 144. Also see Marshall, 'Out of Court'.
76 Abel, *Politics*, vol. 2, introduction, p. 2.
77 Abel, 'Contradictions of Informal Justice', p. 307.
78 Auerbach, *Justice without Law?*, p. 144.
79 Duff, *Trials and Punishment*, p. 298.
80 Rawls, *Theory of Justice*.
81 See Taylor, 'Nature and Scope' and Miller, 'Recent Theories', for broader overviews.
82 Innumerable typologies exist. In *Social Justice*, Miller identifies three distinct criteria for just distribution: needs, rights and desert, pp. 24–31. I believe desert is less relevant in developing countries, as 'one's due' is skewed by inequality at many levels. I propose inequality instead as a more relevant category for distributive justice in developing and war-torn societies.
83 Onora O'Neill, 'Transnational Justice', pp. 279, 298. NB: All references in this chapter to O'Neill are to Onora O'Neill.
84 Sadurski, *Giving Desert its Due*, p. 173.
85 Miller, *Social Justice*, pp. 127–8, citing Barry's point made in *Political Argument*.
86 On categorical versus instrumental needs, see Megone, 'What is Need?' On instrumental, functional and intrinsic needs, see Miller, *Social Justice*, pp. 126–36.
87 Beitz, 'Economic Rights', p. 344.
88 Sadurski, *Giving Desert its Due*, p. 159.

89 Miller, *Social Justice*, p. 317.
90 Sen, *Inequality Re-examined*, p. 40. Capabilities are discussed in Nussbaum, 'Human Capabilities'.
91 Teleological, deontological and rights approaches discussed in: Dworkin, *Taking Rights Seriously*, esp. 'Justice and Rights', pp. 150–83; O'Neill, *Faces of Hunger*; Miller, *Social Justice*, chs 1–2.
92 Libertarian justice is exemplified in Nozick, *Anarchy*.
93 O'Neill, 'Transnational Justice', p. 289.
94 See Miller, *Social Justice*, pp. 52–82.
95 UN, *Human Rights*, vol. 1, pp. 1–42.
96 See Miller, *Social Justice*, pp. 65–78; Campbell, *Justice*, pp. 36–65.
97 Argued by O'Neill in *Faces of Hunger*, pp. 97–120; 'Transnational Justice', pp. 284–8; *Justice and Virtue*, pp. 128–36.
98 Sadurski concedes this in *Giving Desert its Due*, pp. 170–1.
99 UN, 'Vienna Declaration', points 5, 10.
100 Steiner and Alston, *International Human Rights*, pp. 268–9.
101 The cultural relativism argument is that human rights are a 'Western' concept that is inapplicable in non-Western traditional cultures which downplay individual liberties in favour of community responsibilities. See e.g. Galtung, *Human Rights*, pp. 1–25; Bauer and Bell, *East Asian Challenge*; I don't discuss this, as rights and their abuse during conflict are of obvious relevance and concern to non-Western developing societies studied here, although conceptions of rights vary between cultures. The Vienna Declaration rejected the cultural argument. It stated: 'While the significance of national and regional particularities and various historical, cultural and religious backgrounds must be borne in mind, it is the duty of States, regardless of their political, economic and cultural systems, to promote and protect all human rights and fundamental freedoms' (point 5).
102 Mamdani, 'Denial of Justice', p. 6; Campbell concurs, *Justice*, pp. 37–8.
103 Commission on Global Governance, *Our Global Neighbourhood*, esp. ch. 2.
104 O'Neill: *Hunger*, pp. 144–63; *Virtue*, pp. 136–53.
105 UN, *Human Rights*, vols 1 and 2; Alston and Steiner, *International Human Rights*.
106 That is, each right carries with it an obligation on an agent to fulfil that right. Brownlie, *Public International Law*, p. 434, citing Judge Huber; ICHRP, *Taking Duties Seriously*.
107 Cited in Miller, *Social Justice*, p. 62.
108 The capabilities approach might offer a way to integrate rights and duties in the philosophic and economic realms. See Nussbaum, 'Human Capabilities'.
109 Both O'Neill and Rawls present their theories as explicit, conscious alternatives to utilitarianism. See O'Neill, *Faces of Hunger*, esp. chs 4–5; Rawls, *Theory of Justice*, pp. 22–33, 180–92. Varieties of utilitarianism in Miller, *Social Justice*, pp. 31–40.

110 On utilitarianism: varied views in Sen and Williams, *Utilitarianism and Beyond*; balanced critique in Rawls, *Theory of Justice*, pp. 161–75, 183–92; sharp critique in O'Neill, *Faces of Hunger* and *Towards Justice*.

111 Rawls, *Theory of Justice*, p. 30.

112 Miller, *Social Justice*, p. 40.

113 On contract, see Rawls, *Theory of Justice*; on fairness and mutual advantage, see Barry, *Treatise*, vol. 1; on desert, see Sadurski, *Giving Desert its Due*, and Campbell, *Justice*; on contribution, see Taylor, 'Nature and Scope'.

114 One such proponent is Beitz, in Beitz et al., *International Ethics*. Dworkin opposes this in 'Justice and Rights'. Rawls qualified his theory and responded to critiques in *Political Liberalism*.

115 Sen's opening query in *Inequality Re-examined*, pp. 1–30.

116 Rawls, *Theory*, pp. 60–5. For critique of primary goods, see Sen, *Inequality Re-examined*, pp. 79–84.

117 Dworkin: 'What is Equality?', part I, p. 185; part II, p. 334.

118 Walzer, *Spheres of Justice*, pp. 18–19. See Miller and Walzer, *Justice, Pluralism and Equality* for varied perspectives; for scathing criticism, see Dworkin, *Matter of Principle*, pp. 214–20.

119 Sen, *Inequality Re-examined*, p. xi; see Nussbaum and Sen, *Quality of Life*.

120 See Sen, *Development as Freedom*. Also, Nussbaum and Glover, *Women, Culture and Development*.

121 Central argument in Sen's *Inequality Re-examined*. As we see in ch. 5, recent studies in political economy confirm that equity and economic growth or efficiency are positively related and not opposed, as believed in classical economic theory.

122 See Rawls's lexical ordering of principles and their justification in *Theory of Justice*, pp. 302–3, 258–332.

123 Dworkin, 'Why Liberals Should Care', 'Do Liberty and Equality Conflict?'

124 Taylor, 'Nature and Scope', p. 53.

125 O'Neill, 'Justice, Capabilities and Vulnerabilities', p. 140.

126 Examples are Barry, *Liberty and Justice*; Beitz et al., *International Ethics*; *Ethics and International Affairs*, a journal which provides a forum for these enquiries.

127 Examples are Hoffman, *Duties beyond Borders*; Beitz, 'Economic Rights'; O'Neill, *Faces of Hunger*.

128 Woodman, 'Legal Pluralism', p. 153.

129 Ibid., pp. 153–4. Also see Tomasi, 'Individual Rights'.

130 McIntyre, *Whose Justice?* In *Spheres of Justice*, Walzer presents a communitarian vision with cosmopolitan shades. NB: Rawls, a liberal, in *Theory of Justice*, concedes that conceptions of justice are specific to political communities.

131 O'Neill, 'Justice, Capabilities and Vulnerabilities', p. 140.

132 See Nussbaum's philosophical compromise position in 'Human Capabilities'.

Chapter 3   Re-establishing Order or Restoring the Rule of Law?

1   An early version of this chapter entitled 'The Rule of Law or the Rule of Might? Restoring Legal Justice in Post-Conflict Societies' appears in Pugh, *Regeneration*.

2   Plunkett, 'Reestablishing Law', p. 63.

3   Plunkett, 'Establishment of Rule of Law'; 'Reestablishing Law'. Endorsed by former Australian Foreign Minister Gareth Evans, who was deeply involved in the Cambodian peace process. See Evans, *Cooperating for Peace*, p. 56, and 'Comprehensive Political Settlement'.

4   Stanley Foundation, *Post-Conflict Justice*, pp. 6–7, provides a long list.

5   UN, 'Assistance to States', pt. 6. 'Centre' refers to the erstwhile UN Centre for Human Rights, now subsumed within OHCHR.

6   Plunkett, 'Reestablishing Law', pp. 68–9.

7   For instance, USAID uses 'administration of justice'; World Bank uses 'judicial reform'.

8   Shihata, 'Judicial Reform', p. 169.

9   Interview with Cornelius De Rover, police reform expert with the Red Cross (in Geneva 30.06.1998). See also De Rover, *To Serve and to Protect*.

10   See Oakley et al., *Policing the New World*; UNITAR, *Role and Functions*; UN OHCHR, *Human Rights and Law Enforcement*.

11   Preston, 'Integrating Fighters', pp. 461, 463.

12   Nathan, 'Human Rights'; Leys, 'State and Civil Society'.

13   Discussed further in Mani, 'Contextualizing Police Reform'.

14   See e.g. Berdal, *Disarmament and Demobilisation*.

15   UN, *El Salvador Agreements*, ch. 2, point 1.

16   ARENA insisted on receiving assistance for PNC only from the USA, but accepted diversified international assistance for the Police Academy. Costa, 'United Nations and Reform', pp. 375–80.

17   This analysis drawn from: Hemisphere Initiatives (HI), *Endgame* and *Salvadoran Peace Accords*; WOLA, 'Recent Setbacks'; Stanley, *Risking Failure* and *Protectors or Perpetrators?* Also helpful were discussions with police reform experts Chuck Call and William Stanley (in Oslo, 5–6.03.1999).

18   Stanley, *Risking Failure*, p. 7.

19   Ibid., p. 2.

20   Costa, 'United Nations and Reform', pp. 368, 375.

21   CSF, 'Seminar Report', pp. 14–18.

22   HRW, *Human Rights Record*, p. 39.

23   Ibid., pp. 36–9.

24   Neild, *Policing Haiti*, p. 39. Some of my interviewees suggested that the USA initially opposed the military's abolition.

25   HRW, *Human Rights Record*, p. 28.

26   Neild, *Policing Haiti*, p. 36; NCHR, *Haiti's Police Reforms*, pp. 1–3.

27   Gros, 'Haiti's Flagging Transition'.

28 My analysis of the rule of law in Haiti in this chapter was greatly helped by interviews and discussions with: Rachel Neild, Senior Associate, WOLA (Washington, DC, 25.09.1997 and 28.10.1998); Ambassador Pierre Lelong, Permanent Representative of Haiti to the UN (New York, 03.10.1997); Ian Martin, former Human Rights Director of the joint OAS/UN Civilian Mission in Haiti (MICIVIH), and subsequently Head of HRFOR (London, 26.02.1997); William O'Neill, National Coalition for Haitian Rights (NCHR; New York, 03.10.1997); Wendy Cue, MI-CIVIH human rights observer (Geneva, 01.07.1998); Ettore de Benedetto, MICIVIH officer responsible for overseeing police reform (Geneva, 01.07.1998). Also, Adama Dieng, UN Independent Expert on Human Rights situation in Haiti (Geneva, 03.11.1997). Many of my interviewees had experience in more than one of the war-torn countries examined, often with different agencies, adding depth and breadth to their insights.

29 Kritz, interview; CSF, 'Seminar Report', p. 8.

30 Hemisphere Initiatives, *Salvadoran Peace Accords*, p. 6.

31 Neild, *Policing Haiti*, pp. 12–18.

32 Stanley, *Risking Failure*, pp. 7–8.

33 Neild, *Policing Haiti*, p. 22.

34 Neild, *Overcoming History*, p. 3.

35 Ibid., pp. 2, 9–12.

36 Repeated observation in Krog, *Country of my Skull*, a riveting journalist's account of the Truth and Reconciliation Commission. However, see Roht-Arriaza's discussion of superior orders, in *Impunity*.

37 Nathan, 'Human Rights', p. 155.

38 WOLA recommended community policing in Haiti, but it was tried in Cap Haitien with only limited success. See Neild, *Overcoming History*, pp. 20–2.

39 See Mani, 'Contextualizing Police Reform'.

40 W. O'Neill, *No Greater Priority*, p. 1.

41 Shihata, 'Judicial Reform', pp. 152–69.

42 UN HRFOR, 'Administration of Justice', p. 2.

43 Ibid., pp. 4–12. My analysis of rule of law and human rights in Rwanda was greatly helped by interviews and discussions with UN HRFOR officials: Ian Martin, Bill O'Neill, Todd Howland (Cambridge, Mass., 26.09.1997), Wendy Cue, Chris Harland, José Luis Herrero, Stephanie Klein-Ahlbrandt and Geoffrey Peterson (Geneva, 28–30.06.1998); also Michel Moussali, Special Representative of the UN Commission on Human Rights for Rwanda (in Geneva, 30.06.1998); Omar Bakhet, former UN Resident Representative in Rwanda (in New York, 30.10.1998). On general human rights issues, Gianni Maggazenni, Head of Technical Cooperation, OHCHR (Geneva, 29.06.1998).

44 CSF, 'Seminar Report', p. 13.

45 MICIVIH, 'Executive Summary'.

46 Maguire et al., *Haiti Held Hostage*.

47 UN, 'Basic Principles on Independence of Judiciaries'; Brody, *Independence of Judges*.

48 Johnstone, *Rights and Reconciliation*, pp. 18–23.
49 The San José Agreement [II 14 h.], signed 26.07.1990, in UN, *El Salvador Agreements*, pp. 7–12.
50 Buergenthal, 'United Nations Truth Commission'; Johnstone, *Rights and Reconciliation*, pp. 65–76. My analysis of rule of law and judicial reform in El Salvador draws on interviews with: Professor Buergenthal, Truth Commission Member (in Washington, DC, 10.09.1997); Ambassador Ricardo Castaneda, Permanent Representative of El Salvador to the United Nations (in New York, 02.10.1997); Ian Johnstone, UNDPA (in New York, 30.09.1998); Todd Howland, human rights lawyer and NGO activist (in Cambridge, Mass., 27.09.1997); Alvaro de Soto, UN chief negotiator for El Salvador (in New York, 09.09.1997).
51 These politics discussed in Popkin et al., *Justice Delayed*, pp. 3–6; Johnstone, *Rights and Reconciliation*, pp. 67–9.
52 Dodson and Jackson, 'Re-inventing Rule of Law'; concurred by several interviewees.
53 UN, 'Assessment of Peace Process', p. 6.
54 Plunkett, 'Establishment of Rule of Law', p. 68. My analysis on Cambodia was assisted greatly by interviews with: Dennis McNamara, Director of Human Rights for UNTAC during its mandate (in Geneva, 02.07.1998); Daniel Prémont, Director, UN Centre for Human Rights in Cambodia, 1994–96 (in Geneva, 02.07.1998), and discussions with the Centre's human rights lawyers: Brad Adams (Washington, DC, 25.09.1997), Peter Rosenblum and James Ross (Cambridge, Mass., 26.09.1997).
55 MICIVIH, 'Prisons en Haïti'; UN HRFOR, 'Report on Human Rights Situation'.
56 A human rights observer noted that prisoners called UN observers 'sister' or 'brother' and concluded that their assistance implied they believed the suspects to be innocent.
57 LCHR, *Prosecuting Genocide*; Ourdan, 'Un tribunal loin du Rwanda'.
58 Ganzlass, 'Restoration of Somali Justice System'.
59 Discussed further in Mani, 'Conflict Resolution' and Mani, 'Restoring Rule of Law'.
60 UN, 'Assistance to States'; improvements in CSF, 'Seminar Report', pp. 30–2.
61 Comment by interviewee.
62 CSF, 'Seminar Report', p. 24.
63 Kumar et al., *Rebuilding Post-war Rwanda*, p. 76.
64 See Gros, 'Haiti's Flagging Transition'.
65 Rohter, 'Political Feud'.
66 Bowcott, 'Violence and Boycott'.
67 CSF, 'Seminar Report', p. 17.
68 Interview with De Rover. He noted that this framework is prevalent in management training but rarely used in international assistance and training where it is equally relevant.
69 UN HRFOR, 'Administration of Justice', p. 6.

70 Interviews with UN HRFOR officials who, with a single exception, noted declining government commitment to rule of law over time.
71 McGreal, 'Tutsi Soldier to lead Rwanda'.
72 Plunkett, 'Reestablishing Law', pp. 64–5.
73 CSF, 'Seminar Report', p. 17.
74 Interview with De Rover.
75 This threefold categorization of states of disrepair is my own conception.
76 Asmal et al., *Reconciliation through Truth*, p. 54.
77 Ibid., p. 55. Mbeki's statement to the UN Special Committee on the Policies of Apartheid, London, 1964.
78 Ibid., p. 54 (Mandela) and p. 55 (Brundtland).
79 The Guatemalan legal and political regime could be considered illegitimate by this standard, for its long-standing exclusion of the majority indigenous population, which the peace agreements sought to overturn. See Armon, Seider and Wilson, *Negotiating Rights*.
80 My analysis of Namibia draws on interviews with Cedric Thornberry, Chef de Cabinet to UN Special Representative of UNTAG, and human rights lawyer involved in Namibia since 1974 (in Geneva, 30.06.1998); Paul Szasz, former Legal Director, UNTAG (New York, 29.09.1998); John Truman, Chief Electoral Officer, UNTAG (New York, 01.10.1997). Also Martin Andjaba, Permanent Representative of Namibia to the United Nations (New York, 03.10.1998).
81 Prempeh, 'New Jurisprudence', p. 139.
82 Cited in Buergenthal, 'UN Truth Commission', p. 318. Interview: Buergenthal.
83 O'Neill, *No Greater Priority*, pp. 1, 4.
84 This threatens to be the most likely scenario in coming years in many countries still embroiled in, or barely emerging from, conflict, like Afghanistan, Democratic Republic of Congo, Sierra Leone and Angola.
85 Tuckman, 'Lynch Mobs'.
86 Observations by various human rights officials interviewed.
87 Argued fully in Mani, 'Contextualising Police Reform'.
88 UN, *El Salvador Agreements*, ch. 1, points E–F, pp. 47–8.
89 NB: ICESCR permits incremental achievement of goals for developing countries (see ch. 2). The Universal Declaration and both covenants address 'all human beings'.
90 CSF, 'Seminar Report', pp. 22–3, 32–3.
91 Background: UN, *United Nations and Cambodia*; Heininger, *Peace-keeping in Transition*.
92 Plunkett argues in 'Establishment of Rule of Law' that the Agreement's remit for rule of law reform could have been more broadly interpreted and undertaken.
93 Observed by interviewee.
94 Plunkett, 'Reestablishing Law', p. 65 and 'Establishment of Rule of Law', p. 73.
95 Human rights officers I interviewed narrated that in the aftermath of UNTAC, American and French lawyers argued bitterly over which of

their legal systems should be implemented in Cambodia. Yet neither side could articulate clearly the differences between their systems or argue convincingly why either was better suited for Cambodia.

96 Interview.

97 Weiland and Braham, *Namibian Peace Process*, pp. 163–80.

98 Interviews: Kritz, US Institute for Peace (see ch. 2); Harland. Both helped Rwanda's government in drafting laws. Organic (Genocide) Law discussed in ch. 4.

99 Common observation by my interviewees and CSF seminar participants.

100 Seider, 'Reframing Citizenship'. Also interviews with: Patricia Cleves, formerly Head of Indigenous Peoples' Unit, MINUGUA, currently World Bank Post-Conflict Unit (Washington, DC, 28.10.1998); Denise Cook, Guatemala Desk Officer, UN DPA (New York, 29.09.2001).

101 Governor Cameron of Tanganyika, cited in Mamdani, *Citizen and Subject*, p. 112.

102 I found scant recent literature on this highly pertinent subject. I have drawn primarily on two sources only: Woodman, 'Legal Pluralism' and Mamdani, *Citizen and Subject*, esp. ch. 4. Greater scholarly analysis of this subject is urgently required.

103 Mamdani, *Citizen and Subject*, pp. 122–8 (p. 122).

104 Woodman, 'Legal Pluralism', p. 157.

105 Mamdani, *Citizen and Subject*, p. 168.

106 Woodman, 'Legal Pluralism', p. 156.

107 Visman et al., *European Union and Conflict Prevention*.

108 Pankhurst, 'Issues of Justice', p. 26.

109 Observation by interviewee.

110 Mamdani, *Citizen and Subject*, p. 130.

111 Woodman, 'Legal Pluralism', pp. 158–9 (p. 158).

112 Plunkett, 'Reestablishing Law', p. 68.

113 O'Neill in interview; CSF, 'Seminar Report', pp. 21–2.

114 Plunkett, 'Reestablishing Law', p. 68. In colonial times over a century ago, customary laws could be practised, through the authority of local chiefs, *except* when they were deemed to 'outrage' Western ideas of 'humanity', 'civilization' or 'morality'. In such cases, Western law prevailed even over native subjects. See Mamdani, *Citizen and Subject*, pp. 115–17. There is the danger of falling into this pattern today – of opting for an eclectic approach to customary laws dictated by standards of morality that are extraneous to the given community.

115 Plunkett, 'Reestablishing Law', p. 63.

116 Mamdani, *Citizen and Subject*, p. 121.

Chapter 4   Punishing Perpetrators or Vindicating Victims?

1 While the arguments and analysis in this chapter are my own, they were stimulated, tested and strengthened by my participation and

discussions with others at relevant conferences. These include: 'How Can Human Rights be Better Integrated into Peace Processes?', Fund for Peace, Washington, DC, 24–5.09.1997 (hereafter Washington Conference); 'Burying the Past', St Anthony's College, Oxford University, 14–16.09.1998 (hereafter Oxford Conference); 'Rebuilding Torn Societies', Academic Council of the United Nations System, UN, New York, 16–18.06.1999 (hereafter ACUNS Conference); 'High Level Round-Table on Truth and Reconciliation', International Institute for Democracy and Electoral Assistance, Stockholm, 1–2.11.1999 (hereafter Stockholm Conference). I have also drawn extensively on the published proceedings of certain conferences I did not attend. Most notable are: HLS (Harvard Law School), *Truth Commissions: A Comparative Assessment*, Report of an Interdisciplinary Discussion sponsored by Human Rights Program, May 1996; Boraine et al., *Dealing with the Past: Truth and Reconciliation in South Africa*. In this new area of enquiry, the most novel perspectives are those emerging at such encounters, and I am grateful to the participants in these conferences for their insights which enriched my own.

2   Ratner and Abrams, *Accountability*, see esp. 'The Progeny of Nuremberg', pp. 162–92; Minow, *Between Vengeance and Forgiveness*, pp. 25–51.

3   Roberts and Guelff, *Documents on Laws of War*; Brownlie, *Basic Documents*.

4   Neier, *War Crimes*, p. 75.

5   Ibid., pp. 111–260; Ratner and Abrams, *Accountability*, pp. 162–92; Benedetti and Washburn, 'Drafting the International Criminal Court Treaty'.

6   Kritz, *Transitional Justice*, vol. 1; McAdams, *Transitional Justice*.

7   NB: Citizens' and victims' groups fiercely opposed these amnesties. Popkin and Bhuta, 'Latin American Amnesties'; Neier, *War Crimes*, esp. 'The Trouble with Amnesty', pp. 96–107; Mejía, 'Amnesty, Pardon'.

8   Brownlie, *Principles of Public International Law*, 'Law of Responsibility', discussed on pp. 432–76.

9   Roht-Arriaza, *Impunity*, pp. 22–70; Orentlicher, 'Settling Accounts'.

10   ICJ, *Right to Reparation*; UN, 'Study Concerning Right to Restitution'.

11   Ratner and Abrams, *Accountability*, pp. 1–23.

12   UN, *Human Rights – International Instruments*, p. 20.

13   ICJ, *Justice not Impunity*, presents human rights perspectives; David Crocker presents a moral philosopher's perspective.

14   Neier, *War Crimes*, pp. 80–5; Minow, *Between Vengeance and Forgiveness*, pp. 10–14.

15   Roht-Arriaza, *Impunity*, pp. 20–1.

16   Mendez, 'In Defense', p. 4; Zalaquett, 'Confronting Human Rights Violations'. Zalaquett was a member of Chile's truth commission. Although a human rights activist, Zalaquett bows before political con-

straints, and advises against trials in cases like Chile where a military backlash is a real threat.

17 RENAMO atrocities in Vines, *RENAMO*, pp. 87–91; UN, *United Nations and Mozambique*. The UN notes that FRELIMO abuses were mainly by 'Government troops acting outside the orders of their commanders', p. 11.

18 UN, 'Situation of Human Rights in Rwanda'.

19 Onishi, 'Survivors Sadly Say, Yes'. These amnesty provisions are hampering the UN's attempt to set up a tribunal for Sierra Leone.

20 Goldman, 'UN Moves on Sierra Leone Court'.

21 Krog, *Country of my Skull*, p. 261.

22 Vines, *RENAMO*, p. 77.

23 When accused of mistreating its detainees, the ANC set up two separate commissions of enquiry between 1992 and 1993, released their results and publicly apologized. The ANC is the only non-governmental body to have set up a 'truth commission'. Hayner, 'Fifteen Truth Commissions', pp. 244–5.

24 In *Reconciliation through Truth*, Asmal et al. argue for 'The Need to Decriminalise the Resistance' (pp. 54–63) and 'The Morality of the Armed Resistance' (pp. 120–5).

25 Johnstone, *Rights and Reconciliation*, p. 37. My analysis of El Salvador in this chapter also draws on interviews and discussions cited earlier (in ch. 3) with Buergenthal, Johnstone, Howland, Weinberg, de Soto and Castaneda, all personally involved in peace negotiations, peacebuilding and/or rectificatory justice measures.

26 Krog, *Country of my Skull*, p. 126.

27 Minow, *Between Vengeance and Forgiveness*, pp. 27–34.

28 Skaar, 'Truth Commissions'.

29 Graybill, 'South Africa's Truth', p. 61; case versus trials in Asmal et al., *Reconciliation through Truth*, pp. 18–23.

30 Africa Watch, *Accountability in Namibia*.

31 Interview with Ambassador Martin Andjaba, Permanent Representative of Namibia to the UN (in New York, 03.10.1998).

32 Nathan, 'Human Rights', pp. 157–9.

33 Africa Watch, *Accountability in Namibia*; Dobell, 'Silence in Context'.

34 Africa Watch, *Accountability in Namibia*, chs 8–9.

35 Ibid., ch. 11.

36 In 1973 the UN General Assembly recognized SWAPO as 'the sole authentic and legitimate representative of the Namibian people' (GA Res. 311 [XXVIII]), Weiland and Braham, *Namibian Peace Process*, p. 208.

37 UN, *UN and Cambodia*, p. 5. Besides academic analyses, a piercing insight into the global legacy of Khmer Rouge's tactics is provided by novelist Fawcett in *Cambodia*.

38 Vickery and Roht-Arriaza, 'Human Rights in Cambodia', pp. 246–8.

39 Reproduced in UN, *UN and Cambodia*, p. 135. See Marks, 'Forgetting "The Policies and Practices"'.

40 Mydans, 'UN Ends Cambodia Talks'.
41 Johnstone, *Rights and Reconciliation*, p. 37; interviews.
42 CSF, 'Seminar Report'.
43 UN, 'Situation of Human Rights in Rwanda'. My analysis of Rwanda in this chapter also draws on interviews (cited in ch. 3) with Martin, Cue, Herrero, Howland, Peterson, Harland.
44 Interviews: Kritz; Harland. Both were involved in the process.
45 Detailed discussion in LCHR, *Prosecuting Genocide*; Schabas, 'Justice, Democracy and Impunity'.
46 CSF Report, pp. 10–14; interviews with HRFOR.
47 An HRFOR officer indicated that Category One alone consisted of 1,946 cases in July 1998.
48 In interview.
49 Mendez, 'In Defense', p. 1; comment by Neier, in Boraine et al., *Dealing with the Past*, p. 3.
50 IRIN, 'Rwandan Genocide Trials', p. 1.
51 Observation by Paul Van Zyl, Executive Secretary of TRC, at ACUNS Conference.
52 Goldman, 'UN Moves on Sierra Leone Court'.
53 Interview with international legal adviser to the special prosecutor; CSF, 'Seminar Report', pp. 18–19.
54 In *Accountability*, Ratner and Abrams conclude that lack of evidence makes trials in Cambodia unlikely, pp. 266–87. However, evidence unearthed and released by the War Crimes Research Office (USA) in July 2001 will facilitate the ongoing attempt to prosecute Khmer Rouge leaders; see Becker, 'Reports Document Khmer Rouge Role'.
55 See e.g. Schuett, 'International War Crimes'. The dilemma is underscored by the prolonged internal debate preceding the extradition of Milosevic.
56 See Ourdan, 'Rwanda, enquête', all four articles.
57 Benedetti and Washburn, 'Drafting'; Neier, *War Crimes*, pp. 252–60.
58 Schuett, 'International War Crimes', p. 92.
59 National trials were conducted under Allied Control Council Law no. 10 of 20.12.1945, repr. in Ratner and Abrams, *Accountability*, pp. 308–9.
60 This debate is summarized in CSF, 'Seminar Report', p. 20.
61 Mydans, 'Khmer Rouge Suspects'.
62 Campbell, 'Justice in Sight'.
63 Comment by Dennis Thompson in HLS, *Truth Commissions*, p. 37.
64 André Du Toit's comment in HLS, *Truth Commissions*, p. 36; Graybill, 'South Africa's Truth', p. 60.
65 Hayner, 'In Pursuit', p. 8; Minow, *Between Vengeance and Forgiveness*, pp. 51, 57–61.
66 Mendez, 'In Defense', p. 2; Zalaquett's comment in HLS, *Truth Commissions*, p. 36.
67 In *War Crimes*, Neier concedes that only a tiny percentage may be tried in each case, but feels this suffices symbolically to establish individual accountability and to vindicate victims, pp. 220–3.

68 HLS, *Truth Commissions*, pp. 13–39; Minow, *Between Vengeance and Forgiveness*, pp. 57–61.
69 Graybill, 'South Africa's Truth', p. 60; Hayner, 'In Pursuit', p. 8; HLS, *Truth Commissions*, pp. 13–38.
70 Hayner, 'Fifteen Truth Commissions', p. 225; HLS, *Truth Commissions*, pp. 39–64.
71 UN, *El Salvador Agreements*, pp. 30, 31.
72 Echoed by all my interviewees.
73 UN, 'L'Administration de Justice', point 17, p. 5.
74 Zalaquett, cited in Boraine et al., *Dealing with the Past*, p. 103.
75 Some scholars question whether there can be a single truth in deeply divided societies. Mamdani asks, 'Whose truth? Which truth? The truth of the minority or the majority? Of the political activist or the population?' Mamdani, 'Denial of Justice?', p. 12. On the ubiquity of TCs see Johnson, 'Truth Commissions Multiply'.
76 Hayner, 'International Guidelines', pp. 173–5.
77 Johnstone, *Rights and Reconciliation*, pp. 34–45 (p. 34); Buergenthal, 'UN Truth Commission', provides an insider's account. Americas Watch, *El Salvador: Accountability*, provides a critique.
78 Thomas Nagel, cited by Wecshler in 'A Miracle, a Universe', p. 492.
79 NB: The peace agreements specified 'the provisions of this agreement shall not prevent the normal investigation of any situation or case, whether or not the Commission has investigated it, nor the application of the relevant legal provisions to any act that is contrary to law'. UN, *El Salvador Agreements*, p. 31.
80 One of my interviewees who closely followed the process noted this and observed that FMLN abuses documented in the report focused on the single faction led by Joaquím Villalobos, who had already been alienated from the FMLN party leadership. There is no implication or evidence that the Commissioners were aware of or complicit in the factionalism and politicization. That they were not nationals may be partly responsible – Castaneda's observation that the Commissioners 'did not realize' the politics and political ramifications involved may be linked to this fact (interview).
81 Two views presented by my interviewees.
82 Some of my interviewees expressed this opinion. However, TC member Buergenthal expresses satisfaction that the report was broadly distributed particularly in informal and pictorial representations and was easily accessible to ordinary people. He also feels the process was inclusive, even though hearings had to be confidential and not public due to political tensions (interview).
83 Opinion shared by most of my interviewees.
84 Wilson, 'Violent Truths'.
85 Comments by Jean Arnault, Chief UN peace negotiator and Head of UN Mission, MINUGUA, at Washington Conference.
86 HRW-Americas, *Haiti: Thirst for Justice*, p. 18. The Commission was announced by the government in December 1994, but the Commissioners

were named only in March 1995, leaving them less than a year to report.

87 Interview with MICIVIH officers.
88 HRW-Americas, *Haiti: Thirst for Justice*, provides a scorching critique, pp. 24–7; Maguire et al., *Haiti Held Hostage*, provides a moderate view, pp. 63–4.
89 HRW-Americas, *Haiti: Thirst for Justice*; Stotsky, 'Haiti: Searching for Alternatives'.
90 On victims, see MICIVIH, *Haïti: Droits de l'homme*.
91 See e.g. Africa Watch, *South Africa*.
92 Dumisa Ntsebeza, TRC Commissioner and Head of TRC's Investigative Unit, presentation at Oxford Conference. This analysis was helped in particular by discussions with Ntsebeza; Charles Villa Vicencio, TRC Researcher (both at Oxford Conference); Leslie Gambie, Counsellor, South African Permanent Mission to the UN (New York, 01.10.1997). I am also grateful to Alex Boraine and Justice Richard Goldstone for positive feedback on my analysis in general and South Africa in particular, at the Stockholm Seminar.
93 Britain, 'Outrage over Amnesty'.
94 Mamdani argues this in 'Denial of Justice' and 'Reconciliation without Justice'. See Krog, *Country of my Skull*, on the white community's varied reactions throughout the TRC process.
95 McGreal, 'South Africa's "Guilty"'.
96 Du Toit cited in HLS, *Truth Commissions*, p. 28.
97 Sean Kaliski is cited in Krog, *Country of my Skull*, p. 129.
98 Graybill, 'South Africa's Truth', p. 62; reiterated by my interviewees.
99 Mamdani, 'Denial of Justice', p. 12.
100 Hayner, 'Fifteen Truth Commissions', p. 170.
101 My views on Mozambique in this chapter were shaped by interviews and discussions with: Ambassador Carlos dos Santos, Permanent Representative of Mozambique to the UN (in New York, 30.09.1997); Priscilla Hayner, TC expert (in New York, 03.09.1997); Miguel de Brito, War-torn Societies Project, Mozambique (in Geneva, 02.07.1998); José Campino, former UN officer in Mozambique (also with UNTAG) (in New York, 01.10.1997).
102 See Armon et al., *Mozambican Peace Process*.
103 Comment by Ramirez at Oxford Conference.
104 This view is not radical. It is echoed by Zalaquett, a great supporter of TCs: 'truth commissions are not a simple recipe for every transitional situation. They are only part of a more complex policy to address the past.' Cited in HLS, *Truth Commissions*, p. 29.
105 André Du Toit says, 'Perhaps we assume in trials that the focus on the perpetrator is compatible with the victim's interests. We assume, then, that the victim desires punishment of the perpetrator. . . I do not believe all victims think this way. Many are more interested in the restoration of their human and civic dignity. This may be difficult to attain in the adversarial context of trials.' HLS, *Truth Commissions*, p. 36.

106 For instance, in the 'interdisciplinary discussion' in HLS, *Truth Commissions*, trials are the only alternative raised. In *Between Vengeance and Forgiveness*, Minow provides about the most thoughtful, balanced, in-depth study of this subject. Yet she too focuses almost exclusively on trials and TCs. She usefully includes a full chapter on reparations, but cautions that reparations should not displace trials and TCs (p. 117). She alludes quickly only in her conclusion to 'other possibilities' like purges and memorials (pp. 136–45). An exception is Zalaquett in 'Confronting Human Rights Violations'. Although he sees truth as the priority, he acknowledges reparation, prevention through institutional reform, punishment including non-custodial punishment, and clemency. David Crocker is also cautiously open-minded in 'Reckoning with Past Wrongs'. A growing receptivity to alternatives may be imminent.

107 Groth, *Namibia*. Dobell reviews the book in 'Silence in Context'.

108 The list was entitled 'Their Blood Waters our Freedom' and released symbolically on Heroes Day, 26.08.1996. The list fell short of the 11,000 Namibians SWAPO so far had claimed died during the struggle. Dobell, 'Silence in Context', p. 382.

109 *Africa Confidential*, 41, 18 (2000), p. 8.

110 ICJ, *Justice not Impunity*; Popkin and Bhuta, 'Latin American Amnesties'.

111 Buergenthal, 'UN Truth Commission', pp. 319–20; interview.

112 Wilson, 'Violent Truths', p. 24.

113 Ibid. Arnault vehemently defended this conditionality in the Washington Conference.

114 Ibid.

115 Campbell, 'Justice in Sight'; Campbell and Tuckman, 'Guatemalan Leader Faces Genocide Charges'.

116 HRW-Americas, *Haiti: Thirst for Justice*; Maguire et al., *Haiti Held Hostage*, pp. 39–41; Arthur, *After the Dance*, pp. 11–15.

117 Graybill, 'South Africa's Truth', pp. 45, 57–9. Ntsebeza explained the procedure at the Oxford Conference. Krog, *Country of my Skull*, provides insights.

118 Zalaquett is cited in Boraine et al., *Dealing with the Past*, p. 106.

119 Many are discussed in Kritz, *Transitional Justice*, vols 1–2, covering mainly Latin American and Central and Eastern European transitions. They are much less discussed today, although Minow is an exception.

120 UN, 'Study Concerning Right to Restitution', para. 27.

121 Brownlie, *Principles of Public International Law*, p. 458. Discussion in Lutz, 'After the Elections'.

122 UN, 'Study Concerning Right to Restitution', para. 26.

123 Brownlie, *Principles of Public International Law*, pp. 458–9.

124 Zalaquett in Boraine et al., *Dealing with the Past*, pp. 47–53.

125 Danieli, 'Preliminary Reflections', p. 580; on education, pp. 580–1.

126 *Keesings*, 2000.

127 Krog notes that responses until December 1998 were disappointingly few in *Country of my Skull*.

128 See Chirwa, 'Collective Memory', on UNESCO.
129 e.g. Schwartz, 'Lustration in Eastern Europe'; Boraine et al., *Dealing with the Past*, pp. 57–86.
130 Johnstone, *Rights and Reconciliation*, p. 33. Discussion with Howland who noted that the work of NGOs was crucial for the Ad Hoc Commission, whose initial 3-month mandate would have rendered a full investigation impossible. A group of NGOs sympathetic to the FMLN conducted a lengthy and sophisticated investigation of human rights records of the military on their own and handed their report to the Ad Hoc Commission, which made significant use of it. Howland worked for the NGO conducting the investigation.
131 Graybill, 'South Africa's Truth', p. 47. See Mbigi and Maree, *Ubuntu*.
132 Despite these limitations, the TC performed creditably and its 1999 report went further than expected.
133 Wilson, 'Violent Truths'; personal account provided by Edgar Ramirez, Director of REMHI, at the Oxford Conference. My analysis was also helped by interviews with Cleves and Cook (cited in ch. 3).
134 This is Ramirez's own account; Wilson, 'Violent Truths', reports over 300 mass graves being identified by 1997, p. 22.
135 *The Economist*, 'A Bishop Dead'.
136 Lanchin, 'Guatemala Admits Killings'; Lanchin, 'Another Prosecutor Flees'.
137 Interviews.
138 This account draws on Honwana, 'Sealing the Past'; Chirwa, 'Collective Memory'; and interviews.
139 Pankhurst, 'Issues of Justice', p. 34.
140 Minow, *Between Vengeance and Forgiveness*, p. 135.
141 Comments by Van Zyl and Graeme Simpson, Director, Centre for the Study of Violence and Reconciliation, Johannesburg, respectively, at ACUNS Conference.
142 Minow, *Between Vengeance and Forgiveness*, pp. 61–70.
143 Du Toit cited in HLS, *Truth Commissions*, p. 28.
144 Jeannette Fourie cited in Krog, *Country of my Skull*, p. 230.
145 Ibid., p. 133.
146 Mamdani, personal correspondence, 03.09.1998.
147 Boraine et al., *Dealing with the Past*, pp. 21–2.
148 Minow, *Between Vengeance and Forgiveness*, p. 82.
149 Kanan Makiya cited in HLS, *Truth Commissions*, p. 33.
150 Smyth's comments at Oxford Conference.
151 Mamdani, 'Justice without Reconciliation'.
152 Du Toit cited in HLS, *Truth Commissions*, p. 32.
153 Neier, *War Crimes*, pp. 210–28 (p. 210).
154 Ibid., pp. 211, 224, 221 in order.
155 Martin made this argument against collective guilt at CSF seminar.
156 Seider at Oxford Conference.
157 Villa-Vicencio at Oxford Conference.
158 Sachs cited in Boraine et al., *Dealing with the Past*, p. 130.

Chapter 5   Alleviating Effects or Targeting Causes?

1   Fitzgerald, 'Paying for War', p. 43.
2   An early version of this argument was presented at the British International Studies Association's 1998 conference, University of Sussex. My appreciation to James Boyce, Wendy Cue and Christien van den Anker for comments on that paper.
3   Causes are discussed in Stewart, 'Root Causes'; Van de Goor et al., *Between Development and Destruction*; UN, 'Causes of Conflict'; Crocker et al., *Managing Global Chaos*; Duffield, *Global Governance*, ch. 5.
4   Smith, *State of War*, pp. 14–15.
5   Stewart, 'Root Causes', p. 1; on horizontal vs. vertical inequality, pp. 17–20; on types of inequality, pp. 12–14.
6   Maguire, *Haiti Held Hostage*, pp. 13–19.
7   Stewart, 'Root Causes', p. 10; mobilization, pp. 7–12.
8   Duffield describes them as 'new barbarism' in *Global Governance*, pp. 109–13.
9   Smith, 'Legitimacy', p. 4; Smith, *State of War*, p. 30.
10 Agerbak, 'Breaking the Cycle', p. 27.
11 De Soysa, 'The Resource Curse'.
12 Keen, *Economic Functions*.
13 See esp. Duffield, 'Political Economy' and *Global Governance*.
14 Berdal and Malone, *Greed and Grievance*; Collier, 'Doing Well out of War'.
15 Keen, 'Incentives and Disincentives', p. 39.
16 Stewart, 'Root Causes', p. 17; 'other factors', pp. 14–17.
17 Duffield, *Global Governance*, esp. pp. 113–28 (p. 115). Strangely, this leading scholar of new wars avoids discussing the more pertinent issue of distributive inequality and its link to poverty in his detailed rebuttal of the development–conflict thesis. NB: I do not disfavour this broader approach to development, as long as it recognizes and addresses the linkages between inequality and conflict, and does not presume a simplistic poverty–conflict causality (see conclusion and ch. 6).
18 Pastor and Boyce, *Political Economy*, p. 30.
19 Andersen, 'Multilateral Development Assistance'.
20 UN, 'Causes of Conflict', p. 79.
21 Stewart summarizes studies by Morrison, Auvinen and Nafziger in 'Root Causes', pp. 18–19.
22 Hintjens, 'Explaining the 1994 Genocide', p. 247.
23 Andersen, 'Multilateral Development Assistance'.
24 Figures in Seider, 'Reframing Citizenship', p. 68; Spence et al., *Promise and Reality*, p. 37.
25 Johnstone suggests that 14 families controlled most land, *Rights and Reconciliation*, p. 11. Boyce suggests the number is closer to 60 families, personal correspondence, 13.01.1999.

26　Costello, 'Historical Background'.

27　UNDP, 'Draft Advisory Note'.

28　Arthur, *After the Dance*, p. 9. Maguire, *Haiti Held Hostage*, pp. 13–19. My analysis of Haiti was assisted by interviews with Marx Aristide, former Director of Washington Office on Haiti (in Washington, DC, 28.10.1998), Francesc Vendrell, senior official at UN DPA, and peace negotiator in El Salvador and Haiti, as also interviews cited earlier, particularly: Lelong, Neild, Cue, Martin, O'Neill.

29　World Bank, *Social Indicators, 1996*, p. 317.

30　Klasen, 'Poverty and Inequality', pp. 7, 13.

31　Fawcett, *Cambodia*, p. 71; Mydans, 'Cambodia's Killing Fields'.

32　Interviews with Ambassador dos Santos, de Brito cited earlier; analyses in Armon et al., *Mozambican Peace Process*; Vines, *RENAMO*.

33　*Africa Confidential*, 'Flood Relief–Debt Relief', p. 5; 'Still Resisting'. Confidential discussion with senior Mozambican diplomat (November 2000).

34　Boyce, 'Reconstruction and Democratization', p. 1.

35　Naim, 'Washington Consensus'.

36　Stiglitz, 'More Instruments'. Stiglitz admits the Consensus's shortcomings and mistakes made.

37　e.g. Colclough and Manor, *States or Markets?*, pp. 238–59.

38　Alesina, 'Political Models', p. 37.

39　Detailed discussion in Carbonnier, *Conflict*, pp. v–vii; Fitzgerald, 'Paying for War', pp. 53–8.

40　Pastor and Boyce, *Political Economy*, p. 19.

41　Carbonnier, *Conflict*, p. viii. Italics in original.

42　Stiglitz's conclusion in 'More Instruments'. Italics added.

43　Béteille, *Social Inequality*, p. 364.

44　Leading development economists then shared this belief. Gunnar Myrdal claimed, 'That in the Western countries social equalization goes together with economic growth in circular causation, and with cumulative effects, is to me quite evident.' Béteille, *Social Inequality*, p. 364.

45　See Boyce, 'Disasters'; Pastor and Boyce, *Political Economy*; Weinberg, 'Role of Multilateral Development Banks'.

46　See detailed survey in Carbonnier, *Conflict*, pp. 44–54.

47　Alesina and Rodrik, 'Distribution, Political Conflict', pp. 23, 40, 46. Their findings apply to democracies, because they rely on voters expressing preferences, and could be stretched to other regimes where citizens have a voice.

48　Persson and Tabellini, 'Growth, Distribution', p. 18. They also present their previous studies.

49　Studies by Bertola, Alesina and Rodrik, discussed in Persson and Tabellini, 'Growth, Distribution', pp. 6–7.

50　Study by Murphy, Shleifer and Vishny, cited in Persson and Tabellini, 'Growth, Distribution', p. 20 n. 14.

51　Pastor and Boyce, *Political Economy*, p. 3.

52 Ibid., p. 31. They also regard as necessary greater investment in 'human, natural and physical capital' and democratization, that is, better distribution of power.

53 Fitzgerald persuasively argues why the orthodox structural adjustment package is counter-productive in wartime economies, in 'Paying for War', esp. pp. 55–8.

54 This section draws on Carbonnier, *Conflict*; Weinberg, 'Role of Multilateral Development Banks'; Boyce, 'Disasters'; Pastor and Boyce, *Political Economy*; Boyce and Pastor, 'Macroeconomic Policy'.

55 World Bank, *Post Conflict Reconstruction*.

56 The World Bank provides a critical self-evaluation and discusses these three cases in Kreimer et al., *World Bank's Experience* – political realities, pp. xvi, 34; case studies, pp. 57–65.

57 My analysis of the Bank and Fund draw on their publications as well as discussions with several leading officials responsible for post-conflict reconstruction and for the countries discussed here (primarily in Washington, DC, 27–8.10.1998). For confidentiality, I don't cite them individually, but appreciate their candour and co-operation which helped my analysis.

58 IMF, 'IMF Assistance to Post-Conflict Countries'.

59 On El Salvador, see all listed articles by Boyce and Pastor; De Soto and Castillo, 'Obstacles to Peacebuilding'. On Mozambique, Hanlon, *Peace without Profit*; Willett, 'Ostriches, Wise Old Elephants'. On Cambodia, see Paris, 'Peacebuilding'; Kreimer et al., *World Bank's Experience*. Interviews and discussions that helped my analysis were with: Marx Aristide; Stephanie Weinberg, IFI expert with intimate knowledge of El Salvador peace negotiations and political economy (in Washington, DC, 28.10.1998); Geoffrey Thale, expert on El Salvador and Guatemala at WOLA (in Washington, DC, 27.10.1998).

60 Fitzgerald, 'Paying for War', p. 58.

61 Richardson and Chery, 'Haiti's not for Sale', pp. 32–3. They note that the Mev family officially submitted only one bid for the cement factory, but was apparently in by proxy on all eight bids submitted by international firms. Rampant tax evasion by the rich, causing resentment among the poor, was also observed by some of my interviewees. Richardson and Chery note one example: of illegal hook-ups responsible for the electricity company's poor performance, only 13 per cent are by the poor while 37 per cent are by the rich (p. 34).

62 Ibid., p. 32. Arthur, *After the Dance*, pp. 33–4.

63 Interview with senior WB official.

64 Kennedy and Tilly, 'Against the Death Plan', p. 11.

65 Ibid., p. 11. Also Richardson and Chery, 'Haiti's not for Sale', p. 55; Arthur, *After the Dance*, p. 33. NB: While Kennedy and Tilly note that all SOEs went into surplus, Arthur lists only flour, cement and port authorities making profits. It should be noted that WB officials were dismissive of this claim, although IMF officials acknowledge that Teleco made profits.

66 Keen, 'Incentives and Disincentives', p. 40.
67 Boyce's observation, based on his research in Cambodia in summer 1998 (correspondence, 13.01.1999).
68 Verhoogen, 'US–Haiti Connection', p. 8. He lists and describes several. NB: Although producing for foreign markets, not all plants are foreign-owned. Many are Haitian-owned, making this point also relevant to export-promotion plants.
69 Arthur, *After the Dance*, pp. 31–2.
70 All figures from IMF, 'Haiti', p. 8, minimum wage: table 11.
71 Verhoogen, 'US–Haiti Connection', p. 10. NB: While this would be considered a violation of workers' rights in most Western societies, it was treated as economic logic in low-income Haiti to follow minimum wage law.
72 Verhoogen, 'US–Haiti Connection', p. 10. Kennedy and Tilly also note that the US government was 'bitterly opposed' to the increase, 'Against the Death Plan', p. 11. The IMF and WB's position on this issue is not documented, and did not emerge in my interviews.
73 Verhoogen, 'US–Haiti Connection', pp. 7–10.
74 IMF, 'Haiti', table 32 (p. 65).
75 Ibid. Tables 35 (p. 68) and 32 (p. 65). Food includes beverages, pharmaceuticals, oil and fats.
76 Kennedy and Tilly, 'Against the Death Plan', p. 10; Arthur, *After the Dance*, pp. 32–3.
77 Richardson and Chery, 'Haiti's not for Sale', p. 32.
78 Fitzgerald, 'Paying for War', p. 58. Although he is speaking of policies applied *during* wartime, this would apply equally to economies *emerging from* political crises or conflicts.
79 Boyce, 'Disasters', pp. 23–8. He notes that WB and IMF help arrange for debt reduction for indebted countries from other creditors, but have long insisted that their own debts be serviced as part of their policy.
80 Interview at WB. NB: At the Washington Conference a participant, Brad Adams, alleged that in Cambodia the post-election government diverted international aid to underwrite the cost of remobilizing the army, reinforcing the Bank's argument.
81 Oxfam International, 'HIPC Leaves Poor Countries'.
82 Paris, 'Peacebuilding', pp. 85–6; Fitzgerald, 'Paying for War', pp. 57–8, on impact of IFI policies.
83 Kreimer, *World Bank's Experience*, pp. xvi, 34, 58.
84 Maguire, *Haiti Held Hostage*, p. 8.
85 Reiterated by interviewees. Kennedy and Tilly, 'Against the Death Plan', p. 43.
86 Argued in Boyce and Pastor, 'Aid for Peace'; Boyce, 'Reconstruction and Democratization'.
87 Foley et al., *Land, Peace and Participation*, p. 8.
88 Ibid., p. 6.
89 Boyce, 'Reconstruction and Democratization', pp. 7–9.
90 Foley et al., *Land, Peace and Participation*, p. 6.

91 Arthur, *After the Dance*, pp. 35–6.
92 An involved UN official I interviewed, Vendrell, noted that unlike in El Salvador where the UN played the lead, in Haiti's negotiations the UN was gradually sidelined by the USA, and played a minor role in agenda-setting. On crisis, Gros, 'Haiti's Flagging Transition'.
93 Comment by Strobe Talbot to the US Senate Foreign Affairs Committee, cited in Arthur, *After the Dance*, p. 36.
94 Interview with an adviser to FMLN during peace negotiations, with long-term involvement in El Salvador, who preferred anonymity.
95 Confirmed by both NGO and IMF interviewees.
96 IMF, 'Haiti'; interviews with Neild and IMF staff.
97 Interview with IMF official involved in Namibia after transition, who noted that relations were mainly smooth.
98 Described by Namibian Foreign Minister in Weiland and Braham, *Namibian Peace Process*, pp. 168–70.
99 Dobell, 'SWAPO in Office'.
100 Leys, 'State and Civil Society', p. 197.
101 Leys, 'The Legacy'; Weiland and Braham, *Namibian Peace Process*, pp. 13–56.
102 SWAPO's position paper for the land conference, cited in Dobell, 'SWAPO in Office', p. 181.
103 Discussed in Dobell, 'SWAPO in Office'; Diescho, *The Namibian Constitution*, pp. 93–5.
104 Dobell, 'SWAPO in Office', pp. 181, 180.
105 *Africa Confidential*, 'Too Dry for Crops', p. 5; BBC, 'Namibia's Black Farmers Urge Land Reform'. BBC reports 35,000 Namibian farmers resettled since 1990.
106 Stiglitz, 'More Instruments'.
107 Wolfensohn, 'A New Framework'; 'A Proposal', p. 7.
108 Discussions with UNDP and WB officials.
109 Wolfensohn, 'The Challenge of Inclusion', p. 6.
110 All my IMF interviewees reflected this new attitude. They underlined the concept of 'quality growth', and the ongoing attitudinal change within IMF.
111 Interview at IMF.
112 Kreimer, *World Bank's Experience*, pp. 33–5.
113 Wolfensohn, 'People and Development', p. 3.
114 World Bank, 'Emergency Recovery Assistance'.
115 Kreimer, *World Bank's Experience*, pp. 53–5; interviews at WB Post-Conflict Unit.
116 Interviews at IMF.
117 Ibid.
118 Discussed in Boyce and Pastor, 'Aid for Peace'. They note that peace conditionality was applied intermittently by IFIs in Bosnia to gain compliance with the Dayton accords.
119 Boyce, 'Reconstruction and Democratization', p. 13. NB: Peace conditionality is an innovative idea, but may carry its own problems when

implemented. I do not personally commend or condemn the idea, but merely note it for the record.

120   Wolfensohn's Foreword in World Bank, *Post-Conflict Reconstruction*.

121   While I am cautiously optimistic, a long-term IFI-watcher, Boyce, remains sceptical about WB/IMF change (correspondence, 13.01.1999) and Oxfam's deputy International Director, Nick Stockton, claims my optimism is misplaced/erroneous.

122   Also in Ethiopia, Sudan and Somalia, which are not examined here. See Macrae and Zwi, *War and Hunger*.

123   Interviews at WB.

124   Paris, 'Peacebuilding', p. 88.

125   Spence et al., *Promise and Reality*, p. 52, citing commentator Carlos Rafael Soto, in the journal *El Gráfico*, on 08.05.1996.

126   Keen, 'Incentives and Disincentives', p. 139.

Chapter 6   Recapturing Justice from the Shadows of War

1   De Soto and Castillo, 'Obstacles to Peacebuilding'; Boyce and Pastor, 'Aid for Peace'; also Armon et al., *Negotiating Rights*; Spence et al., *Promise and Reality*, pp. 46–58. My comparative analysis draws heavily on a range of interviews cited earlier with people on all sides in both cases: NGO activists, UN and IFI officials, whom I do not cite individually.

2   Ironically, this land transfer was much less far-reaching and radical in scope and objective than the land reforms that had been installed – at US instigation, as a counter-insurgency measure – in the late 1970s–early 1980s precisely to stem the rising tide of rebellion and prevent outright warfare. The reforms, though quite progressive despite their anti-insurgency motivation, were implemented only in part and never completed; they never inspired the confidence of rebels and their peasantry sympathizers, and armed conflict erupted nonetheless (see e.g. Weinberg, 'Role of Multilateral Development Banks'). It is noteworthy that US pressure and the threat of imminent armed conflict were sufficient to force the government to implement a land reform at that time, whereas the negotiated end to 12 years of armed conflict was insufficient incentive to attempt reform on such a scale once more.

3   Allegedly, the business community became involved in the Guatemalan peace process only at a late stage, while in El Salvador businessmen played a key role in building momentum for peace, recognizing that peace was essential to revive the slumped economy.

4   Comments by Arnault at Washington Conference.

5   See Spence, *Promise and Reality*; Sanchez, 'Turmoil in Guatemala'.

6   Chester Crocker, former US Assistant Secretary of State for African Affairs, speaking of the Namibian settlement, is cited in Weiland and Braham, *Namibian Peace Process*, p. 45.

7   De Soto speaking at Washington Conference.

8   Ibid.
9   Miall et al., *Contemporary Conflict Resolution*, p. 198.
10 ITN, 'Milosevic Defends Role in Balkan Wars', 25.08.2001.
11 This is my personal analysis based on extensive reading and discussions with involved UN and NGO staff.
12 Asmal et al., *Reconciliation through Truth*, p. 75.
13 Interview with De Rover.
14 Plunkett, 'Reestablishing Law', p. 68.
15 The two processes contrasted starkly. In South Africa it took over two years and involved wide and varied consultations. In Namibia the constitution was drafted and agreed by consensus in just 60 days by the elected Consultative Assembly, with almost no public debate or consultation. Both are progressive and express eloquently their objective of promoting human dignity, justice and rights. Interviews with Paul Szasz, legal director in the office of the UN Special Representative in Namibia during UNTAG (in New York, 02.10.1997); Thornberry; Leslie Gambi, Counsellor, Permanent Mission of South Africa to the United Nations (in New York, 3.10.1997). Also see Weiland and Braham, *Namibian Peace Process*, pp. 163–80, 241–56.
16 The TRC was described as an experiment in restorative rather than retributive justice by Villa-Vicencio at Oxford Conference and Van Zyl at ACUNS Conference.
17 Becker et al., 'Therapy with Victims', p. 589.
18 Harris, *Cases and Materials*, p. 491.
19 Van Boven et al., 'Seminar on Right to Restitution', p. 502.
20 Cragg, *Practice of Punishment*, p. 171.
21 Ibid.
22 Of the many types of informal justice tried in recent decades and discussed in ch. 4, the concept of restorative justice has become popular recently among some proponents of transitional justice, particularly supporters of the TRC, as noted earlier. Restorative justice emerged in the context of penal reform in the UK, parts of the USA, and New Zealand, and has similar aims to reparative justice. It is mainly used to deal with occasional crime in peaceful societies rather than widespread brutal violations in times of conflict. Furthermore, restorative justice is susceptible to the criticisms levelled generally against informal justice, discussed in ch. 4. It is worthwhile to devise a new and distinct concept to draw attention and respond to the specific problems of post-conflict societies, where offenders and victims are numerous and offences are more violent and severe, and where techniques of restorative justice like victim–offender reconciliation are not practicable. Nevertheless, reparative justice development could benefit from the insights and experience of restorative justice.
23 Graybill, 'South Africa's Truth', p. 47; Mbigi and Maree, *Ubuntu*.
24 Asmal et al., *Reconciliation through Truth*, p. 214.
25 Discussions at Stockholm Seminar.
26 Cragg identifies difficulties of reparation (without specific reference to post-conflict cases), in *Practice of Punishment*, p. 172.

27 These concepts cannot be elaborated here. See UNDP, *Human Development Report 1994*; Cockell, 'Peacebuilding and Human Security'; Galtung, *Peace by Peaceful Means*, pp. 127–38, 265–74.
28 See Rawls, *Theory of Justice*, pp. 302–3, 60–83; Mani, 'Restoring Justice'; Woodman, 'Legal Pluralism'.
29 Boyce, 'Disasters'.
30 This point made by Boyce, 'Disasters', and Carbonnier, *Conflict, Post-war Rebuilding*.
31 Kennedy and Tilly, 'Against the Death Plan', p. 45.
32 Hence Paris's title, 'The Limits of Liberal Internationalism'.
33 Lanchin, 'Ex-Marxists Defeat Right'.
34 Interviews: Ambassador Castaneda; Weinberg; Thale.
35 This observation reported by Castaneda in interview.
36 Both quotes from Taylor, 'Conditions of an Unforced Consensus', p. 143.
37 Galtung, *Human Rights*, p. 1. The domination of the Security Council's Permanent Five over the UN, and the domination of the USA over both the Security Council and the BWI bear testimony to Galtung's point, notwithstanding the competent, multicultural, globally representative staff of the UN and BWI.
38 Taylor, 'Conditions of an Unforced Consensus', p. 143.

Bibliography

Abel, Richard, 'The Contradictions of Informal Justice', in Abel, *The Politics of Informal Justice*, vol. 1, pp. 267–313

—— (ed.), *The Politics of Informal Justice*, vol. 1: *The American Experience* (London: Academic Press, 1982)

—— (ed.), *The Politics of Informal Justice*, vol. 2: *Comparative Politics* (London: Academic Press, 1982)

Africa Confidential, 'After Sam, Maybe', 42, 10, 18 May 2001

—— 'Bizimungu Bust-up', 41, 7 (3), 31 March 2000

—— 'Flood Relief–Debt Relief', 41, 6, 17 March 2000, 3–4 (p. 4)

—— 'Kagame under Siege', 42, 13, 29 June 2001

—— 'Still Resisting', 41, 23, 24 November 2000

—— 'SWAPO Steamroller', 41, 2, 21 January 2000

—— 'Talks Break Down', 42, 8, 20 April 2001

—— 'Too Dry for Crops', 41, 14 (2000)

Africa Watch, *Accountability in Namibia: Human Rights and the Transition to Democracy* (New York: Human Rights Watch / Africa, 1992)

—— *Conspicuous Destruction: War, Famine and the Reform Process in Mozambique* (New York: Human Rights Watch, 1992)

—— *South Africa: Accounting for the Past – The Lessons for South Africa from Latin America* (New York: Human Rights Watch, 23 October 1992)

African Rights, *Rwanda: Death, Despair and Defiance* (London: African Rights, 1995)

Agerbak, Linda, 'Breaking the Cycle of Violence: Doing Development in Situations of Conflict', in Eade, *Development in States of War*, pp. 26–32

Alesina, Alberto, 'Political Models of Macroeconomic Policy and Fiscal Reforms', in Haggard, *Voting for Reform*, pp. 37–59

Alesina, Alberto and Dani Rodrik, 'Distribution, Political Conflict and Economic Growth: A Simple Theory and Some Empirical Evidence', in Cukierman et al., *Political Economy*, pp. 23–48

Americas Watch, *El Salvador: Accountability and Human Rights: The Report of the United Nations Commission on the Truth for El Salvador* (New York: Human Rights Watch / Americas, August 1993)

Andersen, Regine, 'How Multilateral Development Assistance Triggered the Conflict in Rwanda', *Third World Quarterly*, 21, 3 (2000), 441–56

Anstee, Margaret, *Report on the International Colloquium on Post-Conflict Reconciliation Strategies* (Stadtschlaining: Austrian Study Centre for Peace and Conflict Resolution, 1995)

Aquinas, St Thomas, *Summa Theologia*, excerpt in Porter (ed.), *Classics in Political Philosophy* (London: Prentice-Hall, 1989)

Aristotle, *Nicomachean Ethics*, tr. and ed. Martin Ostwald (New York: Macmillan Library of Liberal Arts, 1986)

——*The Politics* (Harmondsworth: Penguin, 1981)

Armon, Jeremy, Dylan Hendrickson and Alex Vines (eds), *The Mozambican Peace Process in Perspective*, Accord Issue 3 (London: Conciliation Resources, 1998)

Armon, Jeremy, Rachel Sieder and Richard Wilson (eds), *Negotiating Rights: The Guatemalan Peace Process*, Accord Issue 2 (London: Conciliation Resources, 1997)

Arthur, Charles, *After the Dance the Drum is Heavy – Haiti: One Year after the Invasion* (London: Haiti Support Group, 1995)

Asmal, Kader, Louise Asmal and Ronald Suresh Roberts, *Reconciliation through Truth: A Reckoning of Apartheid's Criminal Governance* (Claremont, SA: David Philip, 1996; Oxford: James Currey, 1997)

Associated Press, 'Haiti Raids Opposition Headquarters', 23 August 2001

Auerbach, Jerold, *Justice without Law?* (Oxford: Oxford University Press, 1983)

Austin, John, *The Province of Jurisprudence Determined* (1832; New York: Noonday Press, 1954)

Barker, Paul (ed.), *Living as Equals* (Oxford: Oxford University Press, 1996)

Barry, Brian, *Liberty and Justice: Essays in Political Theory* (Oxford: Clarendon, 1991)

——*Political Argument* (1965; London: Harvester Wheatsheaf, 1990)

——*A Treatise on Social Justice*, vol. 1: *Theories of Justice* (London: Harvester Wheatsheaf, 1989)

Bauer, Joanne and Daniel Bell (eds), *The East Asian Challenge for Human Rights* (Cambridge: Cambridge University Press, 1999)

BBC, 'Namibia's Black Farmers Urge Land Reform', 21 August 2001

—— 'Opposition Candidate Shot', 24 August 2001

Becker, David et al., 'Therapy with Victims of Political Repression in Chile: The Challenge of Social Reparation', in Kritz, *Transitional Justice*, pp. 583–92

Becker, Elizabeth, 'Reports Document Khmer Rouge Role in Torture and Killings', *International Herald Tribune*, 17 July 2001, p. 5

Beitz, Charles, 'Economic Rights and Distributive Justice in Developing Societies', *World Politics*, 33 (1981), 321–46

Beitz, Charles, Marshall Cohen, Thomas Scanlon, and John Simmons (eds), *International Ethics: A Philosophy and Public Affairs Reader* (Oxford/ Princeton: Princeton University Press, 1985)

Benedetti, Fanny and John Washburn, 'Drafting the International Criminal Court Treaty: Two Years to Rome and an Afterword on the Rome Diplomatic Conference', *Global Governance*, 5, 1 (1999), 1–38

Bentham, Jeremy, *An Introduction to the Principles of Morals and Legislation* (1789; New York: Hafner Press, 1948)

Berdal, Mats, *Disarmament and Demobilisation after Civil Wars*, Adelphi Paper 303 (Oxford: Oxford University Press, 1996)

Berdal, Mats and David Malone (eds), *Greed and Grievance: Economic Agendas in Civil Wars* (Boulder, Colo.: Lynne Reinner, 2000)

Bertram, Eva, 'Reinventing Governments: The Promise and Perils of United Nations Peacebuilding', *Journal of Conflict Resolution*, 39, 3 (1995), 387–418

Béteille, André (ed.), *Social Inequality* (Harmondsworth: Penguin, 1969)

Boraine, Alex, Janet Levy and Ronel Scheffer (eds), *Dealing with the Past: Truth and Reconciliation in South Africa* (Cape Town: Institute for Democracy in South Africa, 1997)

Boutros-Ghali, Boutros, *An Agenda for Peace 1995*, 2nd edn (New York: UN, 1995)

Bowcott, Owen, 'Aristide Bid to Win over Haiti Critics', *Guardian*, 29 November 2000

—— 'Violence and Boycott Mar Haitian Election Campaign', *Guardian*, 23 November 2000

Boyce, James, 'Disasters, Development and the Bretton Woods Institutions', paper prepared for UNDP, Project INT/93/709 (New York: UNDP, April 1994)

—— 'Reconstruction and Democratization: The International Financial Institutions and the Post-conflict Transitions in El Salvador and Guatemala', paper presented at 21st International Congress of Latin American Studies Association, Chicago, September 1998

Boyce, James and Manuel Pastor, 'Aid for Peace: Can International Financial Institutions Help Prevent Conflict?', *World Policy Journal* (summer 1998), 42–9

—— 'Macroeconomic Policy and Peace Building in El Salvador', in Kumar, *Rebuilding Societies*, pp. 287–314

Bratt, Duane, 'Peace over Justice: Developing a Framework for UN Peacekeeping Operations in Internal Conflicts', *Global Governance*, 5, 1 (1999), 63–82

Britain, Victoria, 'Outrage over Amnesty for Apartheid Killer', *Guardian*, 13 June 2000

Brody, Reed (ed.), *The Independence of Judges and Lawyers: A Compilation of International Standards*, special issue 25–6 (Geneva: Centre for the Independence of Judges and Lawyers, April–October 1990)

Brownlie, Ian, *Basic Documents on Human Rights*, 3rd edn (Oxford: Oxford University Press, 1992)
—— *Principles of Public International Law*, 4th edn (Oxford: Oxford University Press, 1990)
Buergenthal, Thomas, 'The United Nations Truth Commission for El Salvador', in Kritz, *Transitional Justice*, pp. 292–325
Campbell, Duncan, 'Guatemalan Rights Worker Attacked', *Guardian*, 6 September 2000
—— 'Justice in Sight for Victims', *Guardian*, 25 May 2000
Campbell, Duncan and Jo Tuckman, 'Guatemalan Leader Faces Genocide Charges', *Guardian*, 7 June 2001
Campbell, Tom, *Justice* (Basingstoke: Macmillan, 1988)
Carbonnier, Gilles, *Conflict, Post-war Rebuilding and the Economy* (Geneva: UNRISD, 1998)
Carnegie Commission on Preventing Deadly Conflict, *Preventing Deadly Conflict* (New York: Carnegie Corporation, 1997)
Chirwa, Wiseman, 'Collective Memory and the Process of Reconciliation and Reconstruction', *Development in Practice*, 7 (1997), 479–86
Chopra, Jarat, *Peace Maintenance: The Evolution of International Political Authority* (London: Routledge, 1999)
—— (ed.), *The Politics of Peace Maintenance* (London: Lynne Reinner, 1998)
Cockell, John, 'Conceptualising Peacebuilding: Human Security and Sustainable Peace', in Pugh, *Regeneration*, pp. 15–34
—— 'Peacebuilding and Human Security: Frameworks for International Responses to Internal Conflict', paper presented at Third Pan-European International Relations Conference, Vienna, September 1998
Colclough, Christopher and James Manor (eds), *States or Markets? Neoliberalism and the Development Policy Debate* (Oxford: Clarendon, 1991)
Collier, Paul, 'Doing Well out of War: An Economic Perspective', in Berdal and Malone, *Greed and Grievance*, pp. 91–111
Commission on Global Governance, *Our Global Neighbourhood* (Oxford: Oxford University Press, 1995)
Corden, Anne, Keith Tolley, and Eileen Robertson (eds), *Meeting Needs in an Affluent Society: A Multi-disciplinary Perspective* (Aldershot: Avebury, 1992)
Costa, Gino, 'The United Nations and Reform of the Police in El Salvador', *International Peacekeeping*, 2 (1995), 365–90
Costello, Patrick, 'Historical Background', in Armon et al., *Negotiating Rights*, pp. 10–17
Cousens, Elizabeth and Chetan Kumar (eds), *Peacebuilding as Politics: Cultivating Peace in Fragile Societies* (Boulder, Colo.: Lynne Reinner, 2001)
Cragg, Wesley (ed.), *The Practice of Punishment: Towards a Theory of Restorative Justice* (London: Routledge, 1992)
—— *Retributivism and its Critics* (Stuttgart: Franz Steiner Verlag, 1992)
Crocker, Chester, Fen Osler Hampson and Pamela Aall (eds), *Managing Global Chaos: Sources of and Responses to International Conflict* (Washington, DC: US Institute of Peace, 1997)

Crocker, David, 'Reckoning with Past Wrongs: A Normative Framework', *Ethics and International Affairs*, 13 (1999), 43–64

Crossette, Barbara, 'UN Diplomats Search for Ways to Avoid Violence in Haiti', *New York Times*, 27 August 1999

CSCE (Conference on Security and Cooperation in Europe), 'Document of the Copenhagen Meeting of the Conference on the Human Dimension of the CSCE', Copenhagen, 5–29 June 1990

CSF (Common Security Forum), 'Seminar Report: Promoting the Rule of Law in Post-conflict Societies', seminar held on 26 September 1997, Harvard University, sponsored by the Common Security Forum, rapporteur Rama Mani

Cukierman, Alex et al. (eds), *Political Economy, Growth and Business Cycles* (London: MIT Press, 1992)

Danieli, Yael, 'Preliminary Reflections from a Psychological Perspective', in Kritz, *Transitional Justice*, pp. 572–82

David, Charles-Philippe, 'Does Peacebuilding Build Peace? Liberal (mis)steps in the Peace Process', paper presented to International Studies Association Annual Convention, Minneapolis, March 1998

De Rover, Cornelius, *To Serve and to Protect: Human Rights and Humanitarian Law for Police and Security Forces* (Geneva: International Committee of the Red Cross, 1998)

De Soto, Alvaro and Graciana del Castillo, 'Obstacles to Peacebuilding', *Foreign Policy*, 94 (1994), 69–83

De Soysa, Indra, 'The Resource Curse: Are Civil Wars Driven by Rapacity or Paucity?', in Berdal and Malone, *Greed and Grievance*, pp. 113–35

Dicey, A. V., *An Introduction to the Study of the Law of the Constitution* (1885; Basingstoke: Macmillan, 1959)

Diescho, Joseph, *The Namibian Constitution in Perspective* (Windhoek: Gamsberg Macmillan, 1994)

Dobell, Lauren, 'Silence in Context: Truth and/or Reconciliation in Namibia', *Journal of Southern African Studies*, 23 (1997), 371–82

—— 'SWAPO in Office', in Saul and Leys, *Namibia's Liberation Struggle*, pp. 171–95

Dodson, Michael and Donald Jackson, 'Re-inventing the Rule of Law: Human Rights in El Salvador', *Democratization*, 4, 4 (1997), 110–34

Duff, R. A., 'Alternatives to Punishment – or Alternative Punishments', in Cragg, *Retributivism*, pp. 43–68

—— 'Penal Communications: Recent Work in the Philosophy of Punishment', *Crime and Justice*, 20 (1996), 1–97

—— *Trials and Punishments* (Cambridge: Cambridge University Press, 1986)

Duffield, Mark, *Global Governance and the New Wars* (London: Zed Books, 2001)

Duffield, Mark, 'The Political Economy of Internal War: Asset Transfer, Complex Emergencies and International Aid', in Macrae and Zwi, *War and Hunger*, pp. 50–69

Dworkin, Ronald, 'Do Liberty and Equality Conflict?', in Barker, *Living as Equals*, pp. 39–58

——*Law's Empire* (London: Belknap Press of Harvard University Press, 1986)

——*A Matter of Principle* (London: Harvard University Press, 1987)

——'Political Judges and the Rule of Law', in Dworkin, *Matter of Principle*, pp. 9–32

——*Taking Rights Seriously* (London: Duckworth, 1977)

——'What is Equality? Part I: Equality of Welfare', *Philosophy and International Affairs*, 10, 3 (1981), 185–246

——'What is Equality? Part II: Equality of Resources', *Philosophy and International Affairs*, 10, 4 (1981), 283–345

——'Why Liberals Should Care about Equality', in Dworkin, *Matter of Principle*, pp. 206–13

The Economist, 'A Bishop Dead', 2 May 1998

——'Cambodia: Royal Assent', 21 November 1998

——'The Reckoning: Pinochet's Legacy to Chile', 18 September 1999

Eade, Deborah (ed.), *Development in States of War* (Oxford: Oxfam UK and Ireland, 1996)

Evans, Gareth, 'The Comprehensive Political Settlement to the Cambodia Conflict: An Exercise in Cooperating for Peace', in Smith, *International Peacekeeping*, pp. 1–14

——*Cooperating for Peace: The Global Agenda for the 1990s and Beyond* (St Leonards: Allen and Unwin, 1993)

Fawcett, Brian, *Cambodia: A Book for People Who Find Television Too Slow* (Vancouver: Talon Books, 1986)

Finnis, John, *Natural Law and Natural Rights* (Oxford: Clarendon, 1980)

Fitzgerald, E. V. K., 'Paying for the War: Macroeconomic Stabilisation in Poor Countries under Conflict Conditions', *Oxford Development Studies*, 25, 1 (1997), 43–64

Flathman, Richard, 'Liberalism and the Suspect Enterprise of Political Institutionalization: The Case of the Rule of Law', in Shapiro, *The Rule of Law*, pp. 297–327

Foley, Michael, George Vickers, and Geoff Thale, *Land, Peace and Participation: The Development of Post-war Agricultural Policy in El Salvador and the Role of the World Bank* (Washington, DC: WOLA, June 1997)

Fuller, Lon, *The Morality of Law* (1964; London: Yale University Press, 1969)

Galtung, Johan, *Human Rights in Another Key* (Cambridge: Polity, 1994)

——*Peace by Peaceful Means: Peace and Conflict, Development and Civilisation* (London: Sage, 1996)

——'Three Approaches to Peace: Peacebuilding, Peacekeeping and Peacemaking', in *Peace, War and Defence: Essays in Peace Research*, vol. 2 (Copenhagen: Christian Ejlers, 1975), pp. 282–304

Ganzlass, Martin, 'Restoration of the Somali Justice System', *International Peacekeeping*, 3, 1 (1996), 113–38

Gaus, Gerald, 'Public Reason and the Rule of Law', in Shapiro, *The Rule of Law*, pp. 328–63

Golding, Martin, *Philosophy of Law* (Englewood Cliffs, NJ: Prentice-Hall, 1975)

Goldman, Anthony, 'UN Moves on Sierra Leone Court', *Financial Times*, 26 July 2001

Goodhand, Jonathan and David Hulme, 'From Wars to Complex Political Emergencies: Understanding Conflict and Peacebuilding in the New World Disorder', *Third World Quarterly*, special issue on Complex Political Emergencies, 20, 1 (1999), 13–26

Graybill, Lyn, 'South Africa's Truth and Reconciliation Commission: Ethical and Theological Perspectives', *Ethics and International Affairs*, 12 (1998), 43–62

Griffiths, Ann (ed.), *Building Peace and Democracy in Post-Conflict Societies*, workshop proceedings, Dalhousie: Centre for Foreign Policy Studies, Dalhousie University, 1998

Gros, Jean-Germain, 'Haiti's Flagging Transition', *Journal of Democracy*, 8, 4 (1997), 94–109

Groth, Siegfried, *Namibia: The Wall of Silence. The Dark Days of the Liberation Struggle* (Cape Town: David Philip, 1995)

Gunson, Phil, 'Guatemala's "Peace without Justice"', *Guardian*, 28 December 1996

Haggard, Steven (ed.), *Voting for Reform: Democratic Liberalization and Economic Adjustment* (New York: Oxford University Press for IBRD/World Bank, 1994)

Hampton, Jean, 'An Expressive Theory of Retribution', in Cragg, *Retributivism*, pp. 1–26

Hanlon, Joe, *Peace without Profit: How the IMF Blocks Rebuilding in Mozambique* (Dublin: International African Institute and Irish Mozambique Solidarity, 1996)

Harris, D. J., *Cases and Materials on International Law*, 4th edn (London: Sweet and Maxwell, 1991)

Hart, H. L. A., *The Concept of Law*, 2nd edn (1961; Oxford: Clarendon, 1994)

—— 'Positivism and the Separation of Law and Morals', in Ronald Dworkin (ed.), *The Philosophy of Law* (Oxford: Oxford University Press, 1977)

—— 'Prolegomenon to the Principles of Punishment', in *Punishment and Responsibility: Essays in the Philosophy of Law* (Oxford: Clarendon, 1968), pp. 1–27

—— *Punishment and Responsibility: Essays in the Philosophy of Law* (Oxford: Clarendon, 1968)

Hayek, Friederich, *The Road to Serfdom* (1944; London: Ark Paperbacks, 1986)

Hayner, Priscilla, 'Fifteen Truth Commissions – 1974 to 1994: A Comparative Study', in Kritz, *Transitional Justice*, pp. 225–61

Hayner, Priscilla, 'In Pursuit of Justice and Reconciliation: Contributions of Truth Telling', presented at conference on Comparative Peace Processes in Latin America, Woodrow Wilson International Center for Scholars, Washington, DC, March 1997

—— 'International Guidelines for the Creation and Operation of Truth Commissions: A Preliminary Proposal', *Law and Contemporary Problems*, 59, 4 (1996), 168–75

Hayry, Mätti, 'In Defence of the Utilitarian Theory of Punishment', in Cragg, *Retributivism*, pp. 129–48

Hegel, G. W. F., *Elements of the Philosophy of Right*, ed. Allen Wood, tr. H. B. Nisbet (Cambridge: Cambridge University Press, 1991)

Heininger, Janet, *Peacekeeping in Transition: The United Nations in Cambodia* (New York: Twentieth Century Fund Press, 1994)

Held, David (ed.), *Political Theory Today* (Cambridge: Polity, 1991)

Hemisphere Initiatives, *Endgame: A Progress Report on Implementation of the Salvadoran Peace Accords* (Cambridge, Mass.: HI, 1992)

—— *The Salvadoran Peace Accords and Democratization: A Three-year Progress Report and Recommendations* (Cambridge, Mass.: HI, 1995)

Henkin, Alice (ed.), *Honoring Human Rights and Keeping the Peace: Lessons from El Salvador, Cambodia and Haiti. Recommendations for the United Nations* (Washington, DC: Aspen Institute, 1995)

—— (ed.), *Honoring Human Rights: From Peace to Justice. Recommendations to the International Community* (Washington, DC: Aspen Institute, 1998)

Hintjens, Helen, 'Explaining the 1994 Genocide in Rwanda', *Journal of Modern African Studies*, 37, 2 (1999), 241–86

HLS (Harvard Law School), *Truth Commissions: A Comparative Assessment*, Report of an Interdisciplinary Discussion sponsored by Human Rights Program, May 1996 (Cambridge, Mass.: Harvard Law School, 1997)

Hoffman, Stanley, *Duties beyond Borders* (Syracuse, NY: Syracuse University Press, 1981)

Honwana, Alcinda, 'Sealing the Past, Facing the Future: Trauma Healing in Rural Mozambique', in Armon et al., *Mozambican Peace Process*, pp. 75–81

HRW-Americas (Human Rights Watch-Americas), *Haiti: Thirst for Justice. A Decade of Impunity in Haiti*, 8/7(B), September 1996 (New York: Human Rights Watch/Americas, 1996)

—— *The Human Rights Record of the Haitian National Police* (New York/ Washington, DC: Human Rights Watch/Americas National Coalition for Haitian Rights (NCHR) WOLA, January 1997)

Hutchinson, Allan and Patrick Monahan (eds), *The Rule of Law: Ideal or Ideology?* (Toronto: Carswell, 1987)

ICHRP (International Council on Human Rights Policy), *Taking Duties Seriously: Individual Duties in International Human Rights Law: A Commentary* (Versoix, Switzerland: International Council on Human Rights Policy, 1999)

ICJ (International Commission of Jurists), *Development, Human Rights and the Rule of Law* (Oxford: Pergamon, 1981)

—— 'The Judiciary and the Legal Profession under the Rule of Law', Congress of Delhi, 1959 (Geneva: ICJ, 1993)

—— *Justice Not Impunity*, report of International Meeting on Impunity of Perpetrators of Gross Human Rights Violations, organized by International Commission of Jurists, with National Consultative Human Rights Commission (France) in Geneva, 2–5 November 1992 (Geneva: ICJ, 1993)

—— *The Right to Reparation for Victims of Human Rights Violations: A Compilation of Essential Documents* (Geneva: ICJ, 1998)

IMF (International Monetary Fund), 'Haiti: Recent Economic Developments' (Washington, DC: IMF, July 1998)

—— 'IMF Assistance to Post-Conflict Countries', information brief (Washington, DC: IMF, 1998)

IRIN (UN Integrated Regional Information Network), 'The Rwandan Genocide Trials: Building Peace Through Justice', *IRIN Special Feature*, 1/97, 19 February 1997

ITN, 'Milosovic Defends Role in Balkan Wars', 25 August 2001

Jacoby, Susan, *Wild Justice: The Evolution of Revenge* (London: Collins, 1985)

Johnson, Tim, 'Truth Commissions Multiply', *Miami Herald*, 20 August 2001

Johnstone, Ian, *Rights and Reconciliation: UN Strategies in El Salvador* (Boulder, Colo.: Lynne Reinner, 1995)

Kant, Immanuel, *Perpetual Peace: A Philosophical Proposal*, tr. Helen O'Brien (London: Sweet and Maxwell, 1927)

Keen, David, *The Economic Functions of Violence in Civil Wars*, Adelphi Paper 320 (London: International Institute for Strategic Studies/Oxford University Press, 1998)

—— 'Incentives and Disincentives for Violence', in Berdal and Malone, *Greed and Grievance*, pp. 19–41

Keesings Report of World Events, May 2000

Kennedy, Marie and Chris Tilly, 'Up against the Death Plan: Haitians Resist U.S.-Imposed Economic Structuring', *Dollars and Sense* (March/April 1996), 6–11

Klasen, Stephan, 'Poverty and Inequality in South Africa', occasional paper, Common Security Forum, Cambridge University, January 1997

Kreimer, Alcira et al., *The World Bank's Experience with Post-conflict Reconstruction* (Washington, DC: WB Operations Evaluation Department, 1998)

Kritz, Neil (ed.), *Transitional Justice: How Emerging Democracies Reckon with Former Regimes*, vol. 1: *General Considerations* (Washington, DC: US Institute of Peace, 1995)

Krog, Antjie, *Country of my Skull* (Johannesburg: Random House, 1998)

Kumar, Krishna (ed.), *Rebuilding Societies after Civil War* (London: Lynne Reinner, 1997)

Kumar, Krishna et al., *Rebuilding Post-war Rwanda*, International Response to Conflict and Genocide: Lessons from the Rwanda Experience, 4 (Copenhagen: Steering Committee of the Joint Evaluation of Emergency Assistance to Rwanda, March 1996)

224 *Bibliography*

Lacey, Nicola, *State Punishment: Political Principles and Community Values* (London: Routledge, 1988)

Lanchin, Mike, 'Another Prosecutor Flees Guatemala', *Guardian*, 1 August 2001

—— 'Ex-Marxists Defeat Right at Polls in El Salvador', *Guardian*, 15 March 2000

—— 'Guatemala Admits Killings', *Guardian*, 11 August 2000

LCHR (Lawyers' Committee for Human Rights), *Prosecuting Genocide in Rwanda: The ICTR and National Trials* (New York: Lawyers' Committee for Human Rights, July 1997)

Lederach, John Paul, *Building Peace: Sustainable Reconciliation in Divided Societies* (Tokyo: United Nations University Press, 1997)

Leys, Colin, 'The Legacy: An Afterword', in Leys and Saul, *Namibia's Liberation Struggle*, pp. 196–203

—— 'State and Civil Society: Policing in Transition', in Leys and Saul, *Namibia's Liberation Struggle*, pp. 133–52

Leys, Colin and John Saul (eds), *Namibia's Liberation Struggle: The Two-Edged Sword* (London: James Currey, 1995)

Linz, Juan and Alfred Stepan, 'Toward Consolidated Democracies', *Journal of Democracy*, 7, 2 (1996), 14–33

Lucash, Frank (ed.), *Justice and Equality Here and Now* (Ithaca, NY: Cornell University Press, 1986)

Lutz, Ellen, 'After the Elections: Compensating Victims of Human Rights Abuses', in Kritz, *Transitional Justice*, pp. 551–65

McAdams, James (ed.), *Transitional Justice and the Rule of Law in New Democracies* (Notre Dame, Ind.: University of Notre Dame Press, 1997)

McGreal, Chris, 'South Africa's "Guilty" Reluctant to Sign up', *Guardian*, 20 December 2000

—— 'Tutsi Soldier to Lead Rwanda', *Guardian*, 25 March 2000

McIntyre, Alasdair, *Whose Justice? Which Rationality?* (London: Duckworth, 1988)

McNamara, Dennis, 'UN Human Rights Activities in Cambodia: An Evaluation', in Henkin, *Honoring Human Rights*, pp. 57–82

McNeil, Donald, 'Tangled War in Congo Now Snares Namibia', *New York Times*, 6 August 1999

Macrae, Joanne and Anthony Zwi (eds), *War and Hunger: Rethinking International Responses to Complex Emergencies* (London: Zed Books, 1994)

Maguire, Robert et al., *Haiti Held Hostage: International Responses to the Quest for Nationhood 1986–1996*, Occasional Paper 23 (Providence, RI: Thomas J. Watson Institute for International Studies, 1996)

Mamdani, Mahmood, *Citizen and Subject: Contemporary Africa and the Legacy of Late Colonialism* (Princeton: Princeton University Press, 1996)

—— 'Reconciliation without Justice', *Southern African Review of Books*, 46 (November–December 1996), 3–5

—— 'When does Reconciliation turn into a Denial of Justice?', address to Human Sciences Research Council, Pretoria, 18 February 1998

Mani, Rama, 'Conflict Resolution, Justice and Law: Rebuilding the Rule of Law in the Aftermath of Complex Political Emergencies', *International Peacekeeping*, 5, 3 (1998), 1–25

—— 'Contextualising Police Reform: Security, the Rule of Law and Post-conflict Peacebuilding', in Tor Tanke Holm and Espen Barth Eide (eds) *Peacebuilding and Police Reform* (London: Frank Cass, 2000), pp. 9–26

—— 'Restoring Justice in the Aftermath of Conflict: Bridging the Gap between Theory and Practice', in Anthony Coates (ed.), *International Justice* (London: Ashgate, 1999), pp. 264–99

—— 'Restoring the Rule of Law in Post-conflict Societies', in Thandika Mkandawire et al., *Common Security and Civil Society in Africa* (Uppsala: Nordiska Africainstitutet, 1999)

—— 'The Rule of Law or the Rule of Might? Restoring Legal Justice in Post-conflict Societies', in Pugh, *Regeneration*, pp. 90–111

Marshall, Tony, 'Out of Court: More or Less Justice?', in Matthews, *Informal Justice*, pp. 25–50

Matthews, Roger (ed.), *Informal Justice* (London: Sage, 1988)

—— 'Reassessing Informal Justice', in Matthews, *Informal Justice*, pp. 1–25

Maynard, Kimberley, 'Rebuilding Community: Psychosocial Healing, Reintegration and Reconciliation at the Grassroots Level', in Kumar, *Rebuilding Societies*, pp. 203–26

Mbigi, Lovemore and Jenny Maree, *Ubuntu: The Spirit of African Transformation Management* (Randburg: Knowledge Resources, 1995)

Megone, C. B., 'What is Need?', in Corden et al., *Meeting Needs*, pp. 12–29

Mejía, Carlos Rodrigues, 'Amnesty, Pardon and Other Similar Measures', in ICJ, *Justice Not Impunity*, pp. 169–82

Mendez, Juan, 'In Defense of Transitional Justice', in McAdams, *Transitional Justice*, pp. 1–26

Merkelbach, B.-H., *Summa theologiae moralis* (Paris: 1938)

Miall, Hugh, Oliver Ramsbotham and Tom Woodhouse, *Contemporary Conflict Resolution: The Prevention, Management and Transformation of Deadly Conflicts* (Cambridge: Polity, 1999)

MICIVIH (UN/OAS Joint Civilian Mission in Haiti), *Häiti: Droits de l'homme et réhabilitation des victimes* (Port au Prince/Geneva: Henri Deschamps, 1997)

—— 'La Police Nationale d'Haïti et les droits de l'homme', report, July 1996

—— 'Les prisons en Häiti', Port au Prince, report, July 1997

—— Working Group on the Justice System, 'Executive Summary: Analysis and Evaluation of the Haitian Justice System', 18 March 1994

Miller, David, 'Recent Theories of Social Justice', *British Journal of Political Science*, 21 (1991), 371–91

—— *Social Justice* (Oxford: Clarendon 1976; 2nd edn 1979)

Miller, David and Michael Walzer (eds), *Justice, Pluralism and Equality* (Oxford: Oxford University Press, 1995)

Minow, Martha, *Between Vengeance and Forgiveness: Facing History after Genocide and Mass Violence* (Boston: Beacon Press, 1998)

Moore, Jonathan, *The UN and Complex Emergencies: Rehabilitation in Third World Transitions* (Geneva: UNRISD, 1996)

Murphy, Jeffrie, *Retribution, Justice and Therapy* (Dordrecht / London: Reidel, 1979)

Murphy, Jeffrie and Jean Hampton, *Forgiveness and Mercy* (Cambridge: Cambridge University Press, 1988)

Mydans, Seth, 'Cambodia's Bygones Resist Being Bygones', *New York Times*, 3 January 1999

—— 'In Cambodia's Killing Fields, Even the Future Died', *New York Times*, 10 January 1999

—— 'UN Ends Cambodia Talks on Trials for Khmer Rouge', *New York Times*, 9 February 2002

Naim, Moises, 'Washington Consensus or Washington Confusion?', *Foreign Policy* (spring 2000), 86–103

Nathan, Laurie, 'Human Rights, Reconciliation and Conflict in Independent Namibia: The Formation of the Namibian Army and Police Force', in Rupesinghe, *Internal Conflict*, pp. 152–68

NCHR (National Coalition for Haitian Rights), *Can Haiti's Police Reforms be Sustained?* (New York / Washington, DC: National Coalition for Haitian Rights with WOLA, January 1998)

Neier, Aryeh, *War Crimes: Brutality, Genocide, Terror and the Struggle for Justice* (New York: Times Books, 1998)

Neild, Rachel, *Overcoming History: Police Reform in Haiti* (Washington, DC: WOLA, February 1998)

—— *Policing Haiti: Preliminary Assessment of the New Civilian Security Force* (Washington, DC: WOLA, September 1995)

Neumann, Franz, *The Rule of Law: Political Theory and the Legal System in Modern Society* (Leamington Spa: Berg, 1986)

Nozick, Robert, *Anarchy, State and Utopia* (New York: Basic Books, 1974)

Nussbaum, Martha, 'Human Capabilities, Female Human Beings', in Nussbaum and Glover, *Women, Culture and Development*, pp. 61–104

—— 'In Defence of Universal Values', 1: 'Feminist Internationalism', Seeley Lectures in Political Theory, University of Cambridge, 9 March 1998

Nussbaum, Martha and Jonathan Glover (eds), *Women, Culture and Development: A Study of Human Capabilities* (Oxford: Clarendon, 1995)

Nussbaum, Martha and Amartya Sen, *The Quality of Life* (Oxford: Clarendon, 1993)

Oakley, Robert, Michael Dziedzic, Eliot Goldberg (eds), *Policing the New World Disorder: Peace Operations and Public Security* (Washington, DC: National Defense University Press, 1998)

O'Donnell, Guillermo, 'Illusions about Consolidation', *Journal of Democracy*, 7, 2 (1996), 34–51

O'Donnell, Guillermo and Philippe Schmitter, *Transitions from Authoritarian Rule: Tentative Conclusions about Uncertain Democracies* (Baltimore: Johns Hopkins University Press, 1986)

O'Neill, Onora, *Faces of Hunger: An Essay on Poverty, Justice and Development* (London: Allen and Unwin, 1986)

—— 'Justice, Capabilities and Vulnerabilities', in Nussbaum and Glover, *Women, Culture and Development*, pp. 140–52

—— *Towards Justice and Virtue: A Constructive Account of Practical Reasoning* (Cambridge: Cambridge University Press, 1996)

—— 'Transnational Justice', in Held, *Political Theory Today*, pp. 279–98

O'Neill, William, *No Greater Priority: Judicial Reform in Haiti* (New York: National Coalition for Haitian Rights, 1995)

Onishi, Norimitsu, 'Survivors Sadly Say, Yes, Reward the Tormentors', *New York Times*, 30 August 1999

Orentlicher, Diane, 'Settling Accounts: The Duty to Prosecute Human Rights Violations of a Prior Regime', in Kritz, *Transitional Justice*, pp. 375–416

Ourdan, Rémy, 'Au pays des âmes mortes', *Le Monde*, 31 March 1998

—— 'La guerre de l'ombre', part 3 of 'Rwanda, enquête sur un génocide', *Le Monde*, 2 April 1998

—— 'La réconciliation impossible', part 4 of 'Rwanda, enquête sur un génocide', *Le Monde*, 3 April 1998

—— 'Les yeux fermés', part 2 of 'Rwanda, enquête sur un génocide', *Le Monde*, 1 April 1998

—— 'Un tribunal loin du Rwanda', *Le Monde*, 4 May 1998

Oxfam International, 'HIPC Leaves Poor Countries Heavily in Debt', briefing paper prepared for IMF/World Bank annual meeting in Prague, 18 September 2000

Pankhurst, Donna, case study paper for Complex Political Emergencies Project, February 1998 p.26; 'Issues of Justice and Reconciliation in Complex Political Emergencies: Conceptualising Reconciliation, Justice and Peace', *Third World Quarterly*, 20, 1 (February 1999), 239–56

Paris, Roland, 'Peacebuilding and the Limits of Liberal Internationalism', *International Security*, 22, 2 (1997), 54–89

Pastor, Manuel and James Boyce, *The Political Economy of Complex Humanitarian Emergencies: Lessons from El Salvador*, UN University (UNU) and World Institute for Development Economics research, working paper 131 (Helsinki: UNU/WIDER, April 1997)

Persson, Torston and Guido Tabellini, 'Growth Distribution and Politics', in Cukierman et al., *Political Economy*, pp. 3–22

Plunkett, Mark, 'The Establishment of the Rule of Law in Post-conflict Peacebuilding', in Smith, *International Peacekeeping*

—— 'Reestablishing Law and Order in Peace-Maintenance', *Global Governance*, 4, 1 (1998), 61–80

Popkin, Margaret and Nehal Bhuta, 'Latin American Amnesties in Comparative Perspective: Can the Past be Buried?', *Ethics and International Affairs*, 13 (1999), 99–122

Popkin, Margaret, Jack Spence and George Vickers, *Justice Delayed: The Slow Pace of Judicial Reform in El Salvador* (Washington, DC: WOLA / HI, Cambridge, Mass., December 1994)

Porter, Jene (ed.), *Classics in Political Philosophy* (London: Prentice-Hall, 1989)

Prempeh, Kwasi, 'A New Jurisprudence for Africa', *Journal of Democracy*, 10, 3 (1999), 135–49

Preston, Rosemary, 'Integrating Fighters after War: Reflections on the Namibian Experience', *Journal of Southern African Studies*, 23, 3 (1997), 453–73

Prunier, Gérard, *The Rwanda Crisis: History of a Genocide* (London: Hurst, 1998)

Pugh, Michael, *Regeneration of War-torn Societies* (Basingstoke: Macmillan, 2000)

Ramsbotham, Oliver, 'Clausewitz in Reverse: The End of a Ten-year Experiment? Reflections on the UN's Post-Settlement Peacebuilding "Standard Operating Procedure", 1988–1998', paper presented at British International Studies Association Conference, Leeds, December 1997

Ratner, Steven, *The New UN Peacekeeping: Building Peace in Lands of Conflict after the Cold War* (Basingstoke: Macmillan, 1995)

Ratner, Steven and Jason Abrams, *Accountability for Human Rights Atrocities in International Law: Beyond the Nuremberg Legacy* (Oxford: Clarendon, 1997)

Rawls, John, *A Theory of Justice* (Oxford: Oxford University Press, 1971)

—— *Political Liberalism* (1993; New York: Columbia University Press, 1996)

Raz, Joseph, *The Authority of Law: Essays on Law and Morality* (Oxford: Clarendon, 1979)

Reiss, Hans (ed.), *Kant: Political Writings* (Cambridge: Cambridge University Press, 1991)

Reuters, 'Protesters Die in Mozambique', Maputo, 13 November 2000

Richardson, Laurie and Jean-Roland Chery, 'Haiti's not for Sale', *Convert Action Quarterly*, 55 (winter 1995–6), 30–7

Roberts, Adam and Richard Guelff (eds), *Documents on the Laws of War*, 2nd edn (Oxford: Clarendon, 1989)

Roht-Arriaza, Naomi (ed.), *Impunity and Human Rights in International Law and Practice* (Oxford: Oxford University Press, 1995)

Rohter, Larry, 'Political Feud Ravages Haiti: So Much for its High Hopes', *New York Times*, 18 August 1998

Rupesinghe, Kumar, 'The Disappearing Boundaries between Internal and External Conflicts', in Rupesinghe, *Internal Conflict and Governance*, pp. 1–26

—— (ed.), *Internal Conflict and Governance* (Basingstoke: Macmillan, 1992)

Sadurski, Wojciech, *Giving Desert its Due: Social Justice and Legal Theory* (Lancaster: D. Reidel, 1985)

Sanchez, Marcela, 'Turmoil in Guatemala', *Washington Post*, 15 August 2001

Saul, John and Colin Leys, *Namibia's Liberation Struggle: The Two-Edged Sword* (London: James Currey, 1995)

Schabas, William, 'Justice, Democracy and Impunity in Post-genocide Rwanda: Searching for Solutions to Impossible Problems', *Criminal Law Forum*, 7 (1996), 523–60

Schuett, Oliver, 'The International War Crimes Tribunal for Former Yugo-slavia and the Dayton Peace Agreement: Peace versus Justice?', *International Peacekeeping*, 4, 2 (1997), 91–114

Schwartz, Herman, 'Lustration in Eastern Europe', in Kritz, *Transitional Justice*, pp. 461–83

Seider, Rachel (ed)., *Central America: Fragile Transition* (Basingstoke: Macmillan / Institute of Latin American Studies, University of London, 1996)

—— 'Reframing Citizenship: Indigenous Rights, Local Power and the Peace Process in Guatemala', in Armon et al., *Negotiating Rights*, pp. 66–73

Sen, Amartya, *Development as Freedom* (New York: Anchor, 2000)

—— *Inequality Re-examined* (Oxford: Clarendon, 1992)

Sen, Amartya and Bernard Williams (eds), *Utilitarianism and Beyond* (Cambridge: Cambridge University Press / Editions de la Maison des Sciences de l'Homme, 1982)

Shapiro, Ian (ed.), *The Rule of Law, Nomos*, special issue 36 (London: New York University Press, 1994)

Shenon, Philip, 'UN Plans Joint War Crimes Tribunal for Khmer Rouge', *New York Times*, 12 August 1998

Sher, George, 'Ancient Wrongs and Modern Rights', *Philosophy and Public Affairs*, 10, 1 (1981), 3–17

Shihata, Ibrahim, 'Judicial Reform in Developing Countries and the Role of the World Bank', in *The World Bank in a Changing World*, vol. 2 (Dordrecht: Martinus Nijhoff, 1996), pp. 147–82

Skaar, Elin, 'Truth Commissions, Trials – or Nothing? Policy Options in Democratic Transitions', *Third World Quarterly*, 20 (1999), 1109–28

Smith, Dan, 'Legitimacy, Justice and Preventive Intervention', paper presented at seminar on 'Preventing Conflicts: Past Record and Future Challenges', Uppsala University, 20–2 August 1997

—— *The State of War and Peace Atlas*, with International Peace Research Institute, Oslo (London: Penguin, 1997)

Smith, Hugh (ed.), *International Peacekeeping: Building on the Cambodian Experience* (Canberra: Australian Defence Studies Centre, 1994)

Spence, Jack et al., *Promise and Reality: Implementation of the Guatemalan Peace Accords* (Cambridge, Mass.: HI, 1998)

Stanley, William, *Protectors or Perpetrators? The Institutional Crisis of the Salvadoran Civilian Police* (Cambridge, Mass.: WOLA / HI, 1996)

—— *Risking Failure: The Problems and Promise of the New Civilian Police in El Salvador* (Cambridge, Mass.: HI / WOLA, 1993)

Stanley Foundation, *Post-conflict Justice: The Role of the International Community*, Vantage conference report (Muscatine: Stanley Foundation, 1997)

Steiner, Henry and Philip Alston, *International Human Rights in Context: Law, Politics, Morals* (Oxford: Clarendon, 1996)

Stewart, Frances, 'The Root Causes of Conflict: Some Conclusions', Queen Elizabeth House working paper 16, Oxford University, June 1998

Stiglitz, Joseph, 'More Instruments and Broader Goals: Moving Toward the Post-Washington Consensus', 1998 WIDER Annual Lecture (Helsinki: WIDER, March 1998)

Stotsky, Irwin, 'Haiti: Searching for Alternatives', in Roht-Arriaza, *Impunity and Human Rights*, pp. 185–97

Taylor, Charles, 'Conditions of an Unforced Consensus on Human Rights', in Bauer and Bell, *The East Asian Challenge*, pp. 124–44

—— 'The Nature and Scope of Distributive Justice', in Lucash, *Justice and Equality*, pp. 34–67

Tomasi, John, 'Individual Rights and Community Values', *Ethics: An International Journal of Social, Political and Legal Philosophy*, 101, 3 (1991), 521–36

Tuckman, Jo, 'Lynch Mobs Alarmingly Active', *Guardian*, 19 July 2001

Tunick, Mark, *Punishment: Theory and Practice* (Oxford: University of California Press, 1992)

Umbreit, Mark, 'Violent Offenders and their Victims', in Wright and Galaway, *Mediation*, pp. 99–112

UN (United Nations), *Agreements on a Comprehensive Political Settlement of the Cambodia Conflict* (New York: UN Department of Public Information, 1992)

—— *El Salvador Agreements: The Path to Peace* (New York: UN Department of Public Information, with UN Observer Mission in El Salvador, 1992)

—— *Human Rights*, vol. 1: *A Compilation of International Instruments* (New York / Geneva: UN, 1988)

—— *Human Rights*, vol. 2: *Regional Instruments* (New York / Geneva: UN, 1997)

—— *The United Nations and Cambodia 1991–1995* (New York: UN Department of Public Information, 1995)

—— *The United Nations and El Salvador 1990–1995* (New York: UN Department of Public Information, 1995)

—— *The United Nations and Mozambique 1992–1995* (New York: UN Department of Public Information, 1995)

—— documents: see list, pp. 233–4

UNDP (United Nations Development Program), Emergency Response Division, *Building Bridges Between Relief and Development: A Compendium of the UNDP Record in Crisis Countries* (New York: UNDP, 1997)

—— 'Draft Advisory Note for the Country Cooperation Framework for Haiti and UNDP 1999–2001' (Port au Prince: UNDP, November 1998)

—— *Human Development Report 1994* (Oxford: Oxford University Press, 1994)

—— *Human Development Report 1999* (Oxford: Oxford University Press, 1999)

—— *Human Development Report 2001* (Oxford: Oxford University Press, 2001)

—— 'Working for Solutions to Crisis: The Development Response' (New York: UNDP, July 1998)

UN HRFOR (UN Human Rights Field Operation in Rwanda), 'Genocide Trials to 31 October 1997, Status Report as of 19 December 1997', HRFOR / STRPT / 59 / 2 / 19 December 1997 / E

—— 'Report on the Human Rights Situation in Rwanda and the Activities of HRFOR, September–October 1997', HRFOR / RPT / 15 / Sept–Oct 1997 / E

—— 'The Administration of Justice in Post-Genocide Rwanda', HRFOR / JUSTICE / June 1996 / E

UNITAR (UN Institute for Training and Research), *The Role and Functions of Civilian Police in United Nations Peace-keeping Operations: Debriefing and Lessons*, report of the 1995 Singapore Conference (London: Kluwer Law International, 1996)

UN OHCHR (UN Office of the High Commissioner for Human Rights), *Human Rights and Law Enforcement: A Manual on Human Rights Training for the Police* (Geneva: UN, 1997)

UNRISD (UN Research Institute for Social Development), *Rebuilding War-torn Societies* (Geneva: UNRISD, March 1995)

UN documents: see list below, p. 233

Van Boven, Theo et al., 'Seminar on the Right to Restitution, Compensation and Rehabilitation for Victims of Gross Violations of Human Rights and Fundamental Freedoms: Summary and Conclusions', in Kritz, *Transitional Justice*, pp. 500–4

Van de Goor, Luc, Kumar Rupesinghe and Paul Sciarone (eds), *Between Development and Destruction: An Enquiry into the Causes of Conflict in Post-colonial States* (Basingstoke: Macmillan, 1996)

Verhoogen, Eric, 'The US–Haiti Connection: Rich Companies, Poor Workers', *Multinational Monitor* (April 1996), pp. 7–10

Vickery, Michael and Naomi Roht-Arriaza, 'Human Rights in Cambodia', in Roht-Arriaza, *Impunity and Human Rights*, pp. 243–51

Vines, Alex, *RENAMO: From Terrorism to Democracy in Mozambique*, 2nd rev. edn (London: James Currey, 1996)

Visman, Emma et al., *The European Union and Conflict Prevention in the Horn of Africa* (London: Safer World, 1998)

Walker, Geoffrey de Q., *The Rule of Law: Foundation of Constitutional Democracy* (Carlton, Victoria: Melbourne University Press)

Wallensteen, Peter and Margareta Sollenberg, 'Armed Conflicts, 1989–98', *Journal of Peace Research*, 36 (1999), 593–606

Walzer, Michael, 'Justice Here and Now', in Lucash, *Justice and Equality*, pp. 136–50

—— *Spheres of Justice: A Defence of Pluralism and Equality* (Oxford: Basil Blackwell, 1983)

Weschler, Lawrence, 'A Miracle, a Universe: Settling Accounts with Tor-turers', extract in Kritz, *Transitional Justice*, pp. 491–9

Weiland, Heribert and Matthew Braham (rapporteurs), *The Namibian Peace Process: Implications and Lessons for the Future*, report of Freiburg symposium, July 1992 (Freiburg / New York: Arnold-Bergstaesser-Institut / International Peace Academy, 1994)

Weinberg, Stephanie, 'The Role of the Multilateral Development Banks in El Salvador: The Interrelation of their Strategies with Peace-Building and Poverty Reduction', substantial research paper presented to American University's International Development Program, April 1998

Willett, Susan, 'Ostriches, Wise Old Elephants and Economic Reconstruction in Mozambique', *International Peacekeeping*, 2, 1 (1995), 34–55

Wilson, Richard, 'Violent Truths: The Politics of Memory in Guatemala', in Armon et al., *Negotiating Rights*, pp. 18–27

WOLA (Washington Office on Latin America), 'El Salvador Peace Plan Update 3: Recent Setbacks in the Police Transition' (Washington, DC: WOLA, February 1994)

—— 'Recent Setbacks in the Police Transition', El Salvador Peace Plan Update 3, 4 February 1994 (Washington, DC: WOLA, 1994)

Wolfensohn, James, 'The Challenge of Inclusion', address to the World Bank Board of Governors, Hong Kong, 23 September 1997 (Washington, DC: WB, 1997)

—— 'A New Framework for Development', lecture at University of Cambridge, 4 March 1999

—— 'People and Development', address to the World Bank Board of Governors, Washington, DC, 1 October 1996

—— 'A Proposal for a Comprehensive Development Framework: A Discussion Draft', internal memorandum, Washington, DC: WB, January 1998

Woodman, Gordon, 'Legal Pluralism and the Search for Justice', *Journal of African Law*, 40, 2 (1996), 152–67

World Bank, 'Concepts', paper by the World Bank Post-conflict Reconstruction Unit, World Bank, Washington, DC, 1998

—— *Conflict Prevention and Post-conflict Reconstruction: Perspectives and Prospects*, seminar report, Paris, April 1998 (Washington, DC: WB, 1998)

—— 'Emergency Recovery Assistance', OP 8.50, World Bank, Washington, DC, August 1995

—— *Post Conflict Reconstruction: The Role of the World Bank* (Washington, DC: WB, 1998)

—— *Social Indicators of Development, 1996* (Washington, DC: WB, 1996)

—— *World Indicators of Development 1997* (Washington, DC: WB, 1997)

Wright, Martin, *Justice for Victims and Offenders: A Restorative Response to Crime* (Winchester: Waterside Press, 1996)

Wright, Martin and Burt Galaway (eds), *Mediation and Criminal Justice: Victims, Offenders and Community* (London: Sage, 1989)

Zalaquett, Jose, 'Balancing Ethical Imperatives and Political Constraints: The Dilemma of New Democracies Confronting Past Human Rights Violations', in Kritz, *Transitional Justice*, pp. 203–16

—— 'Confronting Human Rights Violations Committed by Former Governments: Principles Applicable and Political Constraints', in Kritz, *Transitional Justice*, pp. 3–31

United Nations documents

'Administration de la justice et les droits de l'homme des détenus: questions de l'impunité des auteurs des violations des droits de l'homme (civils et politiques)', final report by M. L. Joinet to the Human Rights Commission, E/CN.4/Sub.2/1997/20, 1997

'Agenda for Peace: Preventive Diplomacy, Peacemaking and Peace-keeping', report of the Secretary-General, A/47/277–S/24111, 17 June 1992

'Agreement on a Firm and Lasting Peace' and 'Agreement on the Implementation, Compliance and Verification Timetable for the Peace Agreements' [in Guatemala], A/51/796; S/1997/114, 7 February 1997

'Agreement on Resettlement of the Population Groups Uprooted by the Armed Conflict and Agreement on the Establishment of the Commission to Clarify Past Human Rights Violations and Acts of Violence that have Caused the Guatemalan Population to Suffer', A/48/954 and S/1994/751, 1 July 1994

'Agreement on Social and Economic Aspects and Agrarian Situation, concluded on 6 May 1996 between the Presidential Peace Commission of the Government of Guatemala and the Unidad Revolucionario Nacional Guatemalteca', A/50/956, 6 June 1996

'Assessment of the Peace Process in El Salvador', report of the Secretary-General, General Assembly A/51/917, New York, 1 July 1997

'Assistance to States in Strengthening the Rule of Law', Commission on Human Rights Resolution 1997/48

'Basic Principles on the Independence of Judiciaries', adopted by the Seventh UN Congress on the Prevention of Crime and the Treatment of Offenders, in Milan, 26 August to 6 September 1985, endorsed in UN General Assembly Resolution A/RES/40/32 of 29 November 1985

'Basic Principles on the Role of Lawyers', adopted by consensus at the Eighth UN Congress on the Prevention of Crime and the Treatment of Offenders in Havana, Cuba, from 27 August to 7 September 1990, noted by General Assembly in Resolution 45/121 of 14 December 1990

'Causes of Conflict and the Promotion of Durable Peace and Sustainable Development in Africa', report of the Secretary-General, United Nations, A/52/871–S/1998/318, April 1998

'Comprehensive Agreement on Human Rights' [in Guatemala], UNDOC A/48/928, S/1994/448, annex I

'Draft Universal Declaration on the Independence of Justice', submitted by Special Rapporteur Dr L. M. Singhvi (India) to the Sub-commission on Prevention of Discrimination and Protection of Minorities at its 40th session, 1988, E/CN.4/Sub.2/1988/20

'Human Rights Today: A United Nations Priority', draft UN briefing paper, 13.08.1998 (OHCHR)

'Inventory of Post-Conflict Peacebuilding Activities', UN Doc.ST/ESA/246, 1995

'Renewing the United Nations: A Program for Reform', report of the Secretary-General, UN Doc. A/51/950, 14.07.1997, July 1997

'Report of Human Rights Area of MINUGUA – The Situation in Central America: Procedures for the Establishment of a Firm and Lasting Peace and Progress in Fashioning a Region of Peace, Freedom, Democracy and Development', General Assembly A/52/330, 10 September 1997

'Report of the Independent Expert on the Human Rights Situation in Haiti', presented by Adama Dieng to the 52nd session of the General Assembly, and the Human Rights Commission at its 54th session, Geneva, 15 September 1997

'Report of the UN Truth Commission for El Salvador: From Madness to Hope', UN Doc. S / 25500, 1993

'The Situation of Human Rights in Rwanda submitted by the Special Representative of the Commission on Human Rights, Mr Michel Moussalli, Pursuant to Resolution 1998 / 69', General Assembly, 53rd session, agenda item 110 (c), 18.09.98

'Study Concerning the Right to Restitution, Compensation and Rehabilitation for Victims of Gross Violations of Human Rights and Fundamental Freedoms', preliminary report, UN Doc.E / CN.4 / Sub.2 / 1990 / 10, 26 July 1990, and final report, UN Doc. E / CN.4 / Sub.2 / 1993 / 8 July 1993

'Vienna Declaration and Programme of Action', UN-Doc.A / CONF.157 / 23 of 12 July 1993, adopted by the World Conference on Human Rights on 25 June 1993

Conferences and seminars

'Burying the Past – Justice, Forgiveness and Reconciliation in the Politics of South Africa, Guatemala, East Germany, and Northern Ireland'. Conference at St Antony's College, Oxford University, 14–16 September 1998

'How Can Human Rights be Better Integrated into Peace Processes?' Conference organized by the Fund for Peace, Washington, DC, on 24–5 September 1997

'Rebuilding Torn Societies'. Conference organized by Academic Council on the United Nations System at United Nations, New York, 16–18 June 1999

'High Level Round Table on Truth and Reconciliation'. Conference at the International Institute for Democracy and Electoral Assistance, Stockholm, 1–2 November 1999

Index